The Constitutional Value of Sunset Clauses

In recent years, sunset clauses have mostly been associated with emergency legislation introduced in the wake of terrorist attacks. However, as this book demonstrates, they have a long history and a substantial constitutional impact on the separation of powers and the rule of law. In addition, the constitutional value of such clauses is examined from certain neglected normative aspects pertaining to concepts such as deliberative and consensus democracy, parliamentary sovereignty and constitutional dialogue.

The work is an amalgam of three perspectives: the historical, the positive and the normative. All three are intertwined and each subsequent part builds upon the findings of the previous one. The historical perspective investigates the historical development of sunset clauses since the first Parliaments in England. The positive perspective examines the legal effect and the contemporary utility of sunset clauses. Finally, the normative perspective analyses their interaction with several models of separation of powers, and their influence on the dialogue between various institutions as it values their impact on the rule of law, formal and substantive.

The detailed examination of this topical subject will be a valuable resource for academics, researchers and policy makers.

Antonios Emmanouil Kouroutakis is Postdoctoral Fellow in the School of Law, Aristotle University of Thessaloniki. He has published on aspects of terrorism, emergencies and constitutional law in both English and Greek.

The Constitutional Value of Sunset Clauses

An historical and normative analysis

Antonios Emmanouil Kouroutakis

Routledge
Taylor & Francis Group
LONDON AND NEW YORK

First published 2017 by Routledge

2 Park Square, Milton Park, Abingdon, Oxfordshire OX14 4RN
711 Third Avenue, New York, NY 10017

Routledge is an imprint of the Taylor & Francis Group, an informa business

First issued in paperback 2018

British Library Cataloguing in Publication Data
A catalogue record for this book is available from the British Library

Library of Congress Cataloging-in-Publication Data
Names: Kouroutakis, Antonios, 1981- author.
Title: The constitutional value of sunset clauses : an historical and normative analysis / by Antonios Emmanouil Kouroutakis.
Description: New York, NY : Routledge, 2016. | Includes bibliographical references and index.
Identifiers: LCCN 2016017214 | ISBN 9781472486448 (hardback) | ISBN 9781315454337 (ebook) | ISBN 9781315454313 (epub) | ISBN 9781315454306 (mobipocket/kindle)
Subjects: LCSH: Sunset reviews of government programs—Law and legislation. | Constitutional law. | Legislation. | Separation of powers. | Rule of law.
Classification: LCC K284 .K68 2016 | DDC 342/.06—dc23
LC record available at https://lccn.loc.gov/2016017214

ISBN: 978-1-4724-8644-8 (hbk)
ISBN: 978-1-138-36675-6 (pbk)

Typeset in Galliard
by Apex CoVantage, LLC

To my wonderful Mother, Argiro Imvriotou

Contents

Preface

I am very happy to write the preface for this book, which emerged out of the doctoral thesis that Dr Antonios Kouroutakis completed at Oxford University. I had the pleasure to supervise Antonios' work during this period.

When he first came to Oxford it was clear that he wished to work on a topic relating to the separation of powers, which is of significance within all legal systems. However it took some time to fix on a topic that had not been exhaustively researched and was also of practical and intellectual interest.

We settled on such a topic towards the end of Antonios' first term in Oxford, and it proved to be an excellent subject for research. It is a testimony to the relative novelty of his research in this area that there has been no in-depth study of such clauses in the UK.

Antonios analysed the historical, legal and normative significance of sunset clauses in legislation, primarily with reference to the UK, but with some reference to other legal systems. These 'sunset' clauses limit the period during which a law remains in force.

The book begins with issues of definition, typology and taxonomy in which Dr Kouroutakis distinguishes the different types of sunset clauses that exist, and their respective legal effect. This is followed by three chapters that embody the historical dimension of the book. The author reveals the use made of such clauses from the medieval period onwards, and the debates concerning such clauses that occupied scholars at the time and thereafter. The way in which such clauses were used as a bargaining tool in medieval lawmaking is especially intriguing. So too are the uses to which such clauses were put in the Stuart period, when they had a marked impact on a plethora of issues, ranging from revenue collection to habeas corpus. There is moreover historical evidence of the way in which sunset clauses were used during times of emergency.

It is a strength of this book that it combines detailed analysis of the historical dimension of the subject, with equally rigorous examination of the more normative aspects of the inquiry. This is readily apparent in the chapter on the separation of powers, where the author considers carefully the way in which sunset clauses affect relations between the legislature and the executive, and also the ways in which the separation of powers impacts on the use of such clauses. The normative dimension of the book is carried forward in the chapter on parliamentary sovereignty, which includes consideration of the way in which sunset clauses can foster dialogue between present and future parliaments. This is followed by two insightful chapters that consider the relationship between sunset clauses and the rule of law, the divide between the chapters turning on that between formal and substantive conceptions of the rule of law.

This book will be of great interest to all those concerned with constitutional law and also to those whose principal concern is legal history. It casts valuable light on a concept that has important practical and normative implications for the workings of the state, both past and present.

Professor Paul Craig,
St John's College, Oxford.

Acknowledgements

This book is based on four years of research at the wonderful facilities of Worcester College, Oxford. I was fortunate to have accessed the finest libraries at Oxford and have used the facilities of the university.

I am extremely grateful to Paul Craig not only for hearing and reading my ideas but even more for his criticisms and comments on them. I am deeply indebted to him for assisting me and guiding my research and inspiring my thoughts during our meetings, which I consider to be the most intellectual moments of my life. Thank you, Paul – I owe to you my way of thinking about law.

I am also grateful to John Allison and Roger Brownsword for their useful comments on several parts of this book that broadened my perspective and improved this manuscript. I have been privileged to discuss with you my ideas.

I cannot refrain from mentioning Stephen Gardbaum and Adam Winkler, who at various stages taught me valuable lessons about being a legal researcher. Your words have proved an enduring influence.

I would like also to thank many teachers, colleagues and friends with whom I had the opportunity to discuss aspects of my work. Most importantly, I have been lucky to have met during the writing of this book Michail Risvas, Corey Johnson, Matthew Astley, Kosmas Kaprinis, Michail Decastros, Maria Ioannidou, Vasiliki Brisimi, Julian Nowag, Ioannis Ladas, Daniel Pascoe, Daniel Alati and Odysseas Repousis. A special mention to Elina Ferlia for her generous support and encouragement.

At Worcester College, Oxford, I thank the staff and, in particular, Cath Fraser for her help and her kindness. At Routledge, I appreciate the assistance of Alison Kirk and the comments of my anonymous reviewers. All errors are attributed to the author alone.

But for my mother, Argiro Imvriotou, without her unconditional love and unlimited support, this book would not have been written. I hope life will give me the time to give back to the world the care and the love that I received from you.

Abbreviations

AC, QB	Law Reports
All ER	All England Law Reports
art	article
Bl Comm	Blackstone, Commentaries on the Law of England
BISD	Basic Instruments and Selected Documents
c	chapter (of statutes)
CE	Court of Exchequer Chamber
Ch/Chrs	Chapter/Chapters
CJ	Chief Justice
cl	clause
Co	Company
Co Ints	Coke, Institutes of the Laws of England
col/cols	column/columns
CUP	Cambridge University Press
EC	European Communities
ECHR	European Convention on Human Rights
ed/eds	editor/editors
edn	edition
Edw	Edward
Eliz	Elizabeth
ER	English Reports
EWHC	High Court, Chancery Division
ff	And following
fn	footnote – (external to the work)
Geo	George
HC	House of Commons
Hen	Henry
HL	House of Lords
HM	Her Majesty's
HRA	Human Rights Act
HMSO	Her (or His) Majesty's Stationery Office
KB	Kings Bench
LQR	Law Quarterly Review
MP/MPs	Member of Parliament/ Members of Parliament
MS/MSS	manuscript/manuscripts

n/nn	footnote/footnotes (internal to the work)
no	number
OUP	Oxford University Press
para/paras	paragraph/paragraphs
PL	Public Law
PRO	Public Records Office
R	The Queen (or King)
Raym	Sir Thomas Raymond's King's Bench and Common Pleas Reports
Ric	Richard
s/ss	section/sections
SC	Supreme Court
SI	Statutory Instruments
SP	State Papers
SS	Publication of the Selden Society
St	Statute (UK Statute)
Stat	Statute (US Statute)
TNA	The National Archives
UK	United Kingdom
UKHL	House of Lords
UKSC	Supreme Court
UN	United Nations
UNHCR	United Nations High Commissioner for Refugees
UNTS	United Nations Treaty Series
US	United States
Vol/vols	volume/volumes
Vict	Victoria
YB	Yearbook

Instruments

Statutes

United Kingdom

9 Edw III st 1 c 1
11 Edw III c 1
14 Edw III st 1 c 21
25 Edw III st 3 c 2
25 Edw III st 5 c 2
42 Edw III c
1 Ric II c 7
4 Ric II c 17
4 Hen IV c 35
9 Hen V st 1 c 2
9 Hen V st1 c 3
9 Hen V st 1 c 4
9 Hen V st 2 c 8
9 Hen V st 2 c 9
9 Hen V st 2 c 10
1 Hen VI c 6
2 Hen VI c 4
2 Hen VI c 21
8 Hen VI c 12
19 Hen VII c 14
1 Hen VIII c 4
1 Hen VIII c 20
1 Eliz c 20
5 Eliz I c 8
13 Eliz I c 1
14 Eliz I c 1
27 Eliz I c 16
23 Eliz I c 2
1 Jac I c 7
1 Jac I c 9
1 Jac I c 18
1 Jac I c 33
3 Jac I c 8
3 Jac I c 10
3 Jac I c 9
3 Jac I c 11
4 Jac I c 2
4 Jac I c 11
7 Jac I c 1
7 Jac I c 4
7 Jac I c 5
7 Jac I c 11
7 Jac I c 13
7 Jac I c 17
7 Jac I c 18
7 Jac I c 20
21 Jac I c 9
21 Jac I c 17
21 Jac I c 18
21 Jac I c 20
21 Jac I c 22
21 Jac I c 28
1 Car I c 7
16 Car I c 8
16 Car I c 12
16 Car I c 22
16 Car I c 25
16 Car I c 29
16 Car I c 31
16 Car I c 36
12 Car II c 18
13 Car II st 2 c 1
14 Car II c 33
15 Car II c 7
16 Car II c 1
25 Car II c 2
25 Car II c 7
1 Jac II c 17

1 Gul&Mar c 3
1 Gul&Mar c 2
1 Gul&Mar c 5
1 Gul&Mar c 13
1 Gul&Mar c 19
4&5 Gul&Mar c 24
Act of Settlement 1701 (12&13 Gul III c 2)
Acts of Parliament (Expiration) Act 1808 (48 Geo III c 106)
Administration of Justice (Emergency Provisions) (Northern Ireland) Act 1939
Administration of Justice (Emergency Provisions) Act 1939
Administration of Justice Act 1774 (14 Geo III c 39)
Aid and Contribution for the Prosecution of the War 1798 (38 Geo III c 16)
Allied Powers (Maritime Courts) Act 1941
American Prohibitory Act 1776 (16 Geo III c 5)
Anti-Terrorism, Crime and Security Act
Anti-Terrorism, Crime and Security Act 2001
Apothecaries Amendment Act 1825
Appeal of Murder, etc. Act 1819 (59 Geo III c 46)
Appropriation Act 1849 (3&4 Vict c 112)
Army and Navy Act 1798 (39 Geo III c 4)
Australian Courts Act 1828 (9 Geo IV c 83)
Bankrupts Act 1705 (4&5 Anne c 4)
Banking (Special Provisions) Act 2008
Banking Act 2009
Bankrupts Act 1706 (6 Anne c 22)
British Ships (Transfer Restriction) Act 1915
Children and Young Persons Act
Civil Contingencies Act 2004
Coastguard Act, 1925
Colonial Trade Act 1760 (1 Geo III c 9)
Constitutional Reform Act 2005
Constitutional Reform and Governance Act 2010
Continuance of Acts 1737 (11 Geo II c 18)
Continuance of Acts, etc. 1753 (26 Geo II c 32)
Continuance of Acts, etc. 1757 (31 Geo II c 35)
Correspondence with Enemies Act 1793 (33 Geo III c 27)
Court of Chancery Act 1763 (4 Geo III c 32)
Courts (Emergency Powers) Act 1939
Courts (Emergency Powers) Act 1943
Currency and Bank Notes Act 1914
Custom, Duties, etc. Act 1763 (4 Geo III c 15)
Customs (War Powers) Act 1915
Customs Act 1772 (13 Geo III c 44)
Debt Relief (Developing Countries) Act 2010
Duties in American Colonies Act 1765 (5 Geo III c 12)
Duties on Income Act 1799 (39 Geo III c 13)
East India Company Act 1767 (7 Geo III c 49)
East India Company Act 1767 (7 Geo III c 57)
East India Company Act 1768 (8 Geo III c 11)
East India Company Act 1769 (9 Geo III c 24)
East India Company Act 1772 (13 Geo III c 9)
Education Act 2002
Emergency Power (Defence) Act 1939
Enlistment Act 1794 (34 Geo III c 43)
Enlistment of Foreigners Act 1804 (44 Geo III c 75)
Enlistment of Foreigners Act 1806 (46 Geo III c 23)
Equality Act 2010
European Union Act 2011
Explanatory Notes to the Statutory Revision Act 1894
Exportation Act 1705 (4&5 Anne c 19)
Finance Act 1894 (57&58 Vict c 30)
Financial Services and Markets Act 2000
Fire Services Act 2003
Fishery Harbours Act 1915
Goods and Services (Price Control) Act 1941
Growth of Coffee Act 1745 (19 Geo II c 23)
Habeas Corpus Suspension Act 1722 (9 Geo I c 1)
Habeas Corpus Suspension Act 1795 (35 Geo III c 3)
Habeas Corpus Suspension Act 1798 (38 Geo III c 36)
Habeas Corpus Suspension Act 1799 (39 Geo III c 15)

Habeas Corpus Suspension Act 1799 (39 Geo III c 44)
Habeas Corpus Suspension, etc. Act 1714 (1 Geo I st 2 c 8)
Habeas Corpus Suspension, etc. Act 1714 (1 Geo I st 2 c 30)
Highgate and Chipping Barnet Road Act 1720 (7 Geo I st 1 c 18)
Holocaust (Return of Cultural Objects) Act 2009
Housing (Emergency Powers) Act
Human Rights Act 1998
Import and Export Control Act 1990
Import, Export and Customs Powers (Defence) Act 1939
Imprisonment (Temporary Provisions) Act 1980
Income Tax Act 1803 (43 Geo III c 122)
Income Tax Act 1806 (46 Geo III c 65)
Income Tax Act 1842 (5&6 Vict c 35)
Income Tax Repeal, etc. Act 1808 (42 Geo III c 42)
Increase of Rent and Mortgage Interest (War Restrictions) Act 1915
Indemnity Act 1727 (1 Geo II c 23)
Indemnity Act 1730 (4 Geo II c 6)
Indemnity Act 1763 (4 Geo III c 31)
John Wilkinson's Estate Act 1794 (34 Geo III c 67)
Land Drainage Act of 1914
Land Tax Perpetuation Act 1798 (38 Geo III c 60)
Land Tax, Forfeited Estates, etc. Act 1702 (1 Anne c 6)
Local Government (Emergency Provisions) Act 1916
Maintenance of Live Stock Act 1915
Manning of the Navy Act 1794 (34 Geo III c 66)
Massachusetts Governments Act 1774 (14 Geo III c 45)
Militia Act 1714 (1 Geo I st 2 c 14)
Militia, etc. Act 1711 (10 Anne c 33)
Moss Troopers Act 1700 (12&13 Gul III c 6)
Munitions of War Act 1915
Murder (Abolition of Death Penalty) Act 1965
Mutiny Act 1716 (3 Geo I c 2)
Mutiny, America Act 1765 (5 Geo III c 33)
National Registration Act 1915
National Registration Act 1939
Navy Act 1740 (14 Geo II c 38)
Negotiations of Notes and Bills Act 1797 (37 Geo III c 32)
Northern Ireland (Emergency Provisions) Act 1973
Northern Ireland (Temporary Provisions) Act 1972
Northern Roads, London Act 1735 (9 Geo II c 39)
Paper Bills of Credit Act 1763 (4 Geo III c 34)
Parliamentary Elections Act 1770 (10 Geo III c 16)
Parliamentary Standard Act 2009
Plantation Trade Act 1695 (7&8 Gul III c 22)
Police (Northern Ireland) Act 2000
Poor Law Amendment Act 1834
Prevention of Terrorism (Temporary Provisions) Act 1974
Prevention of Terrorism (Temporary Provisions) Act 1976
Prevention of Terrorism (Temporary Provisions) Act 1984
Prevention of Terrorism (Temporary Provisions) Act 1989
Prevention of Terrorism Act 2005
Prevention of Violence (Temporary Provisions) Act 1939
Price Control (Regulation of Disposal of Stocks) Act 1943
Price of Coal (Limitation) Act 1915
Price of Goods Act 1939
Provisional Collection of Taxes Act 1968
Quartering Act 1774 (14 Geo III c 54)
Rebellion in America Act 1767 (7 Geo III c 59)
Regulation of Railways Act Short title 1873
Rent of Furnished Houses Control (Scotland) Act 1943
Residence in France During the War Act 1798 (38 Geo III c 79)
Road Traffic (Temporary Restrictions) Act 1991

Sex Discrimination (Election Candidates) Act 2002
Ships and Aircraft (Transfer Restriction) Act 1939
Special Acts (Extension of Time) Act 1915
Statute Law (Repeals) Act 1973
Statute Law Revision Act 1894 (57&58 Vict c 56)
Sugar Colonies, etc. Act 1756 (29 Geo II c 26)
Superannuation Act 1972
Superannuation Act 2010
Suspension of Habeas Corpus Act 1794 (34 Geo III c 54)
Terrorism Act 2000
Terrorism Act 2006
Terrorism Prevention and Investigation Measures Act 2011
Terrorist Asset-Freezing (Temporary Provisions) Act 2010
The Accommodation Agencies Act 1953
The New South Wales Act 1823 (4 Geo IV c 96)
The Parliament Act 1911 (1&2 Geo V c 13)
The Sovereign Grant Act
The Treasonable Practices Act 1796 (36 Geo III c 8)
Tithe Communication Act 1836
Trade Act (14 Geo III c 19)
Trade of Sugar Colonies Act 1732 (6 Geo II c 13)
Trade with France Act 1704 (3&4 Anne c 12)
Treason Act 1817 (57 Geo III c 6)
Unemployment Insurance (Emergency Powers) Act 1939
Union of England and Scotland Act (4&5 Anne c 15)
Union of England and Scotland Act 1704 (3&4 Anne c 6)
Universities and Colleges (Emergency Powers) Act 1915

Canada

Anti-terrorism Act (SC 2001 c 41)

France

Loi n° 60–101 (4 février 1960)

United States

Economic Growth and Tax Relief Reconciliation Act, Pub L No 107–16, 115 Stat 38 (2001)
Ethics in Government Act Amendments, Pub L No 97–409, 96 Stat 2039 (1983)
Ethics in Government Act, Pub L No 95–521, 92 Stat 1867 (1978)
Independent Counsel Reauthorization Act, Pub L No 100–191, 101 Stat 1293 (1987)
Independent Counsel Reauthorization Act, Pub L No 103–270, 108 Stat 732 (1994)
Jobs and Growth Tax Relief Reconciliation Act, Pub L No 108–27, 117 Stat 752 (2003)
Tax Relief, Unemployment Insurance Reauthorisation, and Job Creation Act, Pub L 111–312, 124 Stat 101 (2010)
Uniting and Strengthening America by Providing Appropriate Tools Required to Intercept and Obstruct Terrorism Act, Pub L No 107–56, 115 Stat 272 (2001)
USA Patriot Act, Pub L No. 107–56, 115 Stat 272 (2001)

Statutory instruments

Explanatory Memorandum to The Financial Services and Markets Act 2000 (Market Abuse) Regulations Order 2005 SI 2005/381
Explanatory Memorandum to The Superannuation Act 2010 (Repeal of Limits on Compensation) Order 2010 SI 2010/2996
The Anti-terrorism, Crime and Security Act 2001 (Continuance in force of sections 21 to 23) Order 2003 SI 2003/691
Regional Commissioners Act (Expiry) Order 1946 SI 1946/164
The Anti-terrorism, Crime and Security Act 2001 (Continuance in force of sections 21 to 23) Order 2004 SI 2004/751
The Debt Relief (Developing Countries) Act 2010 (Permanent Effect) Order 2011 SI 2011/1336
The Financial Services and Markets Act 2000 (Market Abuse) Regulations Order 2005 SI 2005/381

The Financial Services and Markets Act 2000 (Market Abuse) Regulations Order 2009 SI 2009/312
The Northern Ireland Act 1998 (Commencement No 5) Order 1999 SI 1999/3209
The Superannuation Act 2010 (Repeal of Limits on Compensation) Order 2010 SI 2010/2996

EU directives and regulations

Council and European Parliament Directive (EC) 2003/6 of 28 January 2003 on insider dealing and market manipulation (market abuse) (2003) OJ L96/16
Council Regulation (EC) No 1225/2009 of 30 November 2009 on Protection against Dumped Imports from Countries not Members of the European Community OJ L343/51
Regulation (EC) No 544/2009 of the European Parliament and of the Council of 18 June 2009 amending Regulation (EC) No 717/2007 on roaming on public mobile telephone networks within the Community and Directive 2002/21/EC on a common regulatory framework for electronic communications networks and services OJ L167/12
Regulation (EC) No 717/2007 of the European Parliament and of the Council of 27 June 2007 on roaming on public mobile telephone networks within the Community and amending Directive 2002/21/EC OJ L171/32

Bills

Anti-terrorism, Crime and Security HL Bill (2001–2) 33
Anti-Terrorism, Crime and Security Bill [49]
Civil Contingencies HC Bill (2003–4) 14
Civil Contingencies HL Bill (2003–4) 77
European Convention on Human Rights (Temporary Withdrawal) HC Bill (2010–2) 308
European Union HL Bill (2010–1) 55
Prevention of Terrorism HC Bill (2004–5) 61
Terrorist Asset-Freezing (Temporary Provisions) HC Bill (2009–10) 62

Constitutions

Basic Law for the Federal Republic of Germany
Constitution New Hampshire (1776)
Constitution South Carolina (1776)
Constitution of Hellenic Republic (1975)
Constitution of Malaysia (1957)
Constitution of the Republic of Albania (1998)
Constitution of the Republic of South Africa (1993)
Constitution of the United States (1787)
French Constitution (1793)
Law on Major Constitutional Provisions of Albania (1991)

International treaties

Agreement on Implementation of Article VI of the General Agreement on Tariffs And Trade of April 12, 1979, BISD 26 S/171
Convention for the Protection of Human Rights and Fundamental Freedoms (adopted 4 November 1950, entered into force 3 September 1953) 213 UNTS 221
International Covenant on Civil and Political Rights, (16 December 1966, entered into force 23 March 1976) 999 UNTS 171
Protection of Human Rights and Fundamental Freedoms (adopted 4 November 1950, entered into force 3 September 1953) 213 UNTS 221

Reports and policy documents

7th Report of Historical Manuscripts Commission
9th Report of Historical Manuscripts Commission
Cabinet Office, Government's Response to the Report of the Joint Committee on

the Draft Civil Contingencies Bill (Cm 6078, 2004)

Committee on Ministers' Powers, Report (Cmd 4060 1932)

Committee upon Expired and Expiring Laws, Report (HC 25 January 1808)

Committee upon Temporary Laws, Expired or Expiring, Report (HC 13 May 1796)

Congressional Research Service, 'Parliament and Congress: A Brief Comparison of the British House of Commons and the US House of Representatives' (Congress, 19 May 2005)

Delegated Powers and Regulatory Reform Committee, Guidance for Departments on the role and requirements of the Committee (HL Nov 2009)

European Commission, Digital Agenda for Europe: what would it do for me? (19 May 2010, MEMO/10/199)

European Union Committee, Mobile Phone Charges in the EU: Follow-up Report (HL 2008–9, 42)

HM Government, Sunsetting Regulations: Guidance (April 2011)

HM Government, Sunsetting Regulations: Guidance (March 2011)

HM Treasury, Budget Report (June 2010)

HM Treasury, Consultation on the abolition of 36 tax reliefs (May 2011)

HM Treasury, Overview of Tax Legislation and Rates (March 2011)

HM Treasury, Overview of Tax Legislation and Rates (March 2011)

HM Treasury, Tax policy making: a new approach (June 2010)

HM Treasury, The new approach to tax policy making: a response to the consultation (December 2010)

HM Treasury, The new approach to tax policy making: a response to the consultation (December 2010)

Home Affairs Select Committee, The Anti-Terrorism, Crime and Security Bill 2001 (HC 2001–2, 351)

Home Affairs Select Committee, The Anti-Terrorism, Crime and Security Bill 2001 (HC 2001–2, 351)

Home Department, The Definition of Terrorism (Cm 7052, 2007)

Home Department, The Definition of Terrorism (Cm 7052, 2007)

Home Department, The government reply to the Twenty-Fourth Report from the Joint Committee on Human Rights, Counter Terrorism Policy and Human Rights (Cm 6920, 2006)

Home Department, The government reply to the Twenty-Fourth Report from the Joint Committee on Human Rights, Counter Terrorism Policy and Human Rights (Cm 6920, 2006)

Home Office, Review of the Operation of the Prevention of Terrorism (Temporary Provisions) Act 1979 (Cm 8803, 1983)

Home Office, Review of the Operation of the Prevention of Terrorism (Temporary Provisions) Act 1979 (Cm 8803, 1983)

Joint Committee on Human Rights, Anti-terrorism, Crime and Security Act Statutory Review and Continuance of Part 4 (2003–4, HL 38, HC 381)

Joint Committee on Human Rights, Counter-Terrorism Policy and Human Rights: Prosecution Pre-Charge Detention (2005–6, HL 240, HC 1576)

Joint Committee on Human Rights, Scrutiny of Bills: Further Progress Report (2002–3, HL 119, HC 765)

Joint Committee on the Draft Civil Contingencies Bill, Draft Civil Contingencies Bill (2002–3, HL 184, HC 1074)

Law Commission, Post Legislative Scrutiny (Law Com No 302, 2006)

Law Commission, Post-Legislative Scrutiny: A Consultation Paper (Law Com No 178, 2006)

Les Documents de Travail du Sénat, 'Les Ordonnances, Série Etudes Juridiques, Bilan au 31 Décembre 2007' (n EJ4)

Mandelkern Group on Better Regulation, Final Report (13 November 2001)

President Reagan, Statement on Signing the Independent Counsel Reauthorization Act of 1987, Independent Counsel

Reauthorization Act of 1987, 2 Pub Papers 1524 (Dec 15, 1987)
Privy Council Office, Guide to Making Federal Acts and Regulations (2nd edn, 2001)
Privy Counsellor Review Committee, Anti-terrorism, Crime and Security Act 2001 Review (HC 2003–4, 100)
Public Administration Select Committee, Taming the Prerogative: Strengthening Ministerial Accountability to Parliament HC (HC 2003–4, 422)
Public Bill Committee, 'Regulatory Enforcement and Sanctions Bill [Lords]' 4th sitting (19 June 2008)
Public Papers of the Presidents, 'Statement on Signing the Independent Counsel Reauthorization Act of 1987' (US Government Printing Office 1989)
Select Committee on the Constitution, Fast-track Legislation: Constitutional Implications and Safeguards, (HL 2008–9, 116-I)
Select Committee on the Constitution, Fast-track Legislation: Constitutional Implications and Safeguards, (HL 2008–9, 116-II)
Select Committee on the Expiring Laws Continuance Act, Report (HC 21 July 1922)
Select Committee on the Expiring Laws Continuance Act, Report (HC 26 May 1925)
Senator Hillary Rodham Clinton, 'USA Patriot Act Reauthorization Conference Report' (16 December 2005, Congressional Record, S13713)
Standing Orders of the House of Commons, Public Business (2012 HC 614)
UNHCR Report of the Special Rapporteur on the promotion and protection of human rights and fundamental freedoms while countering terrorism (22 December 2010) UN Doc A/HRC/16/51

Parliamentary debates

Parliamentary rolls

Rot Parl C 65/7 II 112
Rot Parl C65/25 II 294
Rot Parl C65/25 II 296
Rot Parl C 65/41 III 161
Rot Parl C 65/65 III 485
Rot Parl C 65/65 III 496
Rot Parl C 65/65 III 509
Rot Parl C 65/65 III 511
Rot Parl C 65/67 III 556
Rot Parl C 65/68 III 570
Rot Parl C 65/68 III 572
Rot Parl C 65/68 III 585
Rot Parl C 65/68 III 586
Rot Parl C 65/68 III 589
Rot Parl C 65/74 IV 22
Rot Parl C 65/75 IV 35
Rot Parl C 65/76 IV 63
Rot Parl C 65/84 IV 191
Rot Parl C 65/84 IV items 41–6
Rot Parl C 65/85 IV 202
Rot Parl C 65/85 IV 251
Rot Parl C 65/85 IV 260
Rot Parl C 65/99 V 141–70
Rot Parl C 65/99 V 151
Rot Parl C 65/123 VI 335
Rot Parl C 65/127 VI 442
Rot Parl C 65/128 VI 458
Rot Parl C 65/130 VI 542

Hansard reports

HC Deb 16 June 1808 vol 11 col 912
HC Deb 20 May 1818 vol 38 col 840
HC Deb 01 April 1828 vol 18 col 1430
HC Deb 18 April 1828 vol 18 col 1565
HC Deb 17 June 1847 vol 93 col 696
HC Deb 27 August 1889 vol 340 col 718
HC Deb 10 August 1896 vol 44 col 456
HC Deb 13 July 1897 vol 51 col 81
HC Deb 30 June 1898 vol 60 col 748
HC Deb 26 July 1904 vol 138 col 1234
HC Deb 26 July 1904 vol 138 col 1244
HC Deb 19 July 1915 vol 73 col 1197
HC Deb 19 July 1939 vol 350 col 670
HC Deb 24 July 1939 vol 350 col 1047
HC Deb 24 July 1939 vol 350 cols 1047
HC Deb 24 July 1939 vol 350 cols 1054–5
HC Deb 24 August 1939 vol 351 col 67

HC Deb 24 August 1939 vol 351 cols 102–9
HC Deb 13 July 1965 vol. 716 col 358
HC Deb 13 July 1965 vol. 716 col 408
HC Deb 13 July 1965 vol. 716 col 444
HC Deb 25 November 1974 vol 882 col 35
HC Deb 28 November 1974 vol 882 col 743
HC Deb 21 March 1985 vol 75 col 568W
HC Deb 29 November 1990 vol 181 cols 1059–63
HC Deb 23 March 1999 vol 328 col 240
HC Deb 14 December 1999 vol 341 col 153
HC Deb 14 December 1999 vol 341 col 154
HC Deb 27 July 2000 vol 354 col 1290
HC Deb 19 November 2001 vol 375 col 28
HC Deb 19 November 2001 vol 375 col 62
HC Deb 19 November 2001 vol 375 col 77
HC Deb 21 November 2001 vol 375 col 394
HC Deb 21 November 2001 vol 375 col 397
HC Deb 12 December 2001 vol 376 col 952
HC Deb 12 December 2001 vol 376 col 956
HC Deb 12 December 2001 vol 376 col 959
HC Deb 05 February 2002 vol 379 col 217WH
HC Deb 23 April 2002 vol 384 col 222W
HC Deb 14 May 2002 vol 385 col 589W
HC Deb 04 July 2002 vol 388 col 487
HC Deb 21 January 2004 vol 416 col 1253W
HC Deb 16 November 2004 vol 426 col 1364
HC Deb 17 November 2004 vol 426 col 1368
HC Deb 17 November 2004 vol 426 col 1367
HC Deb 22 February 2005 vol 431 col 186
HC Deb 10 March 2005 vol 431 col 1859
HC Deb 9 November 2005 vol 439 col 298
HC Deb 26 Jul 2007 vol 463 col 1466W
HC Deb 26 January 2009 vol 487 col 22
HC Deb 1 July 2009 Vol 495 col 403
HC Deb 7 April 2010 vol 508 col 1044
HC Deb 7 September 2010 vol 515 col 218
HC Deb 28 March 2011 vol 526 col 34W
HC Deb 11 July 2011 vol 531 col 85
HL Deb 17 April 1916 vol 21 cols 753–6
HL Deb 18 April 1916 vol 21 cols 758–69
HL Deb 26 July 1951 vol 172 cols 1335–73
HL Deb 26 July 1951 vol 172 col 1339
HL Deb 08 December 1953 vol 184 col 1106
HL Deb 17 December 1969 vol 306 col 1138
HL Deb 05 December 1972 vol 337 col 145
HL Deb 06 February 1984 vol 447 col 898
HL Deb 27 January 1987 vol 483 col 1282
HL Deb 10 December 2001 vol 629 col 1198
HL Deb 10 December 2001 vol 629 col 1199
HL Deb 10 December 2001 vol 629 col 1201
HL Deb 10 December 2001 vol 629 col 1202
HL Deb 10 December 2001 vol 629 col 1205
HL Deb 19 June 2003 vol 649 col 1017
HL Deb 19 June 2003 vol 649 col 1025
HL Deb 22 February 2005 vol 669 col 1102
HL Deb 01 March 2005 vol 670 col 132
HL Deb 01 March 2005 vol 670 col 161
HL Deb 01 March 2005 vol 670 col 203
HL Deb 10 March 2005 vol 670 col 1024
HL Deb 10 March 2005 vol 670 col 1040
HL Deb 6 June 2005 vol 672 col 754
HL Deb 21 February 2008 vol 699 col 276
HL Deb 15 June 2011 vol 529 col 809

Manuscripts and public records

MS 449, 257
Stowe MSS, 354
TNA PRO C 49/19/16
TNA PRO SP 16/1/68
TNA PRO SP 16/1/94
TNA PRO SP 16/2/33
TNA PRO SP 16/2/36
TNA PRO SP 16/3/76
TNA PRO SP 16/4/35
TNA PRO SP 16/5/8
TNA PRO SP 16/5/23
TNA PRO SP 16/5/24
TNA PRO SP 16/5/32
TNA PRO SP 16/5/49
TNA PRO SP 16/5/55
TNA PRO SP 16/5/81
TNA PRO SP 16/5/90
TNA PRO SP 16/5/6

Table of cases

United Kingdom

United States

Part I

Positive analysis of sunset clauses

1 Definition, taxonomy and origin of sunset clauses

> Perpetua lex est, nullam legem humanum ac positivam perpetuam esse; et clausula quae abrogationem excludit initio non valet. (It is a perpetual law that no human or positive law can be perpetual; and a clause in a law which precludes the power of abrogation is void ab initio.)
>
> Bacon's Max in Reg 19

The meaning of sunset clauses and their legal effect

Defining sunset clauses

The duration of laws and their perpetual binding force have always been a central concern of philosophers and academics. In *The Concept of Law*, Hart discusses the persistence of law and observes that the Witchcraft Act 1735 was a legislative expression of some centuries ago, but was still in use until the middle of the 20th century.[1] The laws of past generations are the most prominent feature in the statute book and mark the life of present and future generations.

Indeed, while ordinary legislation endures in force until amended or repealed, the inclusion of a sunset clause defines the duration of a law. Therefore such a law is commonly viewed as temporary.[2] For instance, Parliament passed the Terrorist Asset-Freezing Act 2010, which was limited in duration through a sunset clause in section 1, ending on 31 December 2010,[3] and thus in the title the label 'Temporary Provisions' was added in parentheses.[4]

Sunset clauses are statutory provisions providing that a particular law will expire automatically on a particular date unless it is re-authorised by the legislature.[5] Thus, according to Hart's classification between primary and secondary legal rules, a sunset clause belongs in the latter category, given that it is a rule about the duration of the rules.[6]

1 HLA Hart, *The Concept of Law* (Paul Craig ed, 3rd edn, OUP 2012) 64.

2 And on the contrary, legislation without a sunset clause has the presumption of permanence. See Daniel Greenburg (ed), *Craies on Legislation* (8th edn, Sweet & Maxwell 2004) 381.

3 Terrorist Asset-Freezing (Temporary Provisions) Act 2010, s 1.

4 Terrorist Asset-Freezing (Temporary Provisions) Act 2010, s 3.

5 *Black's Law Dictionary* defines a sunset law as follows: 'A statute under which a governmental agency or program automatically terminates at the end of a fixed period unless it is formally renewed'. *Black's Law Dictionary* (Bryan A Garner ed, 8th edn, Thomson West 2004) [sunset law].

6 HLA Hart, *The Concept of Law* (Paul Craig ed, 3rd edn, OUP 2012) 79ff.

Such clauses have been used for a very long time. Despite this, the term 'sunset clause' is a relatively recent term in legal scholarship, established in the US after the Watergate scandal. The term was first proposed by Common Cause, a non-party organisation founded in 1970 with the aim of promoting accountability in the political system.

At that time, the use of a sunset clause was expected to create an incentive for the periodic and comprehensive executive and legislative evaluation of agencies.[7] It is noteworthy that the term 'sunset' was used, as opposed to the term 'sunshine' law.[8] According to the latter, regulatory authorities are required to make available to the public material pertaining to meetings, decisions and records.[9] Further, in contrast with the contemporary definition of the term 'sunset clause', during the 19th century the term 'sunset clause' was used in debtor poor law and referred to the provision authorising obedience after the expiration of the writ commanding arrest.[10]

Nowadays, the term sunset clause connotes a clause limiting the duration of an act. Within the literature such a clause is also described as a time-limitation clause[11] or duration clause,[12] or a temporary provision.[13] However, these terms are not synonymous with the term sunset clause; while there is some overlap between them, they are not identical or coterminous.[14] In relation to a duration clause, it suffices to mention that not all such clauses prescribe an automatic termination date. For instance, the Constitution of Clarendon included a duration clause which prescribed that

> There are, moreover, many other and great customs and dignities of the holy mother church, and of the lord king, and of the barons of the kingdom, which are not contained in this writ. And may they be preserved to the holy church, and to the lord king, and to his heirs, and to the barons of the kingdom, and may they be inviolably observed for ever.[15]

Similarly, there is an overlap between temporary provisions and sunset clauses. In principle, the inclusion of a sunset clause in an act signals its temporal character. Consequently, the correlation between temporary legislation and sunset clauses is not accurate, as temporary legislation does not always contain a sunset clause. This is exemplified by the Indemnity Acts, which are undoubtedly a subset of temporary legislation but have a retrospective character.

7 Bruce Adams, 'Sunset: A Proposal for Accountable Government' (1976) 28 Administrative Law Review 511, 514.
8 Bruce Adams, 'Sunset: A Proposal for Accountable Government' (1976) 28 Administrative Law Review 511, 514.
9 *Black's Law Dictionary* defines 'sunshine law' as follows: 'a statute requiring a governmental department or agency to open its meetings or its records to public access – also termed open meetings law, public meeting law, open door law'. *Black's Law Dictionary* (Bryan A Garner ed, 8th edn, Thomson West 2004) [sunshine law].
10 See Charles E Grinnell, *Poor Debtor Law of Massachusetts* (Little Brown and Company 1883) 207.
11 David Dean, *Law-making and Society in Late Elizabethan England* (CUP 1996) 259.
12 Sir Courtenay Ilbert, *Legislative Methods and Forms* (Clarendon Press 1901) 279.
13 For instance, see Prevention of Terrorism (Temporary Provisions) Act 1989.
14 Further ambiguity is caused by the combination of sunset clauses with other types of clauses such as review clauses or Henry VIII clauses. The analysis of this ambiguity is part of Ch 7.
15 Constitutions of Clarendon in Ernest F Henderson (ed), *Select Historical Documents of the Middle Ages* (University Press of the Pacific 2004) 16.

The most significant example of the use of Indemnity Acts indemnified dissenters who were holding offices, violating the Test[16] and Corporation Acts.[17] According to the Test and Corporation Acts all civil, military and corporation officers were supposed to take the Sacrament of the Church of England, and due to that requirement, dissenters were excluded from offices. Thus in 1728 Sir Robert Walpole introduced the policy of the Annual Indemnity Acts,[18] which were renewed for more than a century until 1828 when the Test and Corporation Acts finally were repealed. An Indemnity Act provided that 'Members of Corporations who have neglected to take the Oath of Office, qualifying themselves by January 1731, indemnified'.[19]

By examining contemporary parliamentary debates, it is assumed that sunset clauses are either ignored or they are to be used only rarely. In particular, the government responded verbatim to the Report of the Joint Committee on the Draft Civil Contingencies Bill (which argued in favour of the use of a sunset clause), stating that 'the inclusion of a provision in an Act that provides for the expiry of the Act after a certain length of time, commonly referred to as a "sunset clause", is relatively unusual and requires careful consideration'.[20]

Moreover, a statement from a Member of Parliament advocating the use of a sunset clause in the Local Government Bill confirms the suspicion that at the dawn of the 21st century, sunset clauses and temporary legislation were treated as an exceptional legislative tool to be used only rarely:

> The Minister will ask why the powers should be time-limited, when so many other powers are not. If that is his approach, it will illustrate the very constitutional point that I seek to make and it will show how far we have fallen from grace. The Minister should be asking why we should not limit the powers in time, because Parliament used to do so regularly.[21]

This picture is similarly represented in the US, Germany and the Netherlands, as Ranchordás accurately remarks that 'in practice, sunset clauses and experimental laws are almost unknown instruments to legal practitioners and represent a minority of the annual production of legislation in the three jurisdictions under analysis'.[22]

However, in the UK, the use of sunset clauses varies. In some fields, such clauses are nonetheless included in a broad spectrum of legislation. For instance, in 2002 the Secretary of State for the Home Department confirmed that his Department had used sunset clauses in five bills introduced by the Home Office.[23] This is not to say that the operation of sunset clauses is restricted exclusively to the Home Department, since sporadic use of sunset clauses is evident across the whole spectrum of legislative activity and when there is a need for a temporary regulation.

16 25 Car II c 2.
17 13 Car II st 2 c 1.
18 Indemnity Act 1727 (1 Geo II c 23).
19 Indemnity Act 1730 (4 Geo II c 6).
20 Cabinet Office, *Government's Response to the Report of the Joint Committee on the Draft Civil Contingencies Bill* (Cm 6078, 2004) 38.
21 HC Deb 23 March 1999 vol 328 col 240.
22 Sofia Ranchordás, *Constitutional Sunsets and Experimental Legislation: A Comparative Perspective* (Elgar 2014) 9.
23 See HC Deb 23 April 2002 vol 384 col 222W.

In fields such as in taxation, their use is evident and a plethora of reports urge their use,[24] but we have to acknowledge that in some other fields sunset clauses are not used at all. This remark is exemplified by the response of the Foreign Secretary to a question regarding sunset clauses in Foreign and Commonwealth Affairs on 21 January 2004. The Foreign Secretary replied that:

> whether a sunset clause is needed in legislation depends on the circumstance of each Bill. In the case of the Foreign and Commonwealth Office (FCO), much of our legislation is to implement HMG's international obligations, so if those obligations do not have a specific time limit, a limit in our domestic legislation would not be appropriate. No Acts of Parliament since 1997 for which the FCO is responsible contained a sunset clause.[25]

Unequivocally, the misconceptions regarding the frequency of sunset clauses and the relatively minimal discussion of such clauses in the UK have resulted in certain neglected normative aspects of such laws. On top of that, not only are sunset clauses an element of the contemporary statute book, but they also have been an integral part of the statute book in the legislative history of the UK.[26]

Indeed, academic literature does not have many reference sources on sunset clauses, and the divergent approaches on the use of temporary laws, recorded in law journal articles, prove that it is a highly controversial topic.

A broader research concerning temporary legislation in the US is published by Gensen, who examines temporary legislation and endorses its use, and he argues that in specific fields such legislation should be the rule and not the exception.[27] In addition, Fagan's analysis of temporary laws is centred around the relationship between legislators and citizens, legislators and special interest groups, and current and future legislators.[28]

Some articles have been published in US journals on the potential of temporary laws (in particular sunset clauses), from the perspective of separation of powers, to enhance the role of the legislature and support its monitoring task over the administration. This idea was originally expressed by Lowi.[29] Adams first argued that such clauses are a tool to restore the balance of power between the legislature and the executive,[30] while Price supports the view that the sunset clause movement in the US is relevant to the growth of bureaucracy and argues that its success depends upon its proper implementation.[31] Further, Davis elaborates on how sunset clauses would meet the objective of reinstating the legislature as co-partner

24 For instance see HM Treasury, *Tax Policy Making: A New Approach* (HM Revenue & Customs 2010).

25 HC Deb 21 January 2004 vol 416 col 1253W. The same statement was repeated in 2007 regarding the past five years. See HC Deb 26 Jul 2007 vol 463 col 1466W. Similarly, in 2002 the Lord Chancellor explicitly stated that no bills of his department in the last five years contained sunset clauses. see HC Deb 14 May 2002 vol 385 col 589W.

26 See Chrs 2–4.

27 Jacob E Gersen, 'Temporary Legislation' (2007) 74 Chicago Law Review 247.

28 Frank Fagan, *Law And The Limits of Government Temporary versus Permanent Legislation* (Elgar 2013).

29 Theodore J Lowi, *The End of Liberalism, the Second Republic of the United States* (2nd edn, WW Norton & Company 1979).

30 Bruce Adams, 'Sunset: A Proposal for Accountable Government' (1976) 28 Administrative Law Review 511.

31 Dan R Price, 'Sunset Legislation in the United States' (1978) 30 Baylor Law Review 401.

with the executive in government, and of combating bureaucracy.[32] Finally, Muskie contends that such clauses are the best vehicle to ensure the proper evaluation of federal agencies.[33]

While there is no discussion at all pertaining to the interaction of sunset clauses with formal and substantive conceptions of the rule of law, in 2001 the Mandelkern report for better regulation endorsed temporary laws in specific areas of regulation.[34] And recently, Ginsburg, Masur and McAdams endorsed temporary laws in policy making as a tool to limit regulation.[35] Also, Ranchordás explored the potential of temporary laws in experimental legislation.[36] But, other authors argue that such clauses do not meet their aim to decrease the amount of regulations,[37] or that they are an inefficient mechanism for oversight.[38]

Their use specifically in emergencies was supported by Ackerman.[39] However, critique of the use of temporary laws in emergencies was raised by Gross,[40] Finn,[41] Ip[42] and Kouroutakis-Ranchordás.[43] In relation to taxation, there has been some support for their use.[44] But there has been some criticism on the ground that they were used as a tool to bypass a procedural budgetary rule.[45]

Legal effect

Sunset clauses have two major legal effects. First, unless re-authorised by the legislature, a sunset clause brings about the expiration of a law on a prescribed date. Expiration, as brought about by a sunset clause, is different from repeal. Second, if a clause prescribes that

32 Lewis Anthony Davis, 'Review Procedure and Public Accountability in Sunset Legislation: An Analysis and Proposal for Reform' (1981) 33 Administrative Law Review 393.

33 Edmund S Muskie, 'Sunset Legislation, Restoring Public Confidence in Government' (1977) 4 Journal of Legislation 11.

34 Mandelkern Group on Better Regulation, Final Report,13 November 2001.

35 Tom Ginsburg, Jonathan S Masur, Richard H McAdams, 'Libertarian Paternalism, Path Dependence, and Temporary Law' (2014) 81 Chicago Law Review 291.

36 Sofia Ranchordás, *Constitutional Sunsets and Experimental Legislation: A Comparative Perspective* (Elgar, 2014); Sofia Ranchordás, 'Sunset Clauses and Experimental Legislation: Blessing Or Curse for Legal Certainty?' (2014) 35 Statute Law Review 1.

37 Vern McKinley, 'Sunrises without Sunsets. Can Sunset Laws Reduce Regulation?' (1995) 18 Regulation 57.

38 Bert A Rockman, 'Legislative-Executive Relations and Legislative Oversight' (1984) 9 Legislative Studies Quarterly 387; Guido Calabresi, *A Common Law for the Age of Statutes* (Lawbook Exchange 1999) 62.

39 Bruce Ackerman, 'The Emergency Constitution' (2004) 113 Yale Law Journal 1029.

40 Oren Gross, 'Chaos and Rules: Should Responses to Violent Crises Always Be Constitutional' (2003) 112 Yale Law Journal 1011.

41 John E Finn, 'Sunset Clauses and Democratic Deliberation: Assessing the Significance of Sunset Provisions in Antiterrorism Legislation' (2010) 48 Columbia Journal of Transitional Law 442.

42 John Ip, 'Sunset Clauses and Counterterrorism Legislation' (2013) PL 74.

43 Antonios Kouroutakis and Sofia Ranchordás, 'Snoozing Democracy: The De-Juridification of Emergencies' (2016) 25 Minnesota Journal of International Law (forthcoming).

44 Martin A Sullivan, 'False Alarms and Real Problems with Budget Gimmicks' (2003) 99 Tax Notes 1129; George K Yin, 'Temporary – Effect Legislation, Political Accountability, and Fiscal Restraint' (2009) 84 New York University Law Review 174.

45 William G Gale, Peter R Orszag, 'Sunsets in the Tax Code' (2003) 99 Tax Notes 1553; Elizabeth Garrett, 'Accounting for the Federal Budget and Its Reform' (2004) 41 Harvard Journal on Legislation 187; Rebecca M Kysar, 'The Sun Also Rises: The Political Economy of Sunset Provisions in the Tax Code' (2006) 40 Georgia Law Review, 335; Manoj Viswanathan, 'Sunset Provisions in the Tax Code: a Critical Evaluation and Prescriptions for the Future' (2007) 82 New York University Law Review 656.

a statute should expire from a certain date, then it is reasonable to assume that it is not valid unless re-enacted. Nevertheless, it will be shown that, in practice, there are exceptions in each instance.

To begin with, note that the expiration, or 'sunset', of an act has the same consequences as if it were repealed.[46] However, as Broom remarks, there is a difference between statutes which expire and statutes which are repealed, since 'although the latter become as if they had never existed (except so far as they relate to transactions already completed under them), yet, with respect to the former, the extent of the restrictions imposed, and the duration of the provisions, are matters of construction'.[47]

To illustrate Broom's remark, it is worth mentioning an early case reported by Sir Thomas Raymond.[48] In 1661, the Deputy Governor of Jamaica enacted laws to tax liquor. In 1663, with the appointment of the new deputy governor, the King granted him the power to enact laws for a period of two years. Accordingly, the new deputy governor passed laws taxing liquor for a two-year period. Upon the expiration of this law, the question arose as to whether the former law of 1661 was to be revived. The Privy Council held that the expiration of an act revives the previous regulation, while repeal does not.[49]

Turning to the second major legal effect, as set out above, the Latin maxim on legal interpretation, *expressio unius est exclusio alterius* (expression of one is the exclusion of the other), applies to sunset clauses. This canon of construction, which is also expressed as *expressum facit cessare tacitum*, means broadly that mentioning one thing may exclude another thing.[50] Hence, the determination that on a certain date the law will expire means that from that date onwards, the law is not valid unless it is re-enacted. However, as will be shown below, this is not always the case.

The application of this maxim is not undisputed. Indeed, it has received robust criticism from several scholars. For example, Posner states that this canon makes sense under the hypothesis of a 'legislative omniscience', implying that all omissions are deliberate.[51] Radin, on the other hand, reverses the principle, stating that 'the question will accordingly be in every case, not whether on the expression of one thing excludes everything else, but whether we are to deny or affirm this rule in this particular case'.[52] In similar vein, Sunstein suggests that the maxim should not be used mechanically.[53]

Furthermore, the application of the maxim by the courts is not always coherent. A series of cases, although recognising the canon of interpretation, reject its application.[54] The House of Lords in an early case ruled that 'there is certainly an axiom of law [. . .]. But that is not of universal application. It depends upon the intention of the parties.'[55] In another

46 Sir Peter Benson Maxwell, *On the Interpretation of Statutes* (4th edn, Sweet & Maxwell 1905) 623.
47 Herbert Broom, *Legal Maxims* (T & JW Johnson Law Booksellers 1845) 38.
48 83 ER 207 (1660) Raym 397.
49 As if 'an Act of repeal is repealed, the first Act repealed is revived'. See 83 ER 207 (1660) Raym 397.
50 See FAR Bennion, *Bennion on Statutory Interpretation* (5th edn, Lexis Nexis 2008) 1250.
51 Richard A Posner, 'Statutory Interpretation – In the Classroom and in the Courtroom' (1983) 50 University of Chicago Law Review 800, 813.
52 Max Radin, 'Statutory Interpretation' (1929–1930) 43 Harvard Law Review 863, 874.
53 Cass R Sunstein, 'Interpreting Statutes in the Regulatory State' (1989) 103 Harvard Law Review 405, 455.
54 *Canadian National Rlys v Canadian SS Lines Ltd* (1945) AC 204 (PC); *Wiseman and Another Appellants and Borneman and others Respondents* (1971) AC 297 (HL).
55 *Saunders v Evans* (1861) 8 HLC 719, 729 (HL).

case the High Court, citing Maxwell on the *Interpretation of Statutes*, found reasonable, proper and applicable in the particular case the statement that:

> Provisions sometimes found in statutes enacting imperfectly or for particular cases only that [. . .] have occasionally furnished ground for the contention that an intention to alter the general law was to be inferred from the partial or limited enactment, resting on the maxim, 'expressio unius est exclusio alterius.' But that maxim is inapplicable in such cases. The only inference which a Court can draw from such superfluous provisions [. . .] is that the Legislature was either ignorant or unmindful of the real state of the law or that it acted under the influence of excessive caution.[56]

Moreover, in *United States v Vonn* the US Supreme Court held that:

> the canon that expressing one item of a commonly associated group or series excludes another left unmentioned is only a guide, whose fallibility can be shown by contrary indications that adopting a particular rule or statute was probably not meant to signal any exclusion of its common relatives.[57]

Beyond this general critique of the maxim, its application in relation to sunset clauses is not always coherent. A characteristic case, from which useful conclusions regarding the construction of sunset clauses can be reached, is *Barnhart, Commissioner of Social Security v Peabody Coal Co*,[58] which questions the consequences of the expiration of a time limitation.

Under the Coal Industry Retiree Health Benefit Act 1992, the Commissioner of Social Security 'shall, before October 1, 1993', assign each coal industry retiree eligible for benefits to an extant operating company responsible for funding the beneficiary's benefits. After 1 October 1993, despite the expiration of the sunset clause, the Commissioner assigned beneficiaries to various operating companies. The operating companies challenged the assignments made to them after the 1 October 1993 deadline. The question for the court was whether the statutory date sets a time limit on the Commissioner's power to assign such beneficiaries to various operating companies and therefore whether a beneficiary not assigned on 1 October 1993 must be left unassigned.

Surprisingly, the court held that the Commissioner's initial assignments made after 1 October 1993 were valid despite not being made in time. The majority reasoned that a statute directing official action needed more than a mandatory 'shall' before the grant of power would be read to expire when the job was supposed to be completed, as the sunset clause meant 'to spur the Secretary to action, not to limit the scope of his authority'.[59] Moreover, Justice Souter, giving judgment as part of the majority, stated that 'if Congress had meant to set a counterintuitive limit on authority to act, it would have said more than it did'.[60]

56 *The State (at the Prosecution of The Minister for Lands and Fisheries) v His Honor Judge Sealy* (1939) 1 IR 21, 32 (HC).

57 (2002) 535 US 55, 65 (US SC).

58 *Barnhart, Commissioner of Social Security v Peabody Coal co. et al* (2003) 537 US 149 (US SC).

59 *Barnhart, Commissioner of Social Security v Peabody Coal co. et al* (2003) 537 US 149 (US SC) 158.

60 *Barnhart, Commissioner of Social Security v Peabody Coal co. et al* (2003) 537 US 149 (US SC) 163.

However, Justice Scalia, in his dissenting opinion, characterised the majority's decision as a disposition upon the Commissioner of Social Security of 'an unexpiring power to assign retired coal miners to signatory operators'.[61] Commenting on the construction given to the sunset clause, Justice Scalia stated that 'this makes no sense. When a power is conferred for a limited time, the automatic consequence of the expiration of that is the expiration of the power.'[62]

Justice Souter circumvented the criticism of Justice Scalia and denied the application of the maxim, holding that no one could disagree with Justice Scalia that:

> when a power is conferred for a limited time, the automatic consequence of the expiration of that time is the expiration of the power [. . .] but his assumption that the Commissioner's power to assign retirees was 'conferred for a limited time' assumes away the very question to be decided.[63]

Having presented the facts and the dicta of this case, it is apparent that the maxim was not applied. *Expressio unius est exclusio alterius* is a linguistic canon, meaning that provisions shall be interpreted in accordance with the rules of grammar.[64] However, the linguistic canons of constructions are not the exclusive interpretive devices to define the meaning of statutes. Judges use various tools and methods, such as legislative history, legislative intent or several constitutional principles.[65]

In principle, therefore, if a clause states that a statute should expire from a certain date, it is reasonable to assume that it is not valid unless it is re-enacted. However, this is not a rule without exceptions. In practice, various factors such as the wording of the provision and its vagueness or the legislative intent can influence and ultimately determine the construction of a sunset clause and the expiration of an act.

Having said that, it is seen that sunset clauses are neither synonymous nor coterminous with duration clauses and temporary provisions. Also, the expiration of an act due to a sunset clause is automatic and instantaneous, without the need for further action, and that expiration of the law is not equivalent to repeal. The expiration of a law, moreover, does not depend exclusively on its wording; rather, other interpretive devices, such as legislative intent, are also taken into account.

Typology of sunset clauses

Identification of the major classifications of sunset clauses is a precondition for understanding their role and the variety of options such clauses provide to the legislature. While the sunset clause occasionally took on a standardised form for short periods, or was part of a

61 *Barnhart, Commissioner of Social Security v Peabody Coal co. et al* (2003) 537 US 149 (US SC) 172.

62 *Barnhart, Commissioner of Social Security v Peabody Coal co. et al* (2003) 537 US 149 (US SC) 174.

63 *Barnhart, Commissioner of Social Security v Peabody Coal co. et al* (2003) 537 US 149 (US SC) 159 (fn 6).

64 Gross defines linguistic canons as the 'rules for interpreting statutory text that are akin to rules of grammar', as opposed to the term substantive canons, which are rules that 'create presumptions about the substantive meaning of statutes': see Frank B Gross, *The Theory and Practice of Statutory Interpretation* (Stanford University Press 2009) 85.

65 Frank B Gross, *The Theory and Practice of Statutory Interpretation* (Stanford University Press 2009) 85.

specific type of legislation, as will be seen in the historical sections of this book,[66] the reality is nonetheless that throughout legislative history, sunset clauses have not had a settled form or a certain place assigned to the operative words and they were used in several types of legislation.[67] Formally speaking, the construction of sunset clauses varies, as there is no specific pattern.

However, systematic research on sunset clauses allows us to identify a variety of sunset clauses, such as: the 'entire' sunset clause compared to the 'sectional'; the 'conditional' compared to the 'unconditional'; the 'direct' compared to the 'indirect'. This typology depends on the construction of the clauses, which produces different results.[68]

Entire and sectional

Until recently, the drafting of a sunset clause was Parliament's concern. With a series of Standing Orders regulating the way Members of Parliament conduct public business, Parliament prescribed that 'the precise duration of every temporary law or enactment shall be expressed in a distinct clause or subsection of the bill'.[69] Hence, the first categorisation of sunset clause, between entire and sectional, is evident from this standing order, which makes a distinction between law and enactment. 'Entire' classifies the sunset clause by reference to the act as a whole, providing the expiration of all sections at the same time;[70] by way of contrast, 'sectional' classifies those sunset clauses which prescribe the expiration of one or some sections only.[71]

As a result, this typology is related to the construction of the clause, especially concerning its scope. A sunset clause may have a more complex construction prescribing different expiration dates for different sections, such as section 15 of the Road Traffic Act which provides that:

> subject to subsections (2), (3) and (5) below, an order under section 14 of this Act shall not continue in force – (a) if it is in respect of a footpath, bridleway, cycle track or byway open to all traffic, for more than six months; and (b) in any other case, for more than eighteen months, from the date on which it comes into force.[72]

Direct and indirect

The second classification of the sunset clause is likewise based on the scope of the provision. A sunset clause is direct when it prescribes the termination of the whole or part of the act which is embodied, while an indirect sunset clause refers to a different act. By way of

66 See Chrs 2–4.
67 Committee upon Temporary Laws, Expired or Expiring, *Report* (HC 13 May 1796) 322.
68 Finn remarks that there are several kinds of sunset clauses, but his analysis is limited to some examples. See John E Finn, 'Sunset Clauses and Democratic Deliberation: Assessing the Significance of Sunset Provisions in Antiterrorism Legislation' (2010) 48 Columbia Journal of Transnational Law 442, 445.
69 Standing Orders of the House of Commons, *Public Business* (2012 HC 614).
70 See for instance The Accommodation Agencies Act 1953, s (2)(4) 'This Act shall cease to have effect on the thirty-first day of December, nineteen hundred and fifty-seven'.
71 Police (Northern Ireland) Act 2000, s 47(2).
72 Road Traffic (Temporary Restrictions) Act 1991, s (15) (1). During the reign of George I, a statute containing two sunset clauses sunsetting two different parts of the legislation in different times was recorded for the first time. See 1 Geo I st 2 c 10.

illustration, a direct sunset clause would provide that 'the duration of the act is three years'. Conversely, an indirect sunset clause is one which provides, for example, that:

> [i]f it has not already been withdrawn by the United Kingdom, a designated derogation ceases to have effect for the purposes of this Act – (a) in the case of the derogation referred to in section 14(1)(a), at the end of the period of five years beginning with the date on which section 1(2) came into force; (b)in the case of any other derogation, at the end of the period of five years beginning with the date on which the order designating it was made.[73]

Indirect sunset clauses are not commonly used in the UK, and the aforementioned example was enacted in 1997. Another paradigm indirect sunset clause is recorded during the Interregnum. The Act stated that:

> no Bill of Tonnage and Poundage shall hereafter pass in Parliament, but such as shall relate and be in Force to compel all Merchants to pay for all Goods and Merchandizes exported or imported from the said First Day of July, 1642, on which Day the former Bill of Tonnage and Poundage expired.[74]

While a plethora of direct sunset clauses are recorded in the statute books, indirect sunset clauses are mainly recorded in constitutional documents. Therefore, the common utility of indirect sunset clauses is recorded in constitutional orders with codified constitutions and a hierarchy of norms.[75]

Conditional and unconditional

The final classification of sunset clauses is related to the expiration date, which might be based upon a condition. A sunset clause is unconditional when the expiration date is certain, and does not depend upon any condition. For instance, the expiration date in the sunset clause is unconditional in section 27 of the Prevention of Terrorism Act 1989, which provides that 'the provisions of Parts I to V of this Act and of subsection (6)(c) below shall remain in force until 22nd March 1990 and shall then expire'.[76] Thus, the expiration date is definite when it is unconditional and, as a result, known in advance.

On the other hand, a sunset clause is conditional when the automatic expiration of the law depends upon a condition such as the end of a war or emergency; for instance, section 2 of the Local Government Act 1916 provides that 'this Act, except the provisions of sections two, three, sixteen, seventeen, eighteen and paragraph (4) of section twenty three thereof, shall have effect only during the continuance, of the present war [. . .]'[77] or the decision of

73 Human Rights Act 1998, s 16(1).

74 See CH Firth and RS Rait (eds), *Acts and Ordinances of the Interregnum 1642–1660* (HMSO 1911) 16 [August 1642: The Ordinance of Parliament, concerning the Subsidy of Tonnage and Poundage].

75 For further examples of indirect sunset clauses in constitutional documents see Ch 8.

76 Prevention of Terrorism Act (Temporary Provisions) Act 1989.

77 Local Government (Emergency Provisions) Act 1916, s (24) (2). This form can have more complicated structures, as exemplified by the Increase of Rent and Mortgage Interest Act 1915, section 5(2), which provides that 'this Act shall continue in force during the continuance of the present War and for a period of six months thereafter and no longer [. . .]'. See Increase of Rent and Mortgage Interest (War Restrictions) Act 1915, s (5) (2).

a Minister, the so-called Henry VIII clause. The Prevention of Terrorism Act of 1974 prescribed that:

> (1) Sections 1 to 8 of this Act shall remain in force until the expiry of the period of six months beginning with the passing of this Act and shall then expire unless continued in force by an order under this section.
>
> (2) The Secretary of State may by order provide a. that all or any of the provisions of those sections which are for the time being in force (including any in force by virtue of an order under this section) shall continue in force for a period not exceeding six months from the coming into operation of the order.[78]

Thus, the expiration date is indefinite when it is based upon a condition. The distinction between unconditional and conditional sunset clauses becomes more complicated where commencement of an act containing a sunset clause depends upon a condition and is therefore uncertain. As a result, the legislator chooses to define the expiration date implicitly in combination with the commencement of the Act. For instance, section 8 of the Imprisonment (Temporary Provisions) Act 1980 provides that 'the provisions of Part I of this Act shall remain in force until the expiry of the period of one month beginning with the date on which this Act is passed [. . .]'.[79] Thus the expiration date is not fixed explicitly, but is instead dependent upon the activation date.

The reason why the legislation might contain either a conditional or an unconditional expiration date depends on the nature of the regulation and its surrounding circumstances. As we shall see in the historical chapters of this book,[80] the early application of sunset clauses was marked by expiration dates that were mainly conditional, such as 'to endure until next parliament', but it will be shown that, with the growth of the rule of law, over time expiration dates have become more definite, and unconditional.[81] This development may have been motivated by practical concerns, but it was also in accordance with the principle of legal certainty and the growth of the rule of law, since those affected could be sure as to the expiration date of the act.[82]

It is readily apparent that a conditional sunset clause in an act engenders concerns regarding its interpretation. Thus when vague expressions such as the end of the war or the end of a particular emergency were used, the identification of the exact expiry date could be difficult. In addition, it was critical to specify the role of the judge in relation to issues of fact, and this had implications from a separation of powers perspective.[83] Conditional sunset clauses are not very common at the present time, but cases concerning the expiration of emergency situations nonetheless provide useful insights.

For example, a case regarding the expiration of an emergency was brought before the Privy Council acting as the highest court in Malaysia.[84] On 15 May 1969, when Parliament was not sitting, the Yang di-Pertuan Agong (hereinafter 'the ruler') proclaimed a state of

78 See Prevention of Terrorism (Temporary Provisions) Act 1974, s 12.
79 Imprisonment (Temporary Provisions) Act 1980, s (8) (1).
80 See Chrs 2–4.
81 See Ch 7.
82 See Ch 7.
83 See Ch 5.
84 According to the Constitution of Malaysia (1957) art 131.

emergency according to Article 150(2) of the Constitution.[85] At the same time and according to his constitutional emergency powers, the ruler issued the Emergency Ordinance, according to which he had the power to issue a series of security regulations.[86] Subsequently, in 1975, even though the Parliament had been summoned four years earlier on 20 February 1971, the ruler issued the Essential Regulations, according to section (2) of which security offences were to be tried without a jury.[87]

The question before the Privy Council was whether the Essential Regulations 1975 were valid.[88] The appellant argued that the emergency had lapsed by 1975, thus the ruler did not have the power to issue the Essential Security Regulations and explicitly pointed out that:

> the test for lapse is whether the circumstances prevailing at the time the emergency was proclaimed were still subsisting at the time the regulations were made: that can be ascertained by comparing the factual situation with the facts set out in the recital to the proclamation.[89]

The Privy Council held that even if Emergency Ordinance, section (2), delegated to the ruler wide powers to make any laws in the future without an express expiry date, the Essential Regulations 1975 were ultra vires, as his power lapsed on 1971 when the Parliament sat.[90] The ruling of the Privy Council was therefore mainly based on procedural grounds.

The UK Supreme Court had, until recently, addressed the expiration of an act only in relation to a Henry VIII clause.[91] A case was brought before the Court of Appeal in 1995 concerning emergency legislation passed in the wake of the Second World War, namely the Import, Export and Customs Powers (Defence) Act.[92] This delegated the power to the government to issue regulations making it a criminal offence to export particular goods to particular countries. It provided that:

> this Act shall continue in force until such date as His Majesty may by Order in Council declare to be the date on which the emergency that was the occasion of the passing of this Act came to an end, and shall then expire except as respects things previously done or omitted to be done.[93]

Nevertheless, no Order in Council was ever made in regard to this Act declaring its expiration, and subsequently the government issued the Export of Goods (Control) Order 1987[94] and the Export of Goods (Control) Order 1989[95] prohibiting the export of several goods with several countries including, among others, Iraq.

85 Constitution of Malaysia (1957) art 150(2): 'if a Proclamation of Emergency is issued when Parliament is not sitting, the Yang di-Pertuan Agong shall summon Parliament as soon as may be practicable, and may, until both Houses of Parliament are sitting, promulgate ordinances having the force of law, if satisfied that immediate action is required'.
86 Emergency (Essential Powers) Ordinance 1969, (Malaysia).
87 Essential (Security cases) (Amendment) Regulations 1975, (Malaysia).
88 *Teh Cheng Poh v Public Prosecutor* (1980) AC 458, 464 G (PC).
89 *Teh Cheng Poh v Public Prosecutor* (1980) AC 458, 464 A (PC).
90 *Teh Cheng Poh v Public Prosecutor* (1980) AC 458, 464 D (PC).
91 About the impact of Henry VIII clause on sunset clause see Ch 7.
92 Import, Export and Customs Powers (Defence) Act 1939.
93 Import, Export and Customs Powers (Defence) Act 1939 s (9) (3).
94 SI 1987/2070.
95 SI 1989/2376.

In essence, the argument for the appellants was that, however broad or loose a construction is to be given to 'the emergency', it cannot rationally be said to have continued up to 1987, and therefore, they claimed, the purported making of the aforementioned orders was an abuse of the powers given by the Act of 1939.

The Court dismissed the arguments of the appellants even though it was common knowledge that the emergency which was the occasion of the enactment was the imminence of the Second World War, with the main counterargument being that Parliament had the opportunity to repeal that Act during all those years but instead chose not to do so.[96]

Founding era

Most discussions of sunset legislation treat this legal concept as a relatively rare and modern innovation in law making, and academics focus more on federalist papers and the founding of the US Constitution.[97] Plutarch, the Greek historian and biographer, in his *Bioi Parallèloi* (Parallel Lives), describes the life of the Athenian law maker Solon and he states that 'all his laws were to have force for a hundred years and they were written on axones or wooden tablets, which revolved with the oblong frames containing them'.[98] According to Plutarch's description, when Solon drafted the Constitution of Athens he urged the Athenians to preserve it for a certain period of time. This description implies the existence of a sunset clause providing that the 'Solonian Constitution' would expire after a hundred years.

Taking into consideration the fact that Athens suffered from political instability, it is more plausible that Solon's intent was not to set a time limit but to urge the Athenians to preserve the new set of laws for an eternity. Hence the time limitation aimed to create a safe harbor and possibly this is the first entrenchment clause subject to a sunset clause recorded in the law books. Alongside with this historical remark, in practice it is argued that a sunset clause with a relatively long effective period might not be differentiated from a permanent law because their effects are similar.[99]

Philosophically, the first reference on the value of sunset clauses is traced in the laws of Plato.[100] But the Roman Empire marks the genesis of sunset clauses.[101] In general, the temporary character of laws was a legal concept already known from the Hellenistic period of Roman jurisprudence. Schulz, citing Cicero, mentions that the most characteristic product of the jurisprudence of that period was the 'edict', which was a *lex annua*.[102] The temporal character of 'edict' was compatible with the tendency of the jurist to prevent the law from being petrified and stabilised.[103] Furthermore, the magistrates, who were annually elected officials exercising executive power,[104] published the *edicta magistratuum* on wooden boards which were destroyed at the end of their term of office.[105]

96 see *R v Blackledge and Others* (Court of Appeal, 22, May 1995, unrep).
97 Jacob E Gersen, 'Temporary Legislation' (2007) 74 Chicago Law Review 247, 249; Sofia Ranchordás, *Constitutional Sunsets and Experimental Legislation: A Comparative Perspective* (Elgar 2014) 18.
98 Bernadotte Perrin (trs), *Plutarch's Lives I* (Harvard University Press 1967) 473.
99 Jacob E Gersen, 'Temporary Legislation' (2007) 74 Chicago Law Review 247, 263 (fn 68).
100 Thomas L. Pangle, *The Laws of Plato* (University of Chicago) 772b–c.
101 For the emergency regime in the Roman period, see Clinton Rossiter, *Constitutional Dictatorship, Crisis Government in the Modern Democracies* (Princeton University Press) 15.
102 Fritz Schulz, *History of Roman Legal Science* (Clarendon Press 1953) 61.
103 Fritz Schulz, *History of Roman Legal Science* (Clarendon Press 1953) 286.
104 G Mousourakis, *The Historical and Institutional Context of Roman Law* (Ashgate Publishing 2003) 286.
105 Fritz Schulz, *History of Roman Legal Science* (Clarendon Press 1953) 88.

During the Classical period, the Roman Empire was governed on the basis of a decentralised administrative model, consisting of individual enactments applicable to each locality.[106] The 'mandata', which was one of the main sources of law of that period, were imperial instructions addressed to provincial governors regulating administrative and judicial matters, and their main characteristic was that they were limited in time and extent for as long as the emperor or their recipient remained in office.[107] Although they had temporal force originally, it became common practice that the next emperor would renew them.[108]

Moreover, the roots of sunset clause are also evident in Roman emergency legislation. As Rousseau points out in his fourth book on 'Social Contact', entitled *On the Dictatorship*, when the Roman Empire was under a state of emergency and the laws were insufficient to guard the order against it, one of the two Consuls was appointed as Dictator for a short term of six months.[109] However, it is not clear whether there was a fixed term of six months. Lintott, citing Livy and Cicero, stresses that the dictatorship was conceived in principle as a brief term in office. Dictators abdicated as soon as they could, although Lintott notes that there was some evidence of the six-month term.[110]

After the 3rd century BC and when the dictatorship fell into disuse, in times of emergency, the Senate had the power to issue a decree, the *Senatus consultum ultimum* (*Final decree of the Senate*), to restore the order.[111] According to this decree, the state of emergency was declared (*tumultus* in latin or *ταραχή* in greek), the consuls were urged to defend the polity, and finally several institutions, such as the senate and the judiciary (*iustitium* in Latin or in Greek αργία), were suspended temporarily.[112] In light of the *iustitium*, Cicero famously observed that *Silent enim leges inter arma* (in times of war, the law falls silent);[113] nevertheless, it is debatable whether the *iustitium* had any set time limit.[114]

Conclusions

The temporary nature of laws as a tool in law making is rooted deeply in our legal civilisation and is traced back in the Roman period. During the previous centuries, a variety of terms were used in order to describe the automatic expiration of laws, but not all of them are synonymous or coterminous; the terms 'temporary provision' and 'duration clause' have a broader application and thus are not identical to the modern term 'sunset clause'. Indeed, 'sunset clause', or 'provision', 'temporary provision', 'time-limitation clause' or 'duration clause' belong to the family of temporary legislation. But what makes 'sunset clause' distinct is its legal effect of imminent and automatic expiration.

That said, the legal effect of automatic expiration due to a sunset clause is not absolutely identical to the repeal of an act. Furthermore, although the reasonable expectation is that

106 Fritz Schulz, *History of Roman Legal Science* (Clarendon Press 1953) 139.

107 G Mousourakis, *The Historical and Institutional Context of Roman Law* (Ashgate Publishing 2003) 286.

108 G Mousourakis, *The Historical and Institutional Context of Roman Law* (Ashgate Publishing 2003) 286.

109 Rousseau, *The Social Contract and Other Later Political Writings* (Victor Gourevitch ed, CUP 1997) 140.

110 Andrew Lintott, *The Constitution of the Roman Republic* (Clarendon Press 1999) 110.

111 C Wirszubski, *Libertas as a Political Idea at Rome during the Late Republic and Early Principate* (CUP 1960) 55.

112 Gregory Kung Golden, *Emergency Measures: Crisis and Response in the Roman Republic* (ProQuest 2011) 89; cf Kevin Attell (trs), *Giorgio Agamben, State of Exception* (University of Chicago Press 2005) 41.

113 Cicero Pro Tito Annio Milone 4.11.

114 Paul Lachlan MacKendrick and Emmett Leslie Bennett, *The Speeches of Cicero: Context, Law, Rhetoric* (Duckworth 1995) 183.

an act will sunset after a certain period, in practice the construction of a clause, and therefore the expiration of an act, depends on various factors which influence its interpretation. These marginal differences make such clause a distinctive tool in the legislative drafting process.

In addition, the variety of sunset clauses and their uses allows us to consider their theoretical framework. Three principal categorisations can be derived from the preceding analysis of sunset clauses. The typology, which is based on the construction of the clause, is the 'entire' sunset clause compared to the 'sectional', the 'direct' sunset clause and the 'indirect', and the 'conditional' sunset clause compared to the 'unconditional'.

The two major variables are the scope of the clause and the expiration date. Although the above categories are clearly defined, they are not mutually exclusive. For instance, a sectional sunset clause can be conditional or indirect at the same time, and, similarly, a direct sunset clause can be entire or unconditional. This is so notwithstanding that the latter variable, and especially the expiration date upon a condition, raises several interpretive issues. The typology of sunset clauses highlights that they are a flexible legislative mechanism that can fulfil a variety of legislative purposes.

Part II

Historical overview of sunset clauses

2 Sunset clauses as an expression of legislative power in medieval England

> A Prince never lacks legitimate reasons to colour over his failure to keep his word. Of this, one could cite an endless number of modern examples to show how many pacts and how many promises have been made null and void because of the faithlessness of princes [. . .]
>
> Niccolo Machiavelli, *The Prince*, Ch 18

Early use of sunsets

Under the royal prerogative

The debate of Coke, Plunknett and McIlwain on the medieval temporary laws

During the late medieval period, the first parliamentary enactments are recorded and the limited sources of that period provoked scholarship which endeavoured to explain the relevant enactment processes. A debate between Coke, Plunknett and McIlwain on the distinction between ordinances and statutes in that period is, in fact, indirectly relevant to the discussion over early uses of sunset clauses.

Coke expressed the view that although every statute is an ordinance, every ordinance is not a statute, because they lack the assent of the Commons or the Lords.[1] On the other hand, McIlwain has explained the difference between ordinances and statutes based on the temporary nature of the former. He explicitly argued that:

> Statutes are enactments 'perpetuelment a durer'. It is their permanence that makes them 'statutes,' and necessitates somewhat greater formality in their promulgation than is necessary in acts of a character less permanent and therefore less important. Ordinances, on the other hand, are temporary provisions, which are not considered to affect the permanent law unless they are re-enacted 'in form of a statute,' as they often were.[2]

However, Plunknett disagrees with the distinction grown by McIlwain and supports the view that during the first century of parliamentary activity, the term 'ordinance' is used

1 Sir Edward Coke, *The First Part of the Institutes of the Laws of England Vol I* (19th edn, J&WT Clarke 1832) 234.

2 Charles Howard McIlwain, 'Magna Carta and Common Law', in Henry Elliot Malden (ed), *Magna Carta Commemoration Essays* (Lawbook Exchange 2005) 122, 145.

interchangeably with the term 'statute', as there is no distinction between them and both indicate parliamentary enactments.[3]

By contextualising the debate between Coke, Plucknett and McIlwain on ordinances and statutes, it is apparent that the temporary nature of the laws has already been a concern of scholarship, and divergent opinions were expressed in relation to the distinction between ordinances and statutes; these opinions were based on the alleged temporary nature of the former.

While nowadays sunset clauses are scattered throughout statute books on a worldwide scale, and despite the fact that the origin of the term 'sunset clause' is traced to the 20th century,[4] the question of how long it was a part of UK parliamentary legislation is a mystery.

Therefore, the central questions are the following: (1) when was the first sunset clause used in legislation, (2) what was the first utility of such clauses in public legislation and (3) how were they developed? These questions, however, are relevant to the emergence of Parliament in the law making of medieval England.

Sunset clauses as a response to parliamentary petitions

Until recently, the orthodoxy among scholars was that the origin of Parliament can be traced back to the mid-13th century. Nonetheless, there is still some disagreement on the reasons that transformed the court of the king into the Parliament.[5] At the inception of the constitutional change and the emergence of Parliament in the legislative process, even if the extent of the influence of Parliament and especially of the Commons in legislation is debatable among academics,[6] it is beyond dispute that Parliament started to have a more active role in legislation through the petition process.

The early use of sunset clauses was associated with amendments made at the king's behest, which reveals the king's unwillingness to allow his royal prerogative to be undermined by

3 See Theodore Plucknett, *Statutes and Their interpretation in the First Half of the Fourteenth Century* (Lawbook Exchange 2005) 33 ('[N]either of these words was as yet a technical term, and neither had any special meaning').

4 For further details, see Ch 1.

5 Pollard argues that 'so long as parliament had mainly to deal with individual petitions, it remained predominantly a court of law; as soon as common petitions supersede individual petitions, parliament becomes a legislative body'. See AF Pollard, *The Evolution of Parliament* (2nd edn, Longmans Green 1926) 118. Pollard, reciting a quotation by Fleta, a pseudonymous author who states that 'habet enim rex curiam suam in consilio suo in parliamentis suis' (The King has his Court counselling him in his Parliament), argues that in the medieval Parliament the judiciary, the executive and the legislature were exercised by the king in Parliament: AF Pollard, *The Evolution of Parliament* (2nd edn, Longmans Green 1926) 24. Richardson focuses on the mixture of legal and political tasks: see HG Richardson, 'The Origin of Parliament' (1928) 11 Transaction of the Royal Historical Society 137, 154ff. Harriss highlights the frequency of the sessions, and argues that it occurred in the 13th century due to the frequency of its sessions, as in a forty-year period there were forty-four assemblies. See GL Harriss, *King, Parliament and Public Finance in Medieval England to 1369* (Clarendon Press 1975) 75. Pasquet emphasises the King's desire for financial support: see D Parquet, *An Essay on the Origins of the House of Commons* (CUP 1925) 177. Maitland stresses the role of consent between the King and the body: see FW Maitland, *The Constitutional History of England: A Course of Lectures* (HAL Fisher ed, CUP 1908) 74. But Maddicott links the genesis of this institution back to the Germanic assemblies in the 10th century: see JR Maddicott, *The Origins of the English Parliament, 924–1327* (OUP 2010) 5.

6 Howard L Gray, *The Influence of the Commons on Early Legislation* (Harvard University Press 1932); SB Chrimes, *English Constitutional Ideas in the Fifteenth Century* (CUP 1936) 236.

permanent legislation. The first use of sunset clauses is dated from the period of Edward III. Edward III, also known as Edward of Windsor, became king at the age of fourteen and he reigned for fifty years.[7] During the reign of Edward III, remarkable developments in law making were recorded. In particular in 1337, during the eleventh year of his reign, the prodigy of Henry VIII clause is recorded,[8] while the first sunset clause is recorded in 1368. A petition made in the name of the 'mayor, aldermen and commons of the city of London and all other cities and boroughs of England' was suggested in the Parliament and the King accepted the petition, at least for a certain period of time, stating that:

> It is agreed that those of London and no other shall sell victuals (and nothing else) at retail only, and this of the king's special grace, until the next parliament, on condition that it shall be properly regulated and governed in the meantime to the common profit; and it is not the king's intention that any prejudice should be incurred by aliens who have franchises by royal charters.[9]

Secondary sources provide us with useful information regarding the surrounding environment, in particular the aforementioned petition aimed to amend the Statute of York of 1335,[10] which was confirmed by the Statute of York in 1351,[11] conferring the freedom to trade throughout England upon all merchants both English and alien. The Londoners had repeatedly sought release from its terms,[12] and, surprisingly, this time their request was approved, although only for a short period of time.

The reason why the King decided to add the sunset clause is unknown. However, looking at the facts, it may be reasonable to infer that the sunset clause was added to the proposed petition by Edward III in order to accept amendment to the Statute of York. In this way, all sides were satisfied. Thus Parliament's request was satisfied, though for a limited time, and the King did not allow the amendment to be final and thus binding on him forever.

While no sunset clause is recorded until the end of the reign of Edward III, the second sunset clause is recorded during the reign of Richard II. Richard II succeeded his grandfather

7 In January 1327, during the first Parliament after the coronation of Edward III, a temporary statute entitled 'Indemnity for those who took part with the King and his Mother' was adopted to last 'till the Day of the Coronation of the same King'. See 1 Edw III st I c I. This indemnity act, which was related to the opposition of Thomas late Earl of Leicester and Lancaster to Edward III's father, Edward II, has a retrospective character and thus the provision specifying the temporary duration is not classified as a sunset clause. For further details see *Cobbett's Parliamentary History of England Vol I* (Hansard 1806) 81ff.

8 A law is entitled 'exportation of Wools prohibited' and provided that '[. . .] no Merchant, foreign or denizen, [. . .] shall [bring or cause to be brought] by himself nor by other, privily nor apertly from henceforth any Wools out of the Realm, till by the King and his Council it be thereof otherwise provided': see 11 Edw III c 1. This clause is probably the origin of a Henry VIII clause and not a sunset clause, as it does not prescribe the automatic expiration of the act and delegates power to the King and the Council to terminate the relevant regulation.

9 Rot Parl C 65/25 II 296. Accordingly, it was enacted as the 42 Edw III c 7 statute entitled 'Londoners privileged to sell at retail victuals only' and providing that 'it is accorder, that they of London and none other shall sell at retail Victuals only, and that of the King's special grace, till the next parliament, upon condition, that it be well ruled and governed in the mean Time to the common Profit: And it is the King's Mind, that no Prejudice he done to Aliens, which have Franchises by the King's Charters'.

10 9 Edw III st 1 c 1.

11 25 Edw III st 3 c 2.

12 Rot Parl C 65/25 II 294.

in 1377 and he reigned until 1399 when he was deposed. His reign was marked by several significant tensions such as the Peasants' Revolt in 1381 and the Appellant crisis in 1387.[13]

In 1383, Richard II summoned two parliaments, as the concern of the King was the defence of the kingdom and he was in need to secure grants of taxation.[14] During the second Parliament, a petition was submitted regarding the procedural issue of the writ of debt,[15] and the King's response was:

> It is agreed that in this particular case and in all others where mainprise is involved and a writ of supersedeas is grantable, if the persons bailed do not appear at all before the justices on the day specified in the said mainprise, and thus the plaintiff is delayed; then let the said mainpernors be answerable to the plaintiff for a certain sum, to be determined at the discretion and advice of the justices; giving just consideration to the sum of the damage and loss suffered by the plaintiff, and the nature of the thing demanded. And this ordinance shall remain on trial only until the next parliament.[16]

The reason behind the Richard II accepting this petition as temporary is unknown. According to secondary sources, during that parliamentary session there was a tension between the King and the Parliament, and despite the fact the King was not willing to accept challenges to his exercise of prerogative, he had to treat some of the petitions with a conciliatory approach.[17]

After the deposition of Richard II, his cousin Henry of Bolingbroke usurped the throne and became King of England, officially known as Henry IV. The new King met hostile opposition during his first parliaments,[18] and possibly this affected his stance towards the submitted petitions. Interestingly, more frequent is the use of sunset clauses during his reign.

In particular, during the third Parliament on September 1402, a common petition was submitted regarding shoemakers and cordwainers in order to allow them to tan leather.[19] In

13 For more details see Nigel Saul, *Richard II* (Yale University Press 1999) 56ff and 176ff.

14 *Cobbett's Parliamentary History of England Vol I* (Hansard 1806) 180.

15 'Also, the commons pray: whereas it is the practice in the kingdom that when a man has sued another by writ of debt, trespass or account, in such a way that the defendant person is attached by writ of capias and led before the justices, and the parties having pleaded and been given a date of trial, on that day the defending party with all his goods and chattels leaves the county, and only the mainpernors answer to our lord the king. May it please our lord the king in this present parliament thus to ordain in such case: first, that the mainpernors have the means to bear the cost of any judgment: and that if they do not appear before the justices on their appointed day, they be charged to answer towards the parties for the defendant, as if he were there in person'. See Rot Parl C 65/41 III 161.

16 Accordingly, the statute 7 Ric II c 17 was enacted entitled 'When mainpernors shall be liable on damages by delay', including the following clause: 'and this ordinance shall endure in Assay till the next parliament only'.

17 Nigel Saul, *Richard II* (Yale University Press 1999) 147.

18 Pollar AJ Pollard, 'Lancastrian Constitution Experiment Revised: Henry IV, Sir John Tiptoft, and the Parliament of 1406' (1995) 14 Parliamentary History 103.

19 Rot Parl C 65/65 III 496. According to Patent Rolls, this petition was submitted also during the reign of Richard II who approved it adding a sunset clause to endure until the next Parliament. This Common petition, which is noticeable due to the wording of this primary source, because this legislation is characterised as 'grant, until the next Parliament, to the shoemakers and cordwainers (allutarios) of London', is not recorded in the Parliament Rolls. See Calendar of Patent Rolls, *Rich II Vol I* (HMSO 1895–909) 132.

practice the aforementioned petition amended a statute dated from the thirteenth year of the reign of King Richard II that provided that no shoemaker shall be a tanner.[20]

According to the parliamentary rolls, the King's answer was the following: 'the king wishes for the assay to be fixed until the next parliament'.[21]

Moreover, the King approved a petition with reference to customs and the export of bullion from the realm, adding the condition that it shall last until the next Parliament.[22] In addition, another common petition was presented regarding alien merchants, and the King's answer was:

> let this be committed to the council, and let the same council have the power by authority of parliament to ordain a remedy for it by their discretion, by whatever means seem to them most profitable for the king and the realm, between now and the next parliament.[23]

Finally, during the fifth Parliament in October 1404, on the common petition regarding the merchants at Ipswich and Yarmouth,[24] the King's answer was 'let the passage of wool, hides and woolfells, with the tonnage of the wool, be at Ipswich as well as at Yarmouth, for a trial period until the next parliament'.

Conclusions

The following conclusions can be drawn from the early statutes containing a sunset clause. First, the sunset clause was proposed by the King as a condition in order to approve the proposed petition and consequently in order to enact the relevant law or to amend existing legislation. Second, it is significant that the relevant petitions had financial implications and their aim was to support a specific target group, for instance the shoemakers or the merchants. At that time, the merchants and traders were not part of feudal society, but their wealth and their role in the economy and the revenues of the King were significant.[25]

Third, it is noteworthy that the King provided the reason for use of the sunset clause, which was mainly the 'trial period'. However, it is questionable whether it was an excuse or a real reason. From the parliamentary rolls of every following year, there is no evidence whether the law was renewed or whether its effectiveness was discussed.[26] That said, the

20 See 13 Ric II Stat 1 c 12.

21 Rot Parl C 65/65 III 496. Accordingly, it was enacted in the statute 4 Hen IV c 35 providing that 'this Statute be put in Assay, and hold Place till the next Parliaments'.

22 Rot Parl C 65/65 III 509; and the statute 4 Hen IV c 16 entitled 'The statutes forbidding exporting of gold and silver' was enacted.

23 Rot Parl C 65/65 III 511.

24 Rot Parl C 65/67 III 556.

25 For more analysis about the role of the merchants see Douglass C North, *Understanding the Process of Economic Change* (Princeton University Press 2005).

26 On several occasions, though, petitions were recorded renewing temporary legislation. For instance: 'This was another petition concerning pleading. The commons of the counties of Hereford, Gloucester and Shropshire which adjoin the marches of Wales, and the commons of the counties of Somerset, Bristol and Cheshire humbly beseech: that whereas at the parliament held at Westminster in the twentieth year of the blessed reign of our present sovereign lord the king it was ordained by the authority of the said parliament that [. . .]', and the King's response was, 'The king wills that the ordinance made in the parliament held at Westminster in the twentieth year of his noble reign [1442] for such distraints taken, to be enforced for seven years, shall take effect and be enforced until the next parliament, and then it shall expire.' See Rot Parl C 65/99 V 151.

parliamentary rolls do not give any insight into Parliament's reaction to the amendment limiting the duration of the proposed statute. Nonetheless, it is probable that the MPs were satisfied with the approval of their petition in spite of its temporary basis, since the adopted temporary legislation still accorded with their interests and ultimately marked a victory for them.

Finally, in relation to the academic debate between Coke, Plunckett and McIlwain on the distinction between ordinances and statutes, it can be seen that the temporariness of laws was not relevant to that distinction. Therefore, McIlwain's argument that the difference between ordinances and statutes was based on the temporary nature of the former is not convincing. Rather, the temporariness of the laws was more relevant to the balance of powers between the King and Parliament.

Sunset clauses as a restriction to Common petitions

The debate of Gray and Chrimes on the influence of the Commons on legislation

Henry IV summoned a parliament for 24 March 1413, but he died on 20 March.[27] The same day, his son became king and thus the Parliament of March 1413 became his first Parliament. During the first Parliament of Henry V in 1413, no sunset clauses are recorded in the enacted laws. However, at the beginning of the second Parliament in April 1414, an unusual petition was submitted by the Commons. The petition provided that:

> [O]ur sovereign lord, [. . .] just as it has always been their liberty and prerogative that no statute of law should be made without their consent [. . .] that from henceforth, as a result of a complaint of the commons concerning any wrongdoing for which they are asking for a remedy through the common speaker, or else by written petition, that no law should ever be made thereon and engrossed as statute and law which changes the sense or meaning of what is requested by the common speaker or of the aforesaid petitions proffered in writing, either through additions or omissions, or by any kind of term or terms, without the assent of the aforesaid commons. Considering, our sovereign lord, that it is only the intention of your commons, if they ask you two or three things, or as many as they wish, verbally or in writing, that it should always be the prerogative of your high regality to grant those that you desire and to refuse the rest.[28]

The background and context to this petition was that during the Parliament of 1413, the King approved several petitions submitted by the Commons, but the final wording of the relevant statutes enacted was divergent. Gray presents the divergence that occurred between the submitted petitions and the relevant enacted statutes.[29] This petition led to a discussion in academia regarding its significance and its contribution to the constitutional history of medieval England.

Gray, examining the amendments to the petitions submitted to the following Parliaments, concludes that it was a turning point in the Commons' struggle to influence legislation, as

27 *Cobbett's Parliamentary History of England Vol I* (Hansard 1806) 318–9.

28 Rot Parl C 65/74 IV 22.

29 Howard L Gray, *The Influence of the Commons on Early Legislation* (Harvard University Press 1932) 265.

the Commons claimed the right to confirm or reject amendments which changed their intent and, at least for a period, their claim was admitted.[30]

However, Gray adds two reservations limiting the effect of this conclusion. First, he explicitly states that the Crown admitted the Commons' claim to confirm or reject amendments at least for a period of time.[31] Second, he argues that the amendments henceforth took the form of limiting the duration of the statutes.[32] Furthermore, he argues that these amendments limiting the duration of statutes were 'minor amendments' and were considered 'as within the king's prerogative, just as the right to reject a commons petition'.[33]

From another point of view, Chrimes focused on the King's reply, which stated that:

> the king of his special grace grants that from henceforth nothing shall be enacted relating to the petitions of his commons which is contrary to what they have requested, whereby they shall be bound without their consent. Saving always to our liege lord his royal prerogative to grant and deny whichever of the aforesaid petitions and requests he desires.[34]

He characterised the King's response as 'even nugatory', because the King not only totally ignored the petitioned claims but also repeated that nothing should be enacted to the Commons' petition which was contrary to his will.[35] Moreover, Chrimes criticised Gray's argument that the amendment sunsetting statutes were insignificant, in order to strengthen his thesis that the royal promise of 1414 was not a landmark in the constitutional history of medieval England.[36]

The common ground in both approaches is the fact that the king has the right to amend legislation initiated by Common petitions, limiting their duration by using a sunset clause. Indeed, during the following Parliaments, Henry V exercised his power to amend legislation proposed by Common petitions, limiting its duration according to his will. A paradigm of the sunset clause's use took place during the absence of the Henry V in France in 1421. In six Common petitions submitted, time limits were imposed to endure 'till the Parliament which shall be first holden after the King's Return into England from beyond the Sea'.[37]

Gray's work reveals considerable information regarding the use of sunset clauses following the reign of Henry VI. During the Parliaments of 1422–51, twenty-nine amendments were made limiting the duration of statutes.[38] Even in the first Parliament of Henry VI, in November 1422, which lasted less than six weeks in the aftermath of Henry V's death,[39] a sunset

30 Howard L Gray, *The Influence of the Commons on Early Legislation* (Harvard University Press 1932) 169.
31 Howard L Gray, *The Influence of the Commons on Early Legislation* (Harvard University Press 1932).
32 Howard L Gray, *The Influence of the Commons on Early Legislation* (Harvard University Press 1932) 282.
33 Howard L Gray, *The Influence of the Commons on Early Legislation* (Harvard University Press 1932).
34 Rot Parl C 65/74 IV 22.
35 SB Chrimes, *English Constitutional Ideas in the Fifteenth Century* (CUP 1936) 162.
36 SB Chrimes, *English Constitutional Ideas in the Fifteenth Century* (CUP 1936) 163.
37 9 Hen V st 1 c 2; 9 Hen V stl c 3; 9 Hen V st 1 c 4; 9 Hen V st 2 c 8; 9 Hen V st 2 c 9; 9 Hen V st 2 c 10.
38 Howard L Gray, *The Influence of the Commons on Early Legislation* (Harvard University Press 1932) 314.
39 See Chris Given-Wilson (ed), *The Parliamentary Rolls of Medieval England 1275–1504 Vol X* (Boydell Press 2005) 2.

clause was recorded. Six Common petitions were submitted in total: the first concerned the proper practice to be pursued in chancery suits;[40] the second, abuses in purveyance;[41] the third, bad behaviour of wild Irishmen who were studying at the University of Oxford;[42] the fourth, the terms and conditions of office of sheriffs;[43] the fifth, the operation of merchant law in the staples;[44] and the sixth, appointments to offices.[45]

The sunset clause added to the fifth common petition related to the 'easement and profit of the Merchants'.[46] It is remarkable that the King's response did not explicitly mention the time limitation of the statute. The King replied that:

> As regards having confirmations according to the desire of this petition, let them have such confirmations without clause de licet as they have duly had in the past. And as regards the rest of the said petition, let it be done as it has been permitted to be done and used previously in similar cases.[47]

Conclusions

The findings on sunset clauses during the reigns of Henry V and Henry VI lead to the following conclusions. First, the frequency of sunset clauses increased. However, this might be related to the fact that the number of statutes enacted by Common petition increased while this legislative process was developing. Gray shows that during the reign of Henry VI, of the 185 statutes enacted, 162 arose from Common petitions.[48] Moreover, it became clear that the sunset clause was an amendment proposed by the King limiting the duration of the statute. As mentioned above, the King's right to accept or reject a petition was absolute, and thus the limitation of an act for a certain period of time is, in effect, a less negative reaction than rejection, and there was always the hope that such legislation might be renewed.

From the legal positivism perspective, the Common petitions aimed either to limit the royal prerogative or to promote a framework favouring a specific group, especially the merchants. But the Crown, as the one holding the sovereign power, was not willing to limit royal rights indefinitely. The King was willing to bind himself in legislation providing financial benefits for certain groups like merchants. It comes as no surprise then that the vast majority of sunset legislation was related to trade and commerce. Indeed, Maitland accurately observed that:

> [L]egislation begins with Magna Carta and goes on through the Middle Ages; one sees in such legislation at once the admitted claim of parliament to set limits to royal rights, and on the other hand the extreme difficulty that there is in getting the king to observe any laws which [are made] against his pecuniary interests.[49]

40 Rot Parl C 65/84 IV [item 41].
41 Rot Parl C 65/84 IV [item 42].
42 Rot Parl C 65/84 IV [item 43].
43 Rot Parl C 65/84 IV [item 44].
44 Rot Parl C 65/84 IV [item 45].
45 Rot Parl C 65/84 IV [item 46].
46 1 Hen VI c 6, 'St 14 Ric II c 2 recited'.
47 Rot Parl C 65/84 IV 191.
48 Howard L Gray, *The Influence of the Commons on Early Legislation* (Harvard University Press 1932) 334.
49 FW Maitland, *The Constitutional History of England* (CUP 1919) 183.

Furthermore, there is no evidence in the parliamentary rolls of any amendment proposed by the Commons or the Lords which limits the duration of a statute proposed by the King or a petition submitted by the Lords.[50] The first Commons' amendment is recorded in 1429, and it referred to misuse of judicial records and was incorporated in the relevant statute.[51] It was attached as a schedule providing that 'les communes sount assertuz a la bille a cest cedule annexe parissint qe les forsprises en cest cedule comprisez soient affermez come parcelle bille' (the Commons asserted in the bill of this schedule which is provided in the annex that the exceptions which are included would be affirmed like this bill).[52] Nonetheless, Gray argues that there is a possibility of an earlier amendment dated from 1406, but no evidence survives.[53]

In conclusion, from the above analysis it is evident that the early use of sunset clauses was an amendment proposed by the King, and there is no evidence that sunset clauses were in the context of the interaction between the Commons and the Lords in the legislative process. The King had the royal prerogative to deny a petition and to veto legislation. As Stubbs stresses, 'it is in the treatment of petitions that the king shows the most strength of will'.[54] The limitation of a statute's duration is undoubtedly a substantial restriction, but it is not a complete rejection. As long as the King had the absolute power to reject a petition *a maiore ad minus*, he had the power to limit its duration. As regards the duration of the sunset clause, the King had absolute power to define it and there is no evidence of any parliamentary reaction to this power.

Early constitutional value

Sunset clauses and the 'Lancastrian constitutionalism'

The discussion thus far has shown that while the legislative role of Parliament was expanded to submit petitions, the King had the absolute power to approve such petitions and could impose a limit on duration. This part will examine the use of sunset clauses during the Lancastrian period. It will focus on two Acts with sunset clauses that led to a fruitful debate among scholars. The first one is the sunset clause in the Act of Henry IV's Parliament, according to which a kind of ministerial responsibility was established.

In 1406, the length-tension relationship between the King and his Parliament reached a peak. That year, a Parliament was summoned which lasted from March until December, the so-called long Parliament, and its end witnessed un unusual temporary bill. In particular, on November 18 the speaker for the Commons, Sir John Tiptoft, submitted a bill containing thirty-one articles and requested their registration in the roll of Parliament.[55] The articles regulated the status of the Council, prescribing, among other things, in article 1 the

50 A fortiori, Chrimes argues that during that period, the Commons did not even have the right to assent to the amendments made by the King to their petitions: see SB Chrimes, *English Constitutional Ideas in the Fifteenth Century* (CUP 1936) 164, fn 1.

51 8 Hen VI c 12.

52 TNA PRO C 49/19/16.

53 Howard L Gray, *The Influence of the Commons on Early Legislation* (Harvard University Press 1932) 195.

54 William Stubbs, *The Constitutional History of England in its Origin and Development Vol III* (first published 1878, CUP 2011) 23.

55 Rot Parl C 65/68 III 585.

confirmation of the members of the council from the Commons,[56] in article 2 a series of restrictions upon the exercise of their authority[57] and in article 6 the advisory role of the council upon grants and appointments.[58]

The ultimate provision, article 31, which signals the temporary character of the Act, provides:

> Also, it was ordained and agreed that all the aforesaid articles and the contents of the same, in the style and manner in which they were pronounced, should come into force and effect from the beginning of this present parliament only until the end of the next parliament.[59]

The Act proved to be a fertile source of controversy among scholars. Addressing the enactment, Stubbs argues that 'these articles comprise a scheme of reform in government, and enunciate a view of the constitution far more thoroughly matured than could be expected [. . .]',[60] while he describes the whole bill as a constitutional experiment and argues for a 'Lancastrian Constitutionalism'.[61]

Likewise, Pollard argues that 'a consensus was reached in Parliament, by mutual consent of Crown and the body of the realm, for limitation to be placed on the freedom of monarch'.[62] In like manner, McFarlane states that 'in fact Lancastrian constitutionalism was not the fruit of a happy partnership between king and Commons but of the concessions made by a would-be autocrat hampered by financial weakness'.[63]

Contrariwise, Brown waters down the theory of 'Lancastrian Constitutionalism', arguing that the reform was dictated by the circumstances and the King's convenience,[64] while Baldwin remarks that 'most of these articles were, indeed, only repetitions of former enactments, which by this time had become familiar'.[65]

Although both sides have sound arguments, the presence of the sunset clause in the bill highlights the significance of the bill. If the bill was just the administrative convenience of the King, what was the reason to make it temporary? While there is no clear evidence that the sunset clause was added by the King, it is more likely that he introduced it for two key reasons.

First, since the law restricted the King's privilege to appoint Council members, the King had a real interest in limiting its duration, and therefore in adding a sunset clause. In fact,

56 Rot Parl C 65/68 III 585.
57 Rot Parl C 65/68 III 586.
58 Rot Parl C 65/68 III 586.
59 Rot Parl C 65/68 III 589.
60 William Stubbs, *The Constitutional History of England in Its Origin and Development Vol III* (first published 1878, CUP 2011) 55.
61 William Stubbs, *The Constitutional History of England in Its Origin and Development Vol III* (first published 1878, CUP 2011) 5.
62 AJ Pollard, 'Lancastrian Constitution Experiment Revised: Henry IV, Sir John Tiptoft, and the Parliament of 1406' (1995) 14 Parliamentary History 103, 117.
63 KB McFarlane, *Lancastrian Kings and Lollard Knights* (OUP 1972) 99.
64 AL Brown, 'The Commons and the Council in the Reign of Henry IV' (1964) 79 English Historical Review 1, 2.
65 James Fosdick Baldwin, *The Kings' Council in England during the Middle Ages* (Clarendon Press 1913) 158.

the aforementioned bill was an innovation because it introduced a premature form of responsibility of the cabinet government to Parliament.

Second, the examination of the drafting process concludes that the sunset clause was an amendment proposed by the King. In particular, according to the parliamentary rolls, the bill was negotiated by the King and the Lords,[66] but a bargain must have taken place during the legislation drafting. According to *Cobbett's Parliamentary History*, this enactment shows 'that whatever indirect steps Henry took to acquire the diadem, he was resolved to keep it; and is a strong instance, that the best laws for the subject have been often gained under the weakest titles of our kinds'.[67]

Furthermore, a similar bill concerning the Council was proposed by the King in May 1406,[68] but it did not satisfy the Commons[69] and was therefore rejected. In addition, the construction of the clause which provided that the duration would be 'only until the end of the next parliament' demonstrates that the King approved this legislation for the first and last time. Finally, the King, while confirming the bill of November 1406, was concerned with his prerogative, as is shown in the parliament rolls.[70]

The inclusion of the sunset clause in the Act thus denoted its impact on the constitutional order and its effect on the balance of powers between the King and Parliament. The sunset clause was a safeguard to the King's prerogative and also signalled the temporary character of the King's need. When the Act expired, the previous constitutional status quo was re-established.

The early interaction with the rule of law

The early constitutional significance of sunset clauses is not limited to the relationship between the King and Parliament. The use of the clause in *ad hominem* legislation reveals its relationship with the rule of law. A fortiori, it would be regarded as anachronistic to evaluate such clauses from the perspective of the modern conception of the rule of law. Having said that, it is also the case that elements of the rule of law were developing progressively even from the 15th century.[71] Suffice to mention here that Bingham outlines the most important historical events in the development of the rule of law, such as habeas corpus and the abolition of torture.[72] Dicey, in comparing the UK with other nations, states that:[73]

> An Englishman naturally imagines that rule of law (in the sense in which we are now using the term) is a trait common to all civilised societies. But this trait is erroneous.

66 Rot Parl C 65/68 III 585.

67 *Cobbett's Parliamentary History of England Vol I* (Hansard 1806) 305.

68 Rot Parl C 65/68 III 572.

69 See Chris Given-Wilson (ed), *The Parliamentary Rolls of Medieval England 1275–1504 Vol VIII* (Boydell Press 2005) 321.

70 Rot Parl C 65/68 III 585.

71 Shklar identifies two models [archetypes] of rule of law: the first associated with Aristotle and the rule of reason, and the second with Montesquieu and the rule of the institutional restraint. See Judith Shklar, 'Political Theory and the Rule of Law', in Allan C Hutchinson and Patrick Monahan (eds), *The Rule of Law; Ideal and Ideology* (Carswell 1987) 1ff. For a more thorough account of the history of the rule of law see Brian Z Tamanaha, *On the Rule of Law: History, Politics, Theory* (CUP 2004).

72 See Tom Bingham, *The Rule of Law* (Allen Lane 2010) 10ff.

73 See AV Dicey, *Introduction to the Study of the Law of the Constitution Vol I* (JWF Allison ed, OUP 2013) 101.

> Most European nations had indeed, by the end of the eighteenth century, passed through that stage of development (from which England emerged before the end of the sixteenth century) when nobles, priest, and others could defy the law.

In particular, it will be shown how the Commons used a sunset clause for the first time to regulate a specific occasion and at the same time to reassure other constitutional players that the legislation would not have further implications in the future.

The Treason Act of 1351,[74] parts of which are still in force, was significant legislation that codified the crime of treason. This Act contained the first definition of the crime of treason, and distinguished between high and petty treason,[75] while the basic and relevant principles of the common law were largely codified in its provisions.[76] In 1424, a petition was recorded which amended this legislation on treason. The petition provided that:

> [T]he commons pray: whereas in the time of the noble King Edward the third since the conquest, in the twenty-fifth year of his reign at his parliament held at Westminster [1351–2], it was declared by statute in the said parliament what matters should be called treason, among which if a man was indicted, appealed, or arrested on suspicion of high treason, and was committed and detained in the king's prison for this reason, and then escaped from such a king's prison, it was not declared in the past whether the escape should be adjudged treason or not; that it shall be ordained and declared by the authority of this present parliament, by statute, that if any person is indicted, appealed or arrested on suspicion of high treason, as is said above, and is committed and detained in the king's prison for any reason, and escapes voluntarily from the said prison, that such an escape shall be adjudged and declared treason, if such a person is duly convicted of this according to the law of this land. And let the lords of the fee in such a case have the escheats and forfeitures of the lands and tenements of those held of such persons thus convicted, as they do of those who are convicted of petty treason. And this statute shall take place and effect from 20 October last until the next parliament.[77]

This petition altered the scope of the statutes of treason and broadened the definition of the term. Specifically, it included within the definition of treason the case of a detainee who, while suspected of treason, escapes. In addition, this petition requires close attention, as it was the first petition with a sunset clause and this raises a number of important questions. More specifically, the main question is why the petition was time-limited through a sunset clause and, indeed, why the Commons added the time limitation.

The petition, which was approved by the King,[78] has attracted the interest of scholars due to the possible connection and the obvious application of this regulation to the curious case of Sir John Mortimer, which was discussed at an earlier stage of the same parliamentary session. In short, Sir John Mortimer, who was regarded as a threat to the King according to

74 25 Edw III st 5 c 2.

75 For further analysis on the Act, see JG Bellamy, *The Law of Treason in England in the Later Middle Ages* (CUP 2004) 59ff.

76 Samuel Rezneck, 'The Early History of the Parliamentary Declaration of Treason' (1927) 42 English Historical Review 497.

77 Rot Parl C 65/85 IV 260.

78 2 Hen VI c 21.

his Council,[79] was arrested in 1421 by order of Henry V on suspicion of treason. In 1422 he escaped, but he was subsequently recaptured.[80] In February of that year, Sir John Mortimer escaped once again, and as soon as he was recaptured he was brought before parliament, operating as a court, and he was condemned to death for treason.[81]

The complexities of the case are accurately presented by Williams.[82] The controversy surrounds the issue of whether the statute was adopted in relation to the case of Sir John Mortimer and, if so, whether the enactment took place before the escape or after. According to *Chronicles of London*, the aforementioned petition was adopted before the escape of Sir John Mortimer.[83] However, according to *Cobbett's Parliamentary History*, the aforementioned petition was proposed *ex post facto*.[84]

Coke, referring to this particular case, does not mention the statute at all, and he claims that Sir John Mortimer 'was indicted of high treason for certain words'.[85] Hale regarded this petition as independent to the case of Sir John Mortimer but relevant to its precedent. He argues that Sir John Mortimer was condemned according to the power of the Parliament to interpret the Statute of Treason with a Parliamentary Declaration which was 'a particular judgement of parliament in that particular case, to which it was particularly applied'.[86]

On the other hand, Powell correlates the aforementioned petition with the case and argues that 'although prepared to make a special case for Mortimer, the Parliament of 1423–24 was obviously reluctant to allow a permanent statutory extension of the scope of treason'.[87]

In general, the sources concerning the drafting of the petition are limited, and firm conclusions cannot be drawn. But the comprehensive analysis of data and the evaluation of the reports, in conjunction with the wording of the clause, shed light on the case. The aforementioned petition was recorded as the last petition of the same Parliament, while its force was retrospective from the 20th of October – that day was the first day on which Parliament was summoned.[88]

The retrospective character of the law denotes the motivation to include a sunset clause. It is more probable that the Commons wanted to treat the particular case of Sir John Mortimer as exceptional and to limit its impact on the precedent. Therefore, Hale is correct when he remarked that the judgment itself in Mortimer's case was not at all binding in other cases 'because it is checked and control[e]d as to any such effect by the general act of parliament of 2 H[en] 6 which was to continue only to the next parliament'.[89]

79 Charles Lethbridge Kingsford (ed), *Chronicles of London* (Clarendon Press 1905) 342.

80 Charles Lethbridge Kingsford (ed), *Chronicles of London* (Clarendon Press 1905) 281–3, 342.

81 Charles Lethbridge Kingsford (ed), *Chronicles of London* (Clarendon Press 1905) 342; Rot Parl C 65/85 IV 202.

82 See CH Williams (ed), *YB 1 Hen VI Vol 50, 27* (SS 1933).

83 See Charles Lethbridge Kingsford (ed), *Chronicles of London* (Clarendon Press 1905) 283.

84 See *Cobbett's Parliamentary History of England Vol I* (Hansard 1806) 350.

85 See Sir Edward Coke, *The Fourth Part of the Institutes of the Laws of England: Concerning the Jurisdiction of the Courts* (Printed for E and R Brooke 1797) 37.

86 Hale, PC vol I 269. For more analysis on the Parliamentary Declaration on Treason see Samuel Rezneck, 'The Early History of the Parliamentary Declaration of Treason' (1927) 42 English Historical Review, 497.

87 Edward Powell, 'The Strange Death of Sir John Mortimer: Politics and the Law of Treason in Lancastrian England', in Rowena E. Archer and Simon Walker (eds), *Rulers and Ruled in the Late Medieval England* (Hambledon Press 1995) 92.

88 Hale, PC Vol I 269.

89 Hale, PC Vol I 269.

The petition expanding the definition of treason sought to create a special legal regime through *ad hominem* legislation. The Commons' reaction was to restrict the duration of the legislation.

Therefore, the precedent of the Mortimer case could not apply to future cases and the legal framework of treason was not distorted permanently. This sunset clause is therefore of great importance, because it was the first sunset clause proposed by the Commons, and because its purpose was to limit the impact of the Mortimer case on the rule of law.

The use of sunset clauses in the *interna corporis*

Common petitions subjects to sunsets

Henry VII defeated Richard III in the War of the Roses and established the House of Tudors and a new dynasty[90] during which the legislative process evolved and matured. By the middle of the 15th century, the legislative procedure became more definite, as the consent of King, Lords and Commons was necessary for the passage of a bill.[91] Towards the end of the Tudor era, the enactment of legislation became an ever more collective process, while different actors expressed different interests and the reaching of a consensus involved mutual compromise and a conciliatory spirit.

Even if at the beginning of the 15th century the term House of Commons was not used in the modern institutional sense, there is no doubt among the scholars that the existence of two distinct houses in Parliament was clearly understood.[92] The precise time when the split between the two houses, Lords and Commons, occurred is a point of controversy. However, there is evidence that the division existed from the middle of the 14th century.[93] At the same time, Parliament itself established its status as a part of the government, and formed procedures.[94] Thus, Myers acknowledges that 'the whole trend of fifteenth century was for the necessary participation of king, lords and commons in parliamentary acts'.[95]

During the reign of Henry VII and his first Parliament, the Commons presented a petition containing a sunset clause. The petition was entitled 'An act against importing Gascon wine, except in English, Irish or Welsh men's ships', and the sunset clause provided that 'this act and ordinance to last from now until the beginning of the next parliament, saving always to the king all his prerogative'.[96] However, at the same session, another petition aimed to renew an act and expand its duration.[97]

90 For further information see AJ Pollard (ed), *The Wars of the Roses* (Macmillan 1995).

91 AR Myers, 'Parliament 1422–1509' in RG Davies and JH Denton (eds), *The English Parliament in the Middle Ages* (Manchester University Press 1981) 148.

92 SB Chrimes, 'House of Lords' and House of Commons' in the Fifteenth Century' (1934) 49 English Historical Review 494.

93 FW Maitland, *The Constitutional History of England* (CUP 1919) 175.

94 AR Myers, 'Parliament 1422–1509', in RG Davies and JH Denton (eds), *The English Parliament in the Middle Ages* (Manchester University Press 1981) 145.

95 AR Myers, 'Parliament 1422–1509', in RG Davies and JH Denton (eds), *The English Parliament in the Middle Ages* (Manchester University Press 1981) 149.

96 Rot Parl C 65/123 VI 335.

97 The petition was entitled 'An act against foreign merchants bringing girdles, ribbons, lace, etc. into this realm' and the sunset clause provided: 'Afterwards, in the parliament held by Richard III, late in deed and not by right king of England, the same was granted and ordained to be and remain good, valid and effectual until the end of the said four years then next ensuing. The said four years contained in the said

During this period, numerous petitions were submitted with a sunset clause. This means that the draft of the petitions was debated before its submission. Suffice to mention the Parliament of 1495, where five petitions were presented with a sunset clause, namely: 'An act against riots and unlawful assemblies'; 'An act for pulling down weirs and structures'; 'An act for writs of attaint to be brought against jurors for untrue verdicts'; 'An act against perjury, unlawful maintenance and corruption in officers'; and 'An act that sheriffs shall return adequate jurors'.[98]

While discussing some measures concerning law enforcement during the same period (the reign of Henry VII) which were limited due to a sunset clause, Chrimes states, 'why it was deemed appropriate to enact important measures of this kind temporarily only, is a mystery, but it hardly testifies to the firm intentions of the government'.[99] In fact, from the numerous petitions on the same subject (riotous assembly) which have been proposed in the following years during different sessions,[100] it is plausible that the sunset clause was related to the fact that there was not a single point of view in the Commons and the Lords.[101]

There are some indications that sunset clauses were the product of debate before such petitions were filed. Indeed, while a detailed account of the Houses, namely the Commons and the Lords, did not exist, there are sources that can enlighten us in relation to the preparation and drafting of petitions. An illustration is the case of 'liveries'.

A petition presented in 1504 concerning unlawful retaining, which was also known as liveries or maintenance (of army from nobles), requires distinctive focus. The petition was presented with a time-limitation clause to endure during the life of Henry VII. The sunset clause provided that 'the same act shall continue and endure during the life of our said sovereign lord the present king, and no longer'.[102]

---

first act will end and expire at the feast of Easter 1487. May it please your said wisdoms to pray our sovereign lord the king to ordain, by authority of this present parliament, that the said act and ordinance and all of it that touches or concerns the foregoing, be and remain good, valid and effectual until the end of the said four years, and from the end of the same four years until the end and term of the following twenty years': see Rot Parl C 65/123 VI 335. Another example was recorded in 1495, although this time the aim was to make the law perpetual: 'And because the said act of parliament was ordained to remain in effect only until the first day of this present parliament, may it therefore please your most noble grace, by the advice and assent of the lords spiritual and temporal assembled in this present parliament, and by authority of the same, in consideration of the things stated, to ordain, decree and enact that the said act and ordinance, made and ordained in the said last parliament, may always stand, continue and endure in its full strength and effect': See Rot Parl C 65/127 VI 442.

98 Rot Parl C 65/128 VI 458.

99 SB Chrimes, *Henry VII* (University of California Press 1972) 187.

100 In 1504, thirteen petitions were submitted treating the issue of riotous assembly from a different point of view: see Rot Parl C 65/130 VI 542.

101 Cavill argues that the most probable explanation is that the MPs had reservations as to the substance of these laws. See PR Cavill, 'Debate and Dissent in Henry VII's Parliaments' (2006) 25 Parliamentary History 160, 171.

102 Rot Parl C 65/130 VI 542.

From the wording of the petition, it is evident that it derived from a King's initiative:

> The king our sovereign lord calls to mind that where previously various statutes for the punishment of such persons who give or receive liveries, or retain any person or persons, or are retained with any person or persons [. . .] and moreover, our said sovereign lord the king ordains, decrees and enacts by the said authority that no person, of whatever estate or degree or condition, either personally, or anyone else on his behalf by his command or agreement or assent, shall secretly or openly give any livery or sign, or retain any person.[103]

The matter of retaining nobles was of great concern for the kings of that period.[104] As Stubbs points out, the custom of livery was an important element among the conflicts of the previous years.[105] Several statutes were passed regulating the issue.[106] Nonetheless, their enforcement was unsuccessful, mainly because the kings occasionally used the liveries as a standing army, and thus they were not inclined to adopt legislation to abolish it.[107]

According to this petition, the retaining was prohibited unless it was licensed by Henry VII.[108] Cavill claims that a reason for the adoption of the act was the misbehaviour of Lord Bergen's retinue in Kent and Sussex.[109] Elton describes this statute as the 'chief instrument in the Tudor campaign against baronial independence',[110] and Cameron observes that 'The statute of 1504 was the first occasion on which the right of noblemen to retain was called into question. It must therefore be seen as a direct attack upon feudal privilege [. . .].'[111] Henry VII apparently preserved his own standing army, and thus he was in favour of a mere regulation. Contrariwise, the Lords would have been against that regulation.

The petition was approved,[112] and although there is no evidence in relation to the drafting of the sunset clause, it is more probable that Parliament, and especially the Lords, argued in favour and succeeded to impose the first sunset clause on the King's legislation. It is worth mentioning the conclusion of Cameron, who states, 'The relief felt by these nobles when Henry VII's death left them with the problem of coping with an eighteen year old boy can only be imagined. It took Henry VIII and Wolsey just six years to reach a situation in which they also felt it necessary to curb the power of these same nobles.'[113]

103 Rot Parl C 65/130 VI 542.

104 The first statute regulating the liveries is adopted by Richard II in 1377 during the first year of his reign. See 1 Ric II c 7.

105 William Stubbs, *The Constitutional History of England in its Origin and Development Vol III* (first published 1878, CUP 2011) 535.

106 Regarding the precedent legal regime see A Cameron, 'The Giving of Livery and Retaining in Henry VII' (1974) 18 Renaissance and Modern Studies, 17, 22.

107 John A Wagner, *Encyclopedia of the Wars of the Roses* (ABC-CLIO 2001) 20.

108 For further detail regarding the new regulation and the innovation it introduced see A Cameron, 'The Giving of Livery and Retaining in Henry VII' (1974) 18 Renaissance and Modern Studies, 17, 25.

109 PR Cavill, *The English Parliaments of Henry VII 1485–1504* (OUP 2009) 77.

110 GR Elton, *The Parliament of England: 1559–1581* (CUP 1986) 137.

111 A Cameron, 'The Giving of Livery and Retaining in Henry VII' (1974) 18 Renaissance and Modern Studies 17, 34.

112 19 Hen VII c 14.

113 Cameron, 'The Giving of Livery and Retaining in Henry VII' (1974) 18 Renaissance and Modern Studies 17, 35.

However, with the establishment of a detailed account of the work of the two Houses, the indication that the petitions were debated prior to the submission, and that the sunset clause was a product of the debates, becomes trustworthy.

Sunset clauses as a bargaining tool in medieval law making

In 1509 the Lords introduced the 'Lords' Journal', with narrative description of the procedures in the House of Lords, and in 1547 the Commons introduced theirs.[114] The practice of three readings of the bills in each House appeared in the journals, and from the reign of Henry VIII it was regarded as an established rule.[115] In effect, the most interesting part of this thrice-reading process in each House was the interaction between the two Houses, which constituted a negotiation process.

In 1509, during the first Parliament of Henry VIII, the Commons drafted a series of bills either repealing, explaining or limiting statutes by which the previous King 'took advantage of the people', as is explicitly stated in *Cobbett's Parliamentary History*.[116] Specifically, the Commons drafted a bill on time limitation of penal laws according to which the benefit of forfeitures for penal laws was reduced.[117] When the bill was sent to the Lords, during the first reading on 4 February, an amendment was added granting a special framework for crimes against the King and sent back to the Commons for approval. It stated that:

> The Bill concerning the Actions and the information of the People was sent with the command of the Lords amended into the lower house for a second reading, because Lords, it is neither just nor equity, actions against the King to be punished only within one year, but it is decided that actions against the Royal Majesty should be punished within four years, and against the others (will be punished) as it is prescribed in the bill.[118]

During the second reading of the bill on 8 February, the Lords confirmed it as it is stated in the *Journal of House of Lords*, namely 'the Bill concerning the Actions of the People, to whom the Lords assent'.[119] However, on 22 February, the Lords sent back the bill to the Commons containing a sunset clause. The text was as follows: ***Billa de Actionibus Popularibus mittitur in Domum Inferiorem, et additur Actui ut duret usque ad proximum Parliamentum*** (The Bill concerning the Action of the People is sent into the lower House, and that it will last until next Parliament is added to the Act).[120]

114 Howard L Gray, *The Influence of the Commons on Early Legislation* (Harvard University Press 1932) 15.

115 William Stubbs, *The Constitutional History of England in Its Origin and Development Vol III* (first published 1878, CUP 2011) 459.

116 *Cobbett's Parliamentary History of England Vol I* (Hansard 1806) 477.

117 *Cobbett's Parliamentary History of England Vol I* (Hansard 1806) 478.

118 *Journal of the House of Lords Vol 1 1509–1577* (1802) 6. (*Billa de Actionibus et Informationibus Popularibus, lecta secunda vice, missa fuit, ex mandato Dominorum, in Domum Inferiorem reformanda, quia Domini neque justum neque equum judicarunt Regiam Actionem extinguendam uno anno tantum, sed decreverunt Regie Majestati in prosequenda sua Actione quadriennium concedendum, ceteris vero prout in Billa continebatur*).

119 *Journal of the House of Lords Vol 1 1509–1577* (1802) 6 (*Billa de Actionibus Popularibus, cui Domini assenserunt*).

120 *Journal of the House of Lords Vol 1 1509–1577* (1802) 8.

The Commons accepted the limitation, and the statute entitled an 'Acte thath Informacons uppon Penall Statute shalbe made within three Yeres' was enacted.[121] Interestingly, one of the two prototypes of the bill preserved in the Parliament Office is endorsed with the phrase *Le roy se advysera* (The king will consider this further).[122] With the King's reluctant reaction in mind, the following conclusions are reached.

First, the right to amend a bill by limiting its duration was no longer a monopoly of the King's prerogative. The power of the Lords to amend legislation submitted by the Commons is an indication of its upgraded status in the parliament. Mackie accurately points out that during the reign of Henry VIII, the King imposed his policy through the Lords, and he would introduce important legislation in the Lords, while the Lords claimed the power to scrutinise bills submitted by the Commons.[123] As long as the Lords had the power to reject a bill, as they did for instance in 1534 in a bill regulating the sewers, *Billa a Domo Communi transmissa, concernens Proclamationem Actus de Sewers nuper editi siendam, semel et denuo est lecta, et per Dominos est rejecta* (the Bill transmitted from the House of Commons concerning the Proclamation of the Sewers' Actions lately be announced and once again read, and rejected lately by the Lords),[124] the power to limit its duration can be seen as a less dramatically negative reaction.

Second, any legislative restriction on the King's prerogative was likely to be accepted if it had a time limit. This was exemplified with the bill proposed by the Commons concerning the time limitation of penal acts introducing penal procedures. Their aim thorough the time limitation of penal laws was to set restrictions on King's discretion to prosecute its subjects. Both amendments (the former to introduce a distinctive framework in favour of the King and the latter to limit the duration of the Act) proposed by the Lords reduced the impact of the legislation on the King's discretion. Consequently, the sunset clause imposed by the Lords was in accordance with, and indeed was serving, the King's interest. At the expiration of the Act, the limitation would be removed and thus the sovereign would preserve his original power to prosecute without restrictions.

During the reign of Elizabeth I, the legislative process was further developed; in case of disagreement between the Lords and the Commons during the three-stage reading process, the bill was disputed and amended in a committee, forming a 'committed stage'.[125] In addition, another institutional change pertained to the role of the Speaker. The Speaker became the representative and spokesman of the House, while regulating the order of business in the House of Commons.[126]

By the end of 16th century, the committees were appointed not on a de facto basis, but they were standing committees to deal with constantly recurring topics.[127] During the same period, the Committee for Continuance of Statutes was established, with the main focus being on the continuance of expiring laws, and by 1601 this committee had merged with the Committee for Repeal of Statutes.[128] A plethora of statutes contained sunset clauses. In the Law Report concerning Public General Acts, numerous acts entitled 'expiring laws

121 1 Hen VIII c 4.
122 *The Statutes of the Realm, Vol III* (Tanner Richie Publishing 1817) 2 (fn 3).
123 JD Mackie, *The Earlier Tudors 1485–1558* (Clarendon Press 1952) 437.
124 *Journal of the House of Lords 1509–1577 Vol 1* (1767–1830) 79.
125 WS Holdsworth, *A History of English Law Vol IV* (3rd edn, Methuen 1945) 178.
126 WS Holdsworth, *A History of English Law Vol IV* (3rd edn, Methuen 1945) 176.
127 WS Holdsworth, *A History of English Law Vol IV* (3rd edn, Methuen 1945) 178.
128 Wallace Notestein, *The House of Commons 1604–1610* (Yale University Press 1971) 8.

continuance acts' are recorded. In fact, the first Expiring Laws Continuance Act, which was a new method of monitoring expiring laws, dates from 1536.[129]

It is noteworthy that during the first years of Elizabeth I's reign, statutes contained a sunset clause to last for the rest of her life. For instance, in order to protect the Queen from any act of treason after the Pope's call for the 'reconversion of England', Parliament enacted a new Treason Act having effect only during Queen's lifetime.[130] Nonetheless, during the last Parliaments, for sensitive reasons no sunset clause to last for the Queen life was included, as Dean acknowledges.[131] Specifically, out of six Parliaments, thirty-one statutes carried a sunset clause to endure the most 'till the next parliament', while seven were to sunset between three and ten years.[132]

As long as Parliament as an institution was consolidating and the legislative process was flourishing, the regulatory efficiency of the enacted legislation was of growing concern to legislators. As More stated in a speech in the Commons in 1601, 'it is good to have Tryall of Lawes, before wee make them perpetuall [. . .] it were god to Lymittt the Contynuance of this Lawe, and that the deffectes therein might been examined'.[133]

Interestingly, the correlation between good laws and sunset clauses is apparent from the 16th century. However, there is no evidence to demonstrate that the committees scrutinised the expiring laws, while it seems that interest in good laws was not the first priority that made legislators include a sunset clause.[134]

In line with the above remarks on the rule of law, Elton argues that the reason for the time limitation of the statutes was the fact that repealing earlier statutes was 'a clumsy and a rather expensive way of modifying the law in order to suit an interest'.[135] Indeed, as will be demonstrated below, the innovation during the reign of Elizabeth I was the active involvement of interest groups in the legislative process.[136]

In 1584–5, a statute was enacted entitled 'Act touching Artificers usinge the cuttinge of Leather'.[137] It contained a sunset clause 'to continue for the space of sixe yeeres next after this present Session of Parliament and from thence so the ende of the Parliament then next following'. This Act, which repealed an earlier act enacted in 1563,[138] imposed penalties on the 'Curriers', who treated leather with oil and tallow. According to Dean,[139] the Act of 1563, which did not recognise the 'Curriers' as leather-using craftsmen, provoked

129 GR Elton, *Reform and Renewal, Thomas Cromwell and the Common Weal* (CUP 1973) 163.

130 13 Eliz I c 1. A similar sunset clause was included in 14 Eliz I c 1 and 23 Eliz I c 2.

131 David Dean, *Law – Making and Society in Late Elizabethan England* (CUP 1996) 259.

132 David Dean, *Law – Making and Society in Late Elizabethan England* (CUP 1996) 259.

133 David Dean, *Law – Making and Society in Late Elizabethan England* (CUP 1996) 276.

134 It is worth mentioning an act adopted during the parliament of November 1414, which contained a sunset clause. The wording of the Act demonstrates the interest of the monarch in the efficiency of the specific law. The Act, which pertained to the sweaters, clippers and counterfeiters of the currency, provided that 'this ordinance and provision will retain their force and effect, by the aforesaid authority, until the next parliament; in such a way that, if it seems to the king and to the lords and commons who are to come and gather at that next parliament that the same ordinance and provision are sufficient for the aforesaid purpose, then they should be established in that next parliament as a statute to last perpetually'. See Rot Parl C 65/75 IV 35.

135 GR Elton, *The Parliament of England: 1559–1581* (CUP 1986) 134.

136 For instance, it was recorded that 'Englishmen vied for the limited parliamentary time, available to obtain legislation dealing with economic and social matters': see David Dean (n4) 133.

137 27 Eliz I c 16.

138 5 Eliz I c 8.

139 David Dean, *Law – Making and Society in Late Elizabethan England* (CUP 1996) 143.

competition between two companies, the 'Curriers' and the 'Cordwainers'. Both of them, expressing their own interests, promoted bills during the Parliament of 1584–5 in order to amend the Act of 1563. The final bill was against the Curriers' interest, but they managed to add a sunset clause limiting the negative development.

The involvement of lobbyists in the legislative process is recorded even from the reign of Henry VI. During the second Parliament in October 1423, in a statute concerning trade and commerce,[140] the parliamentary rolls reveal the first element of the legislative process involving interaction between the Commons, the Lords and the lobbyists.[141] Their co-operation, however, was aimed at the submission of a Common petition. The merchant delivered it to the Lords, and the latter handed it to the Commons in order to have their advice.

Besides the involvement of interest groups in legislation and the use of sunset clauses as a mechanism to deal with and cater for conflicting interests, Elton argues that such clauses were used extensively in order to enhance the status of the Parliament, adding that:

> in any case, Parliament possessed a more acceptable means to provide against possible mistakes: instead of making permanent laws which might justifiably be repealed, it could and did make laws valid for a trial period and the subject to scrutiny before continuance.[142]

Useful information regarding temporary legislation and the use of sunset clauses can be gleaned from the enactment of the Expiring Laws Continuance Acts. As Dean states:

> [T]he expiring laws continuance act not only reopened old wounds, but they provided the opportunity for further adjustment or amendment. As we have seen in several cases, sometimes the opponents of a measure were forced to secure a time limitation clause as a last resort; to fight the next battle in the committee for the continuance bill was cheaper than promoting an entire bill of repeal.[143]

The multifaceted role of sunset clauses is shown in an anonymous manuscript dating back to the early Stuart period and attributed to a member of the Commons, which provides us with useful information. The passage, which belongs to the Stowe manuscripts collection, was entitled 'Policies in Parliaments', and states that:

> In all penall bills tis held good policye to make them indure but for a tyme, for if it want that clause and be found ill for the state of the comons, it cannot notwithstanding be repealed exept both the Lords and the king consent, whereas otherwise if it stand upon continuance, it is altogather in the hands of the Commons for the dissolving of it, for they may chuse, whether the[y] will continue it, or not.[144]

140 2 Hen VI c 4; 'Recital of an Ordinance of 36 Edw III respecting Merchandises of the Staple'.
141 Rot Parl C 65/85 IV 251: 'another petition, containing five articles, was delivered to the said lords in the same parliament by the merchants of the staple; which petition was then handed over to the said commons by the same lords in order to have their advice on it: which commons redelivered the same petition, with their common petitions, with two parchment schedules attached to it'.
142 GR Elton, *The Parliament of England: 1559–1581* (CUP 1986) 134.
143 David Dean, *Law – Making and Society in Late Elizabethan England* (CUP 1996) 276.
144 Stowe MSS, 354 f 30.

Commenting on this manuscript, Dean asserts that 'since the continuance act still needed approval from the Lords and the royal assent, presumably, the author means that it came under less scrutiny than a single, and new bill of repeal'.[145] Nonetheless, the procedure according to which temporary bills were renewed had an impact on the role of the Lords and on the extent of their intervention. Although Dean is correct in saying that the continuance bill shall be approved from the three estates as a whole, the Commons did, however, have a privilege from the drafting of the continuance bill, and thus they exercised the power to choose which acts would or would not be renewed. Indeed, Lambert admits that 'during the first part of Elizabeth's reign the expiring laws bill began in the Lords but in 1584 and regularly from 1597 it began in a Commons committee'.[146]

Thus sunset clauses were a useful bargaining tool in the hands of legislators throughout the negotiation process. The use of the sunset clause was no longer a royal privilege, but rather an effective negotiation tool. In addition, the Commons had a slight procedural advantage following the inclusion of a sunset clause, as the drafting of the expiring laws bill was their task. This advantage, though, was not decisive, as the Lords could amend the expiring laws bill.

Conclusions

The historical analysis of sunset clauses began in this chapter with the first Parliaments of the late medieval period. Unfortunately, the information available regarding the late medieval period is limited, and the parliamentary rolls do not provide us with sufficient information regarding parliamentary proceedings. Due to the lack of evidence, irrefutable conclusions cannot be reached. However, secondary sources provide us with useful information regarding the origin of the statutes, allowing some firm conclusions to be drawn.

The above analysis, which was based on the apposition of original sources, was designed to show the constitutional value of such clauses during their early use. The limited development of the concept of the rule of law did not favour the study of the interaction between these two concepts. However, as regards the balance of power between the King, the Commons and the Lords, it was shown that the use of this clause accords with the legislative power of each actor.

In chapter 18 of *The Prince*, entitled 'How a Prince Should Keep his Word', Machiavelli famously deduces that a prince never lacks legitimate reasons to break his promise.[147] Indeed, the sovereign, who was supreme law maker with a monopoly of power, had the authority to introduce any kind of legislation and to amend it accordingly. However, when the sovereign power lost this exclusive legislative authority and was bound by the law, any perpetual restriction was deemed incompatible with the interest of the sovereign.

Thus, during the early medieval history of England, when Parliament became an active part of the legislative process, the royal prerogative to amend legislation by adding a sunset clause provided the necessary flexibility and elasticity to the sovereign. The Crown, in limiting the duration of the legislation, complied with the request of the subjects on the one

145 David Dean, 'Pressure Groups and Lobbies in the Elizabethan and Early Jacobean Parliaments' (1991) 11 Parliaments, Estates and Representation, 139, 143 (fn 14).

146 Sheila Lambert, 'Procedure in the House of Commons in the Early Stuart Period' (1980) 95 English Historical Review 753, 780.

147 Niccolo Machiavelli, *The Prince* (Peter Bondanella tr, OUP 1998) 61.

hand, and on the other hand preserved its right to repeal such legislation so as to administer the dominium according to its interest.

This chapter has also considered the way in which sunset clauses could be used to enhance the rule of law, through the case of Sir John Mortimer. Although there are some references as to how such clauses promote good laws, there is no evidence to show that such clauses enhanced the review of expiring legislation.

By the end of the reign of Tudors, the system of government which emerged was that of a mixed government, although not completely articulated.[148] The legislative procedure evolved and became a more multi-party process. The legislative power was shared between different actors: the Crown, the House of Lords and the House of Commons. The power to amend legislation by adding a sunset clause was no longer an exclusive royal prerogative, and as a result, the use of sunset clauses was transformed so that it became a bargaining tool in forming a common ground to reach consensus.

148 MJC Vile, *Constitutionalism and the Separation of Powers* (2nd edn, Liberty Fund 1998) 43.

3 Sunset clauses in a period of transition

> By the virtue of the [legislature] the prince or magistrate enacts temporary or perpetual laws, and amends or abrogates those that have been already enacted.
>
> Montesquieu, *The Spirit of Laws*, Book 11, 6

Sunset clauses in a period of tension

Continuity of temporary legislation and the increase in uncertainty

The era of the Stuarts and the new political circumstances

By the dawn of the 17th century, Parliament had confirmed its role in the legislative process and its constitutional position as an indispensable element of the State. Two major approaches have been recorded among scholars as to the conceptualisation of Parliament's role in legislation in the era of the Stuarts. On the one hand, Sir John Neale and Wallace Notestein identify a contentious relationship between Parliament and the Crown, while on the other hand Sir Geoffrey Elton and Michael Graves emphasise the consensual role of Parliament.[1]

Tanner recognises the institutional development of Parliament and attributes its consolidation to the Tudor period, describing it as one of the great constitutional achievements.[2] Judson remarks that '[t]he Stuarts inherited governmental machinery geared to legal forms and constitutional ideas premised upon the supremacy of law and not of power in human affairs'.[3] The crucial constitutional development of the Stuart period, though, was the rise of a definite opposition to the monarch.[4] According to Zagorin, two conditions allowed the opposition movement to take shape: 'one was the further growth of parliament under the Tudors, the other the change circumstances prevailing after the accession of James I'.[5]

1 For further discussion on the two approaches see David Dean, 'Pressure Groups and Lobbies in the Elizabethan and Early Jacobean Parliaments' (1991) 11 Parliaments, Estates and Representation 139, 143.

2 JR Tanner, *English Constitutional Conflicts of the Seventeenth Century 1603–1689* (CUP 1928) 5.

3 Margaret Atwood Judson, *The Crisis of the Constitution: An Essay in Constitutional and Political Thought in England 1603–1645* (Rutgers University Press 1988) 47.

4 Williams M Mitchell, *The Rise of the Revolutionary Party in the English House of Commons 1603–1629* (Columbia University Press 1957) 27.

5 Perez Zagorin, *The Court and the Country* (Routledge & Kegan 1969) 75. Zagorin mentions that during the reign of Elizabeth, there were opposition groups, but they were a small number and they were loyal to Elizabeth. Perez Zagorin *The Court and the Country* (Routledge & Kegan 1969) 77. Russell,

When King James came to England, he found a set of conditions largely corresponding with his beliefs on governance, but the institutional role of Parliament and its share of powers were discordant with these beliefs.[6] As a consequence, a political discussion developed concerning the nature and location of the highest powers of government.[7] This debate included the relationship of the Crown and the Commons, and the relationship of both with the State.[8]

An unexpected development during the reign of the first two Stuarts was the reduction of legislation passed by the Parliament and approved by the King.[9] The main reason was that both James I and Charles I dissolved the Parliament when it did not comply with their will, with the hope that the next one would better represent their point of view.[10] Four Parliaments took place under the auspices of King James I, and five Parliaments under the auspices of King Charles I. Among them, the first Parliament of James I – that of 1604–10 – passed 97 public and 130 private acts.[11] Between 1610 and 1640, the Parliament of 1614 passed no legislation at all; the parliament of 1621 passed only one act, the 1621 Subsidy Acts; the Parliament of 1624 passed thirty-five public and thirty-eight private acts, with no public bills introduced by the House of Lords;[12] and those of 1625 and 1628 passed only eight public acts each.[13]

Uncertainty from the expiration of temporary laws

The use of sunset clauses was quite frequent during the reign of James I. According to *The Statutes of the Realm*, twenty-six acts containing a sunset clause were passed,[14] with the most remarkable one to take effect upon a contingency aiming for the 'speedye recoverye of manye thousands acres of Marshe Groundes and other Ground within the Counties of Norffolke and Suffolke, latelye surrounded by the Rage of the Sea in divers parts of the said Counties; and for the prevencion of the danger of the like surroundinge hereafter', which was provided to last for seven years.[15]

though, denies the existence of a divided Parliament into supporters of government and opposition. Conrad Russell, 'Parliamentary History in Perspective: 1604–1629' (1976) 61 History 1, 3.

6 WS Holdsworth, *A History of English Law Vol VI* (Methuen 1924) 13.

7 Jeffrey Goldsworthy, *The Sovereignty of Parliament, History and Philosophy* (Clarendon Press 1999) 78. Goldsworthy argues that there was a consensus on the idea that the governmental powers derive from God, but when, how and to whom these powers were conferred, were all subjects of debate.

8 Thomas L Moir, *The Addled Parliament of 1614* (Clarendon Press 1958) 7.

9 Judson categorises the prerogatives of the king to summon and dismiss parliament at his pleasure as the 'head of the state' being the most controversial. See Margaret Atwood Judson, *The Crisis of the Constitution: An Essay in Constitutional and Political Thought in England 1603–1645* (Rutgers University Press, 1988) 24.

10 WS Holdsworth, *A History of English Law Vol VI* (Methuen 1924) 14,15.

11 Alan GR Smith, *The Emergence of a Nation State* (Logman 1984) 257.

12 Kevin Sharpe, 'Introduction: Parliamentary History 1603–1629: In or out or Perspective?', in Kevin Sharpe (ed), *Factions and Parliament Essays on Early Stuart History* (Clarendon Press 1978) 41.

13 Alan GR Smith, *The Emergence of a Nation State* (Logman 1984) 273. According to Smith, the failure to pass legislation was due to a variety of factors: the lack of government legislative programmes, the time consumed by high political matters such as impeachment proceedings, and the early dissolution.

14 *The Statutes of the Realm Vol IV Part II* (Tanner Ritchie Publishing 2007). Among them, eleven acts referred to penal issues (1 Jac I c 7; 1 Jac I c 9; 1 Jac I c 18; 3 Jac I c 8; 3 Jac I c 10; 7 Jac I c 1; 7 Jac I c 4; 7 Jac I c 5; 7 Jac I c 13; 7 Jac I c 17; 21 Jac I c 17) and ten referred to trade issues and agriculture (3 Jac I c 9; 3 Jac I c. 11; 4 Jac I c 2; 4 Jac I c 11; 7 Jac I c 11; 7 Jac I c 18; 21 Jac I c 9; 21 Jac I c 18; 21 Jac I c 20; 21 Jac I c 22).

15 7 Jac I c 20.

At that time, Francis Bacon, who was the Attorney General of England and Wales and afterwards Lord High Chancellor, favoured the temporary character of the laws. He had expressed the maxim ***perpetua lex est, nullam legem humanum ac positivam perpetuam esse; et clausula quae abrogationem excludit initio non valet,*** meaning it is a perpetual law that no human or positive law can be perpetual; and a clause in a law which is *ab initio*.[16] In addition, he undertook an initiative to reform the law digest and especially to review all obsolete statutes; thus he introduced a 'variety of devices which would allow for legal change without sacrifice of legal certainty'.[17]

The tension between James I and Parliament and the reduction in the number of parliamentary acts highlighted a critical dimension of the sunset legislation – mainly, the renewal of legislation containing a sunset clause. In 1610, on the continuance of the statutes, Hakewill, describing how statutes are enacted, mentions that 'bills for the revivall, repeal or continuance of statutes, are usually drawn by lawyers being members of the house, appointed thereunto by the house upon some motion to that purpose made, which is usual at the beginning of every parliament'.[18]

But the so-called Addled Parliament of 1614 produced no statutes because James I dissolved it after it had been sitting for just a few weeks.[19] The main reason was that the Commons was not keen to grant him the subsidies he was requesting.[20] The dissolution of the Addled Parliament led to different conclusions in academia concerning the fifty-eight temporary acts which were due to expire that session. According to the *Journal of the House of Commons*, on 8 April a committee was appointed in order to consider all expiring acts,[21] and on 24 May Mr Moore produced a report according to which the statutes were divided into six parts, and a request was made for the nomination of six subcommittees to evaluate them.[22]

On the one hand, Hinton claims that the acts lapsed, and he stresses that they were not even renewed in the Parliament of 1621.[23] On the other hand, Moir argues that none of the temporary acts lapsed, because the Lord Chancellor declared that 'according to its terms this assembly was to be no parliament, but it was dissolved and annihilated as though no such thing had ever been'.[24] According to the findings, it was commonly accepted that if the Parliament were assembled without passing legislation, the assembly of the members of

16 Francis Bacon, *The Elements of the Common Laws of England* (Printed for C and J Rivington 1826) 63.

17 See David Lieberman, *The Province of Legislation Determined: Legal Theory in Eighteenth Century Britain* (CUP 1989) 183.

18 William Hakewill, *The Manner How Statutes Are Enacted in Parliament by Passing of Bills, Collected Many Years Past Out of the Journals of the House of Commons* (Printed for John Benson 1641) 4.

19 Samuel R Gardiner, *The First Two Stuarts and the Puritan Revolution* (2nd edn, Longmans Green 1877) 21.

20 Samuel R Gardiner, *The First Two Stuarts and the Puritan Revolution* (2nd edn, Longmans Green 1877) 20.

21 *Journal of the House of Commons 1547–1629 Vol I* (1802) 456–7: 'This Parliament not called for Making of Laws; rather for the Execution. – Moveth for Continuance of Statutes which else must die this Session. – That Bill Two Parts; Continuance, and Repeal. – Joined both together. – Many other worthy to be repealed. – A Committee to be well chosen, of Lawyers, and other Gentlemen of Experience; and that this Committee may subdivide itself, and in every, Lawyers, and others, to consider of all Statutes, for Repeal of obsolete, unprofitable, and pernicious Statutes. – This to extend as well to Branches of Statutes, as to whole Statutes.'

22 *Journal of the House of Commons 1547–1629 Vol I* (1802) 496: 'Mr. Moore reporteth the Proceedings of the Committee for Statutes. – That the Heads should be distributed into Six several Parts, and several Sub-Committees to be appointed for every Part.'

23 RWK Hinton, 'The Decline of Parliamentary Government under Elizabeth I and the Early Stuarts' (1957) 13 Cambridge Historical Journal 116, 129.

24 Thomas L Moir, *The Addled Parliament of 1614* (Clarendon Press 1958) 145.

the Parliament did not constitute a parliamentary session but a convention, and as a result the expiring laws did not expire but continued until the first next session.[25]

The issue of the expiring acts became more complicated after the Parliament of 1621, which ended up with two signed acts, the 'Act for the Grant of two entire Subsidies granted by the Temporalty' and the 'Act for Confirmation of the Subsidies granted by the Clergy'.[26] On 6 January 1622, the King dissolved parliament due to the Commons not co-operating in considering a continuance bill, declaring that the assembly of Parliament shall be taken as a convention and not as a session.[27] The dissolution of Parliament resulted in the expiration of seventy acts without renewal.[28] As Jones acknowledges, the immediate result was uncertainty as to whether the expiring acts were to be considered effective.[29] A case was brought before the Court of the Common Pleas upon the statute of 35 Elizabeth c I for the adjuration of secretaries.[30] The court met twice, and on the second occasion it neglected to step in, declaring that 'all the judges were not in the interim, the grand Secretary and the Attorney General were to inform the King that the statute is obscure, and had not been put in jure, and that we could not agree'.

Finally, the Parliament of 1624 solved the whole issue, passing an act repeating the expiring acts by prescribing that:

> [. . .] by virtue of this Act be adjurned ever since the Session of Parliament in the Seventh yeere of his Majestics Raigne of England to have been of such force and effect as the same were the last day of that Session, and from thenceforth until the end of the first Session of the next Parliament.[31]

The solution to the constitutional crisis regarding the renewal of expiring acts was utilised again during the first Parliament of Charles I. An act was passed pertaining to temporary legislation, entitled 'an Act, that this Session of Parliament shall not determyne by his Majesties Royall assent to this and some other Actes', which provided that:

> All Statutes which are to have continuance until the End of the present Session are to remain in force; Proviso if the present Session determine by Dissolution. And that all Billes and matters whatsoever, depending in the same Parliament, not fully determined or enacted before such Adjournement, shall remaine and contynue in the same state and plight, as they are, or shalbe the day of the said Adjournement: And that all Statutes and Acts of Parliament, which are to have contynuance unto the end of this p[re]sent

25 WJ Jones, *Politics and the Bench, The Judges and the Origins of the English Civil War* (George Allen & Unwin 1971) 157.

26 *The Statutes of the Realm Vol IV Part II* (Tanner Richie Publishing 2007) 1208. However, the text of the statutes is not included.

27 James F Larkin and Paul Hughes (eds), *Stuart Royal Proclamations Vol 1* (Clarendon Press 1973) 527: 'A Proclamation Declaring his Majesties pleasure concerning the dissolving of the present Convention of Parliament'.

28 WJ Jones, *Politics and the Bench, The Judges and the Origins of the English Civil War* (George Allen & Unwin 1971) 80.

29 WJ Jones, *Politics and the Bench, The Judges and the Origins of the English Civil War* (George Allen & Unwin 1971) 81.

30 *The Reports of that Reverend and Learned Judge Sir Richard Hutton* (2nd edn, Richards and Edward Atkins 1682) 61 [The Vacation after Hil 20 Jac].

31 21 Jac I c 28.

> Session, shall be of full force after the said Adjournement, untill this p[re]sent Session be fully ended and determined. And if this Session shall determine by dissolucion of this p[re]sent Parliament, then all the Acts aforesaid, shalbe contynued untill the end of the first Session of the next Parliament.[32]

This statute aimed to remove any doubts regarding the continuance of the temporary acts expiring during the Parliament of 1625 in the event of non-renewal due to dissolution. In fact, the session of the Parliament of 1625 did end in dissolution without further action having been taken; however, the temporary acts continued until the end of the first session of the next parliament.

The dissolution of the parliaments during that period without having temporary legislation renewed revealed another critical dimension of sunset legislation with implications for the balance of powers. As Gensen and Posner have pointed out, 'often decisions about the timing of a new law are just as critical as decisions about its content'.[33] Sunset legislation has two temporal considerations: first, adoption of the legislation; and second, termination with the prospect of renewal. The value of sunset legislation with a stipulation for termination is the fact that the decision making process is lengthened through postponement to a desirable moment in the future. Benefits of sunset legislation thus include confirmation of the institutional capacity to renew or not renew a specific regulation. As a result, the continuance bill is not a typical procedure, and its importance depends on the constitutional environment.

More specifically, on the one hand the Crown was dependent on Parliament for the renewal of the temporary legislation, and on the other hand Parliament's task of renewing the legislation was made difficult by the King's dissolution. When, during the era of King James I, the constitutional balance between the Crown and Parliament was in tension, interdependence between those two institutions was not possible. This constitutional tension resulted in the non-renewal of the temporary legislation.

Sovereignty and sunsets in the king's revenue

Sunsets in the king's revenue

During the era of the first Stuarts, the parliamentary workload was concentrated on the financial needs of the King.[34] King James I imposed a new policy levying impositions made without parliamentary assent. This policy was affirmed by the Bate case decision of 1606;[35] however, this new policy levying imposition disrupted the long-established involvement of Parliament in this field.

In general, the king's revenue since the 12th century was categorised into ordinary and extraordinary, with the latter deriving from unusual sources or being collected as an

32 1 Car I c 7.

33 Jacob E Gensen and Eric A Posner, 'Timing Rules and Legal Institutions' (2007) 121 Harvard Law Review 543.

34 Another issue in the agenda was related to concerns over the influence of Catholicism. In particular, the Gunpowder Plot in 1605 raised the concern of the Commons against Catholics, and as Ruigh reveals, frequent petitions were submitted during the reign of King James seeking more stringent enforcement of the statutes against recusants. See Robert E Ruigh, *The Parliament of 1624 Politics and Foreign Policy* (Harvard University Press 1971) 6.

35 For more details see Pauline Croft, 'Fresh Light on Bate's Case' (1987) 30 The Historical Journal 523.

additional contribution when the king had to govern out of the ordinary times and the former income did not suffice for his needs.[36] In particular, the grant of money was a 'voluntary grant – gift of the subjects from his own property to the king'[37] and as Harriss accurately points out, in the medieval history of England 'the granting of taxation was an expression of the political harmony between the King and the subjects'.[38]

However, '[l]eaders of the parliamentary opposition naturally found this doctrine a strong bulwark in their stand against the king'.[39] Interestingly, sunset clauses were a dominant component in legislation concerning the king's revenue during the emergence of the Commons and the Lords in the legislative process. An example that shows the connection of sunset clauses with the amount of grant is the 'tallage',[40] an extraordinary levy, and suffice to cite here a reference from the Calendar of Patent Rolls that shows that connection:

> Grant to the Jews of England, except Isaac de Norwico and Ursel and his brothers, heirs of Hamo de Hereford, that of the 10,000 marks which they owe to the king for the last tallage, they may pay at the Exchequer at Michaelmas next 500, at the following Easter 500, and if they answer well the said 1,000 and other arrears which they owe to the king, then they may pay in like manner 1,000 in the eighteenth year, and after that 2000 yearly, at the same terms, until the said 10,000 marks.[41]

Correspondingly, the same pattern, that of granting levies to the king for a certain period, was followed also in parliamentary business. For instance during the second parliament of the 14th year of Edward III, a statute passed which was entitled 'a subsidy granted to the King on Wool, Woolfells, and other Merchandise exported for a certain period'.[42] It is remarkable that in 1415[43] the Commons and the Lords granted the subsidy on wool to the King for the rest of his life without further parliamentary action, instead of for a year or so. This practice was followed during the first and last Parliaments of Richard III in 1484, during the reign of Henry VI in 1453 and during the reign of Edward IV in 1465.[44]

36 Sydney Knox Mitchell, *Studies in Taxation under John and Henry III* (Yale University Press, 1914) 1.

37 Margaret Atwood Judson, *The Crisis of the Constitution: An Essay in Constitutional and Political Thought in England* 1603–1645 (Rutgers University Press 1988) 39.

38 GL Harriss, *King, Parliament and Public Finance in Medieval England to 1369* (Clarendon Press 1975) 31.

39 Margaret Atwood Judson, *The Crisis of the Constitution: An Essay in Constitutional and Political Thought in England 1603–1645* (Rutgers University Press 1988) 39.

40 For the list of extraordinary levies see Sydney Knox Mitchell, *Studies in Taxation under John and Henry III* (Yale University Press 1914) 2.

41 Calendar of Patent Rolls, *Henry III Vol 3* (HMSO 1901–13) 12.

42 14 Edw III st 1 c 21. This Act was considered as a defining moment in the history of indirect taxation because after several efforts Parliament managed to bring the taxation on wool subsidy under its auspices. See George Unwin, *Finance and Trade under Edward III* (Frank Cass 1962) 157; GL Harriss, *King, Parliament and Public Finance in Medieval England to 1369* (Clarendon Press 1975) 446. During the following years, the subsidy on wool was granted every time it was asked, though normally for a few years at a time: see AL Brown, *The Governance of Late Medieval England 1272–1461* (Stanford University Press 1989) 68.

43 Rot Parl C 65/76 IV 63; [Grant of the subsidy on wool and other merchandise to the king for his lifetime, and a tenth and fifteenth also granted to the king].

44 AR Myers, 'Parliament 1422–1509', in RG Davies and JH Denton (eds), *The English Parliament in the Middle Ages* (Manchester University Press 1981) 147.

The use of sunset clauses in the king's revenue was mainly a reaction to practical needs. It is indisputable that the parliamentary grant of levies was traded in return for the king's affirmative response to the common petitions. The limited duration of the grants implies the existence of this parliamentary interest. Moreover, it was mainly a mechanism to define the amount of the grant rather than to impose a monitoring on expenditure. Finally, even if the lack of resources was a reason for the king to summon Parliament,[45] there is no evidence that the use of sunset clauses in the king's revenue exerted parliamentary pressure to the king to so summon it.

Eventually, by the turn of 17th century, the extensive use of sunset clauses in specific grants formed a custom and a pattern according to which some grants were categorised as perpetual and others as temporary. Coke points out this pattern, saying that:

> Subsidies taken in their generall sense for Parliamentary Aides are divided into perpetuall and temporary: perpetuall into three parts, viz. into Custuma antiqua, sive magna, custuma nova sive parva, and into custome of Broad cloth. Temporary, whereof there are three kindes, viz. 1. of Tonnage and Poundage of ancient time granted for a year or years incertainly, and of latter times for life. 2. A Subsidie after the rate of 4s. in the pound for lands, and 2 s. 8 d. for goods. And 3 for an Aide called a Fifteenth, And of these in order.[46]

As shown above, a sunset clause in king's revenue was an instrument to meet practical needs, in particular to quantify the amount of the grant. There is no evidence that the Commons at the time had the power to refuse the king the grant of levies or impose time constraints to force the king to convene future Parliaments. Nonetheless, the use of these clauses meant the de facto dependence on parliament of each king, and progressively a tradition was established according to which the kings, the Commons and the Lords co-operated in taxation.

To sum up, in the field of king's revenue, Parliament was part of the procedure. Parliament, and specifically the Commons, had the power to define the duration of the sunset clauses. The Parliament, holding the power to levy direct and indirect tax, demanded the king's response to Common petitions.[47] As a result, the underlying concept was a quid pro quo agreement. The use of the sunset clause in taxation served as a mechanism in order to determine the amount of grant, but it also permitted the submission of new petitions during subsequent Parliaments.

The crisis over a sunset clause in the bill on tonnage and poundage

Despite the fact that James I and (later on) Charles I were willing to circumvent Parliament's role in taxation, Parliament was not willing to relinquish its privilege to assent to taxation.[48] To this direction, sunset clauses were used by the Commons in order to assert authority over taxation and to circumscribe the power of the Crown.

45 MV Clarke, *Medieval Representation and Consent* (Longmans Green 1936) 267.

46 Sir Edward Coke, *The Fourth Part of the Institutes of the Laws of England: Concerning the Jurisdiction of the Courts* (Printed for E and R Brooke 1797) 28.

47 The role of sunset clauses in the king's revenue developed later during the 17th century.

48 Harold Hulme, 'Charles 1 and the Constitution', in William Appleton Aiken and Basil Duke Henning (eds), *Conflict in Stuart England: Essays in Honour of Wallace Notestein* (New York University Press 1960) 89, 92

King Charles I succeeded his father in March 1625 and summoned Parliament with the hope of no contentious business[49] and with the aim of obtaining a grant of supply.[50] At the same time, members of the Parliament did not want a long session, since the city of London was suffering from a plague epidemic and they were concerned about whether the session would conclude before the plague became devastating.[51]

As regards the King's request for a grant of supply, ever since the reign of Henry VI duties on exports and imports, known under the name of 'tonnage and poundage', had been granted by Parliament for the lifetime of each successive sovereign in the first session of their reign.[52] However, during the reign of Henry IV, these duties were granted only for a limited period.[53] In general, the duties on tonnage and poundage were obtainable without the argument of necessity requisite for extraordinary taxation because they were associated with the constant needed for protection in the seas and foreign trade.[54] However, during that session the Commons were not willing to approve the grant for the lifetime of Charles I.

Sir Walter Earle proposed two motions: first, that 'the Narrow Seas may be better garded then they have bene; it beings the consideration upon which this graunt was first made, and that for want hereof divers shipps have bene of late taken upon our owne shore'; and second, that 'it might not nowe passe for the Kinges life, till the pointe of the pretermitted costome be examined, which is fownded upon this graunte and in the meane tyme be limitted for a yeare.'[55] Both motions were seconded by Sir Robert Phillipps, who added that:

> [I]t might so be past as not to exclude the question of other impositions. Untill H. the 6ths tyme this graunte had never other then a temporary limitation. Kinges ever received it as a guift of the subject, and were therwith contented without changinge them with any other waye of imposition: for if they had any such power it were altogether unneedfull to pass.[56]

Even if the Solicitor General, Sir Robert Heath, opposed the motion – he argued that 'it had continued so many discents, and might be distastfull to the Kinge, who would be as inclinable to doe matters of grace to us as any of his ancestors'[57] – Earle's motions were approved, and the one-year sunset clause was included in the bill. Consequently, the

49 Conrad Russell, *Parliaments and English Politics: 1621–1629* (Clarendon Press 1982) 217: 'The king wanted two things from the parliament, a grant of supply commensurate with the enterprise he had undertaken and the life grant of Tonnage and Poundage which had been made to all new kings since the fifteenth century.'

50 Roger Lockyer, *Buckingham the Life and Political Career of George Villiers, First Duke of Buckingham* (Longman 1984) 245.

51 Conrad Russell, *Parliaments and English Politics: 1621–1629* (Clarendon Press 1982) 203; Maija Jansson and William B Bidwell (eds), *Proceedings in Parliament 1625* (Yale Center for Parliamentary History 1987) 3.

52 Samuel R Gardiner, *History of England from the Accession of James I to the Outbreak of the Civil War 1603–1642 Vol V* (Longmans, Green 1883) 364. For instance, 1 Hen VIII c 20; 1 Eliz c 20; 1 Jac I c 33.

53 Rot Parl C 65/68 III 570.

54 Linda S Popofsky, 'The Crisis over Tonnage and Poundage in Parliament in 1629' (1990) 126 Past and Present 44, 49. The germ of this policy can be allocated to the 15th century.

55 Samuel R Gardiner, *Debates in the House of Commons in 1625* (Camden Society 1873) 43.

56 Samuel R Gardiner, *Debates in the House of Commons in 1625* (Camden Society 1873) 43.

57 Samuel R Gardiner, *Debates in the House of Commons in 1625* (Camden Society 1873) 43.

temporal Tonnage and Poundage Bill was sent to the upper house and the first reading of the bill took place on 9 July.[58]

Despite its progression, the bill was rejected by the Lords due to its limited duration, as is shown in *Cobbett's Parliamentary History*.[59] Russell argues, however, that after the first reading, the Lords simply left the bill to 'fall asleep'.[60] Another point of view, propounded by Hulme, is that the cause of the Lords' decision not to pass the bill is unknown.[61] The *Journal of the House of Lords* does not provide sufficient information for accurate conclusions to be drawn, although it is explicitly noted that the bill was read three times before its rejection.[62]

The reason why the House of Commons confirmed the one-year sunset clause is not clear. Lockyer argues that the attitude of the Commons during the Parliament of 1625 was not particularly co-operative and might have been different if only they had been given more specific information about the King's policies.[63]

More precisely, Gardiner argues that Sir W. Earle was concerned about the fact that through the name of pretermitted customs, the Crown Lawyers included in the parliamentary grant of tonnage and poundage new impositions expanding the amount of the grant.[64] The pretermitted customs were founded on an interpretation of the tonnage and poundage grant and they differed from the new impositions, which were collected without any pretence of parliamentary authority.[65] Hence, Earle proposed the one-year sunset clause in order to give time for the examination of the scope of the pretermitted customs.[66] The statement by Phillipps, who included the question of other impositions when he seconded Earle's motion, accords with that interpretation.

Moreover, Harrison remarks that the Commons would have required the early approval of the one-year bill on tonnage and poundage as the necessary precondition towards a more comprehensive financial settlement.[67] Although Russell admits that the common interpretation of the sunset clause in the Tonnage and Poundage Bill was to diminish the king's revenue, he expresses a different point of view. He argues that the Commons approved Earle's

58 *Journal of the House of Lords 1620–1628 Vol III* (1767) 462.

59 *Cobbett's Parliamentary History of England Vol II* (Hansard 1807) 6.

60 Conrad Russell, *Parliaments and English Politics: 1621–1629* (Clarendon Press 1982) 229. According to Russell, 'it is very hard to be certain which bills were halted by opposition in the Lords, since the Lords rarely formally rejected a bill they did not like: they allowed it to fall asleep'. See Conrad Russell, *Parliaments and English Politics: 1621–1629* (Clarendon Press 1982) 42.

61 Harold Hulme, 'Charles 1 and the Constitution', in William Appleton Aiken and Basil Duke Henning (eds), *Conflict in Stuart England: Essays in Honour of Wallace Notestein* (New York University Press 1960) 89, 101.

62 *Journal of the House of Lords 1620–1628 Vol III* (1767) 490.

63 Roger Lockyer, *Buckingham the Life and Political Career of George Villiers, First Duke of Buckingham* (Longman 1984) 245.

64 Samuel R Gardiner, *History of England from the Accession of James I to the Outbreak of the Civil War 1603–1642 Vol V* (Longmans Green 1883) 364.

65 Samuel R Gardiner, *Debates in the House of Commons in 1625* (Camden Society 1873) 43 (fn b). For instance through the grant of tonnage and poundage, Edmund Nicholson, projector of the pretermitted customs granted in 1618, had argued that the collection of customs on cloth made of wool as well as on wool itself was allowed. See Maija Jansson and William B Bidwell (eds), *Proceedings in Parliament 1625* (Yale Center for Parliamentary History 1987) 313 fn 8.

66 Samuel R Gardiner, *History of England from the Accession of James I to the Outbreak of the Civil War 1603–1642 Vol V* (Longmans Green 1883) 364.

67 GA Harrison, 'Innovation and Precedent: a procedural reappraisal of the 1625 Parliament' (1987) 102 English Historical Review 51.

motion with the purpose of supporting the king's revenue with the pretermitted custom and impositions. The bill's complexity and the fact that there was no available time at the session due to the plague threat were the crucial elements prompting the inclusion of the one-year sunset clause.[68]

Reviewing primary sources, such as anonymous diaries and state papers, allows us to delve deeper into the intention of the Commons in adding the one-year sunset clause to the Tonnage and Poundage Bill and thereby departing from well-grounded tradition. According to an anonymous diary describing the process in the Parliament of 1625:

> the reasons that moved the house not to grant it for life, as it was in King James his tyme, was for that the kinges Councell in the Parliament of 18 Jacobi [recte 1624] did picke out reasons out of that Act for the ptennitted customs and other impositions wch lay and were imposed on the subts. very grievous unto them, and they had not tyme to examine and redress them.[69]

We may conclude that one reason was that it was the intention of the Commons to re-examine the scope of the goods upon which the tax of tonnage and poundage was applied, because there was no available time at the original session.

The state papers reveal further useful information regarding the reasons for the inclusion of the sunset clause. Before and during the Parliament of 1625, numerous reports were sent from state officials describing incidents of pirates cruising unchecked off the coast of Cornwall.[70] Sir W Earle, who was a representative of the West Country towns, was deeply concerned about that fact.[71] Moreover, a belated report of 2 August, sent by Sir James Bagg to Buckingham, reveals that West Country towns had complained to their Members of Parliament about the unguarded sea and the presence of Turkish pirates.[72] As the management of the specific grant which aimed to safeguard the seas proved inefficient due to the inclusion of a one-year sunset clause in the Tonnage and Poundage Bill, it is assumed that the time limitation was related to matters of tax accountability as well.

Even without reference to the original and primary aim of the Commons in amending the Tonnage and Poundage Bill by limiting its duration, the inclusion of the one-year sunset clause was clearly a significant amendment with important implications in respect of the allocation of authority to approve or refuse taxation. Gardiner accurately states that:

> the question of tonnage and poundage was the question of the sovereignty of England. Charles could not govern the country without this money, and if the claim of the Commons was admitted they might demand anything they liked as the price of their grant.[73]

68 Conrad Russell, *Parliaments and English Politics: 1621–1629* (Clarendon Press 1982) 227.

69 MS 449 257.

70 TNA PRO SP 16/1/68, TNA PRO SP 16/1/94; TNA PRO SP 16/2/33, TNA PRO SP 16/2/36; TNA PRO SP 16/3/76; TNA PRO SP 16/4/35; TNA PRO SP 16/5/8, TNA PRO SP 16/5/23, TNA PRO SP 16/5/24, TNA PRO SP 16/5/32, TNA PRO SP 16/5/49, TNA PRO SP 16/5/55, TNA PRO SP 16/5/81, TNA PRO SP 16/5/90.

71 Maija Jansson and William B Bidwell (eds), *Proceedings in Parliament 1625* (Yale Center for Parliamentary History 1987) 313. Sir W Earle states at the debates of the Commons on 5 July that 'the Turkish pirates come into our seas and take our ships at our doors'.

72 TNA PRO SP 16/5/6.

73 Samuel R Gardiner, *The First Two Stuarts and the Puritan Revolution* (2nd edn, Longmans Green 1877) 62.

The way in which the Commons treated the issue of tonnage and poundage in the years that followed confirms the fact that the Commons was struggling to control the grant of taxation and to safeguard their subsequent authority.

Once the temporary Tonnage and Poundage Bill failed to pass in the House of Lords, the King issued a proclamation to collect the grant on tonnage and poundage without parliamentary consent.[74] In response, in May 1628, Parliament passed the Petition of Rights, which (among other things) confirmed the principle that taxation can be imposed only by Parliament, while the Commons refused once again to grant tonnage and poundage.

In addition, the Commons submitted a 'remonstrance' using the Petition of Rights as a basis against the practice of the Crown collecting the tonnage and poundage, and stated explicitly that 'the receiving of Tonnage and Poundage, and other impositions not granted by Parliament, is a breach of the fundamental liberties of this kingdom, and contrary to your Majesty's royal answer to the said Petition of Right.'[75] The issue of tonnage and poundage was also a matter of discussion until the Long Parliament, because of the case of John Rolle, a Member of Parliament whose goods were seized when he refused to pay tonnage and poundage.[76]

Having said that, a one-year sunset clause in the Tonnage and Poundage Bill was a key part of the tension between the King and the Commons, and reinforced the precept of the English Civil War, 'no taxation without representation', which reveals their conceptual and constitutional value.

Eventually, in 1640, Parliament passed a series of legislation granting the tonnage and poundage. It is noteworthy that the first piece of legislation contained a 20-day sunset clause; the second, a 25-day sunset clause; the third, a 110-day sunset clause; the fourth, a two-month sunset clause; the fifth, a 55-day sunset clause; the sixth, a 38-day sunset clause; and the last, a 2-month sunset clause.[77] These sunset clauses both confirm the increasing role of the Commons to grant the tonnage and poundage and also exemplify the Commons' effort to monitor the King's expenditure.

Sunset clauses in the era of balance of powers

The political circumstances after the restoration

The sudden death of Oliver Cromwell in September 1658 and the subsequent collapse of the republican government under Richard Cromwell led to the restoration of the constitutional order as it was before the Civil War.[78] As Craig accurately remarks, 'the restoration of the monarchy in the person of Charles II did not restore the previous constitutional status quo',[79] and as Holdsworth further points out, Parliament possessed a more central role in

74 Samuel R Gardiner, *The Constitutional Documents of the Puritan Revolution 1625–1660* (Clarendon Press 1906) 49 ['Commission for raising Tonnage and Poundage with Impositions'].

75 Samuel R Gardiner, *The Constitutional Documents of the Puritan Revolution 1625–1660* (Clarendon Press 1906) 70 ['The Remonstance against Tonnage and Poundage'].

76 Linda S Popofsky, 'The Crisis over Tonnage and Poundage in Parliament in 1629' (1990) 126 Past and Present 44, 49 62.

77 16 Car I c 8; 16 Car I c 12; 16 Car I c 22; 16 Car I c 25; 16 Car I c 29; 16 Car I c 31; 16 Car I c 36.

78 The Statute Book is a blank from the close of the 16th year of Charles I (1640–1) to the year of the Restoration, the so-called 12th year of Charles II (1660).

79 Paul Craig, 'Public Law, Political Theory and Legal Theory' (2000) PL 211, 215.

the government 'with an initiative of its own, and an acknowledged right to survey the whole field of political action'.[80] To put it simply, the last Jacobean era was a period when the balance of powers between Parliament and the King was restored, albeit with increasing influence from the Commons. As a result, government after the restoration was more parliamentarian.[81] The new balance of powers which emerged was based on the theory of a balanced constitution.[82]

As regards the position of the King, and in particular the relation between royal prerogative and the law, Vile asserts that '[t]he battle between King and Parliament had resulted in two fundamentally important modifications of this doctrine. First, the King, although he still had powerful and important prerogatives, must acknowledge the supremacy of the law, and, therefore, of the legislature.'[83]

Many primary sources provide us with information regarding the use of sunset clauses in legislation, such as the statute book, the *Journal of the House of Lords*, the *Journal of the House of Commons*, the *Cobbett's Parliamentary History* Reports, and the *Hansard* Reports. Nevertheless, the vast majority of temporary acts from 1714 until 1760 are excised. Sir Charles Robertson explains the lack of the whole text of these acts, as they do not affect the principles, structure or machinery of government.[84] But in 1796 a report on expired and expiring temporary laws was drafted, providing us with a full record of temporary legislation.[85]

Sunset clauses are associated with major constitutional issues during this period that the doctrine of parliamentary sovereignty was in the making, such as the suspending powers of the Crown, the institutionalisation of Parliament as an indispensable machinery in the government but also with rule of law concerns which are not distant to the contemporary problems such as the suspension of habeas corpus, and the use of temporary legislation to facilitate the adoption of innovative legislation such as the new land tax and the first bankruptcy law.

Sunset clauses for the revival of the suspending powers of the crown

One of the main constitutional issues emerging during the reigns of Charles II and James II was the extent of the suspending powers of the king according to his prerogatives. The origin of the suspending power of the monarch derived from the middle ages and was a reserve power permitting the king to correct the deficiencies of the ordinary law.[86] However, as Holdsworth states, the 'Tudors and the earlier Stuarts do not seem to have made any great use of that power, and no discussion arose concerning it during that period'.[87]

80 WS Holdsworth, *A History of English Law Vol VI* (Methuen 1924) 162.
81 GR Elton, *Studies in Tudor and Stuart Politics and Government Vol II* (CUP 1974) 158.
82 Regarding the concept of 'balanced government' and the process according to which it emerged, see MJC Vile, *Constitutionalism and the Separation of Powers* (2nd edn, Liberty Fund 1998) 58.
83 MJC Vile, *Constitutionalism and the Separation of Powers* (2nd edn, Liberty Fund 1998) 58.
84 See Sir Charles Grant Robertson, *Select Statutes, Cases and Documents to Illustrate English Constitutional History* (4th edn, Methuen 1923) 194.
85 Committee upon Temporary Laws, Expired or Expiring, *Report* (HC 13 May 1796).
86 Regarding the concept of 'balanced government' and the process according to which it emerged, see MJC Vile, *Constitutionalism and the Separation of Powers* (2nd edn, Liberty Fund 1998) 218.
87 MJC Vile, *Constitutionalism and the Separation of Powers* (2nd edn, Liberty Fund 1998) 220.

A bill introduced into the House of Lords in 1662–3, giving the monarch wide suspending power, had failed to pass.[88] Another effort took place in 1672 and, remarkably, the bill again failed to pass. On the latter occasion, the bill introduced into the House of Lords was more specific than previously: the suspending power was limited to certain named statutes and it contained a five-year sunset clause limiting its duration.[89] It appears that the sunset clause in the bill was used in an effort to create a common ground of consensus so that the proposed bill would be passed by Parliament.

Despite the failure of the bill, Charles II and James II exercised their prerogatives, which were in substance a repeal of the suspended law. The 1672 Declaration of Indulgence issued by Charles II and the 1687 Declaration of Indulgence, together with the amendment issued by James II, suspended all penal laws against Catholic and Protestant nonconformists. However, it is significant that while the reaction of the Commons in 1673[90] forced Charles II to withdraw the Declaration of Indulgence,[91] the reaction of the Commons in 1788 was more co-operative. Indeed, the Commons declared that 'the king, with the assent of the lords, might make such sufferance touching the Statute of Provisors lately passed, as should seem to him reasonable until the next parliament'.[92]

The whole issue was permanently resolved in 1689 with the adoption of the Bill of Rights[93] that contained a clause prohibiting the suspension of laws without parliamentary consent: 'That the pretended power of suspending the laws or the execution of laws by regal authority without consent of Parliament is illegal'.

Sunsets for more frequent parliaments

The well-established practice during the last period of Charles I regarding the short-term sunsetting of the tonnage and poundage legislation was kept under the rule of Charles II.[94] Notably, with regard to the relationship between the House of Commons and the House of Lords, the former advanced its role in taxation. Porritt accurately argues that in the field of taxation, the Commons had established a privileged role.[95] In fact, the Lords exercised

88 *7th Report of Historical Manuscripts Commission* 167–8.

89 *9th Report of Historical Manuscripts Commission Part II* 25.

90 Journal of the *House of Lords 1666–1675 Vol XII* (1767) 539–40.

91 Journal of the *House of Lords 1666–1675 Vol XII* (1767) 551.

92 FW Maitland, *The Constitutional History of England: A Course of Lectures* (HAL Fisher ed, CUP 1908) 306.

93 1 Gul&Mar c 5 [An Act declareing the Rights and Liberties of the Subject and Setleing the Succession of the Crowne.

94 Similarly, the practice of involving sunset clauses in the delegation of powers was continued as well. Nonetheless, there was no parliamentary intervention on the matter, as the colonial policy was under the royal prerogative. It is worth mentioning the commission given to the newly appointed Governor of Jamaica, Sir Thomas Modyford Bart. The new governor was instructed, among others, to limit the duration of all laws with a two-year sunset clause. The commission explicitly granted the power to the governor to 'call Assemblies, and with their consent to make laws, reserving to himself a negative voice; also to levy monies: said laws to agree with those of England, and to be in force for two years only, except they be confirmed by the King'. W Noel Sainsbury (ed), *Calendar of State Papers Colonial, America and West Indies Vol 5* (HM Stationery Office 1994, Digital version at British History Online) [656].

95 Edward Porritt, *The Unreformed House of Commons, Parliamentary Representation before 1832 Vol I* (CUP 1909) 545.

only a limited power upon money bills, as they could not amend bills on taxation, and, moreover, they could not amend the duration of a sunset clause.

Consequently, the Commons claimed the aforementioned principle of the privileged role of the House of Commons concerning money bills in order to block the Lords' initiatives upon the levy of money.[96] A Commons report to the Lords on 20 March 1671, concerning an amendment to the Bill for Impositions on Merchandize, was emblematic. It stated:

> [T]hat the Power exercised by the House of Peers, in making the Amendments and Abatements in the Bill, intituled, An Act for an additional Imposition on several foreign Commodities, and for Encouragement of several Commodities and Manufactures of this Kingdom, both as to the Matter, Measure, and Time, concerning the Rates and Impositions on Merchandize, is a fundamental, inherent, and undoubted Right of the House of Peers; from which they cannot depart.[97]

The short time limitation in taxation is acknowledged by Holdsworth, who recognises that 'in the first place, the revenue granted to the king in perpetuity decreased, and that granted annually for a limited term increased', and points out that 'in the second place, the rule of strict appropriation universally applied to the annual or limited grants, resulted in securing for the House of Commons permanent control over the amount and kind of expenditure which the crown could incur'.[98] In addition, it is claimed that the short-term sunsetting of tax legislation was a mechanism to guarantee that frequent Parliaments would occur.[99]

During the first Parliament of William III and Mary II, many temporary acts were passed and, according to Holdsworth, 'were made necessary by the exigencies of the situation'.[100] The first Mutiny Act was passed according to the Bill of Rights clause which prohibited the raising of a standing army without parliamentary consent.[101] The Mutiny Act contained a one-year sunset clause,[102] and its renewal became regular practice for around two centuries.[103] The importance of this sunset clause is highlighted by Holdsworth, who claims that the annual renewal of the standing army 'has proved to be one of the strongest sanctions for parliamentary annual session'.[104]

96 Contrariwise, the Lords developed the principle of not incorporating irrelevant bills in money bills, as the Commons were keen to incorporate irrelevant bills to money bills in order to prevent amendment in the House of Lords. See *Cobbett's Parliamentary History of England Vol VI* (Hansard 1810) 360.

97 *Journal of the House of Commons 1667–1687 Vol IX* (1802) 239.

98 WS Holdsworth, *A History of English Law Vol VI* (Methuen 1924) 252.

99 Gilbert Burnet and Thomas Burnet, *Bishop Burnet's History of His Own Time Vol II* (Thomas Ward 1724–34) 43.

100 WS Holdsworth, *A History of English Law Vol VI* (Methuen 1924) 194.

101 1 Gul&Mar c 5 [An Act declareing the Rights and Liberties of the Subject and Setleing the Succession of the Crowne.

102 1 Gul&Mar c 5 [An Act for punishing Officers or Soldiers who shall Mutiny or Desert Their Majestyes Service].

103 FW Maitland, *The Constitutional History of England: A Course of Lectures* (HAL Fisher ed, CUP 1908) 329. In fact, it was renewed during the second session of the first Parliament of William III. However, it was not renewed during the third session as, according to Ogg, the Commons did not approve the necessity of a standing army at that moment: see David Ogg, *England in the Reigns of James II and William III* (Clarendon Press 1955) 441.

104 WS Holdsworth, *A History of English Law Vol VI* (Methuen 1924) 241.

Other writers,[105] though, have stressed that the annual calling of parliaments is explicable on the basis of the king's need to secure further subsides. Montesquieu famously remarked, 'If the legislative power enacts, not from year to year, but forever, on the raising of public funds, it runs the risk of losing its liberty, because the executive power will no longer depend upon it.'[106]

Focusing either on the annual Mutiny Act or on several annual subsidies, each author admits that the use of sunset clauses in legislation was a useful mechanism which imposed the need for frequent parliamentary sessions. Without doubt, the frequency of the parliamentary sessions was a significant concern which was encapsulated also in the text of the Bill of Rights of 1689.[107]

Consequently, another use of the sunset clause emerged, having ramifications for the institutional co-operation of the government and its interdependence. The lack of a specific framework regulating the summons of Parliament[108] was in practice replaced with the use of sunset clauses in important legislation, which made the monarchs' ruling without parliaments ineffective.

Sunsets and the first Habeas Corpus Suspension Act

The reign of the first two Stuarts after the Restoration proved to be one of the most erratic periods in British history, starting with a revolution and concluding in another. The Glorious Revolution which was based on the successful co-operation of Whigs and Tories against James II led to the succession of the throne by William of Orange and Mary II.[109] A parliamentary convention was summoned in order to offer the throne and draft the major constitutional documents of the settlement. Several sunset clauses were recorded in a plethora of legislation,[110] with the most notable an act to suspend the habeas corpus.

Specifically, in the immediate wake of this transition, during the first year of the reign of William and Mary, the first act to suspend the habeas corpus was recorded,[111] just ten years after the Habeas Corpus Act was adopted.[112] The political environment that caused this development was the fact that the new regime faced exigency due to the supporters of James II, also known as Jacobites, who aimed to restore the reign of James II.[113]

105 David Hayton, 'Contested Kingdoms. 1688–1756', in Paul Langford (ed), *The Eighteenth Century* (OUP 2002) 40; HT Dickinson, 'The British Constitution', in HT Dickinson (ed), *A Companion to Eighteenth-Century Britain* (Blackwell 2002) 13.

106 Montesquieu, *The Spirit of the Laws* (Anne Cohler and others trs, CUP 1989) 164.

107 1 Gul&Mar c 5 [An Act declareing the Rights and Liberties of the Subject and Setleing the Succession of the Crowne.

108 In 1664 the Triennial Parliaments Act '16 Car II c 1' passed; however, due to the lack of a mechanism to enforce the calling of Parliaments, Charles II was able to complete the last four years of his reign without Parliament.

109 WS Holdsworth, *A History of English Law Vol VI* (Methuen 1924) 163.

110 I.e 1 Gul&Mar c 3; [An Act for preventing all Doubts and Questions concerning the Collecting the Publique Revenue]; 1 Gul&Mar c 13 [An Act for Reviveing two former Acts for Exporting of Leather].

111 1 Gul&Mar c 2 [An Act for Impowering His Majestie to Apprehend and Detaine such Persons as He shall finde just Cause to Suspect are Conspireing against the Government].

112 31 Car II c 2 [An Act for the better secureing the Liberty of the Subject and for Prevention of Imprisonments beyond the Seas].

113 For further details see Amanda L. Tyler, 'The Forgotten Core Meaning of the Suspension Clause' (2012) 125 Harvard Law Review 901, 934.

This drew significant attention at the debates in the House of Commons and House of Lords.[114] Given that it was the first time that a sunset clause was used for the suspension of the habeas corpus remedy, it is noteworthy that the sunset clause is set out twice in the text of the statute.[115] On the one hand, in the body of the Act it is stated that 'every Person or Persons [. . .] may be detayned in safe Custodie till the Seventeenth Day of Aprill in the Yeare of Our Lord One thousand six hundred eighty and nine, without Baile or Mainprize [. . .]'; while on the other hand, there is a sunset provision entitled 'continuance of Act', which is continuance sunsetting the Act as a whole on 17 April.

The latter was an amendment proposed in the House of Commons,[116] and this pleonasm expresses the significance of the sunset clause in the habeas corpus. Indeed, another amendment proposed during the same session, which failed to pass, reaffirms the consternation which members of the House felt concerning the suspension of habeas corpus. However, during the same session, two acts renewing the suspension of the habeas corpus were passed, the first until 5 May and the second until 23 October.[117]

According to Thomson,[118] 'the passing of the Act desired by the Commons implied that henceforth extraordinary powers could only be conferred upon the executive by Parliament and for such time and in such manner as Parliament pleased'.

Sunset clauses and early innovative legislation

In 1702 upon the death of William III, Anne, the daughter of James II, became Queen. At the turn of the century, normality was restored and parliamentary business contributed a significant amount of work to legislative action.

During the first year of the reign of Anne, a new policy was initiated in the field of taxation. An act was passed imposing a land tax,[119] which contained a one-year sunset clause, and which continued for approximately a century, until 1798, when it became perpetual.[120] Furthermore, due to the hostilities against France and the outbreak of the War of the Spanish Succession, Parliament adopted an act 'for Prohibiting all Trade and Commerce with France',[121] which was intended to last for the duration of the war.

In addition, another innovation is recorded in 1705, this time concerning bankruptcy law, as an act was adopted introducing the discharge of a bankrupt's exiting liabilities.[122] The act was temporary, due to a three-year sunset clause,[123] and signalled a shift from creditor

114 *Journal of the House of Lords 1685–1691 Vol XIV* (1767–1830) 222.
115 For more discussion about the Habeas Corpus Suspension Acts see Chrs 4 and 8.
116 The Convention Parliament (William): The convention becomes a Parliament – begins 20/2/1689', *The History and Proceedings of the House of Commons 1680–1695 Vol 2* (1742) 280.
117 1 Gul&Mar c 5 [An Act for Impowering His Majestie to Apprehend and Detaine such Persons as He shall finde just Cause to Suspect are Conspireing against the Government]; 1 Gul&Mar. c 19 [An Act for Impowering His Majestie to Commit without Baile such Persons as He shall finde just Cause to Suspect are Conspireing against the Government].
118 Mark A Thomson, *A Constitutional History of England 1642–1801* (Methuen 1938) 286.
119 Land Tax, Forfeited Estates, etc. Act 1702 (1 Anne c 6).
120 Land Tax Perpetuation Act 1798 (38 Geo III c 60).
121 Trade with France Act 1704 (3&4 Anne c 12).
122 See Jay Cohen, 'The History of Imprisonment for Debt and its Relation to Development of Discharge in Bankruptcy' (1982) 3 Journal of Legal History, 153, 156; John C McCoid, 'Discharge: The most important development in Bankruptcy history' (1996) 70 American Bankruptcy Law Journal 163, 164; Vanessa Finch, *Insolvency Law, Perspectives and Principles* (CUP 2002) 9.
123 Bankrupts Act 1705 (4&5 Anne c 4), s 17.

assistance to debtor assistance.[124] Interestingly, the motivation behind this enactment is recorded in *ex parte Burton.*[125] In that case, Lord Hardwicke mentions that:

> the statute of the 4 and 5 Ann. which was temporary at first, and never intended to be a perpetual law [. . .] was made in consideration of two long wars which had been very detrimental to traders, and rendered them incapable of paying their creditors.[126]

McCoid, who focuses on the further development of the law, recognises that this temporary legislation might have related to the War of the Spanish Succession. However, he argues that:

> While that is certainly a possibility, Parliament's not-much-later readiness to enlarge both the time frame and the coverage, as well as to alter its terms, seems to correspond more to experimentation than to any perception of a particular short-term need. Moreover, the idea of an experiment fits comfortably in the pattern formed by the sporadic efforts to deal with the problem of insolvency made previously by the Privy Council, Chancery, Interregnum Council, and Parliament.[127]

Although the principal focus of the Act was to prescribe the appropriate behaviour of bankrupts, this new framework was, as McCoid argues,[128] abused. Suffice to mention the story of Thomas Pitkin and Thomas Brerewood. As Kaderns notes, 'the two conspirators had managed to make off with over 50,000 pounds, around 150.000.000 US Dollars in modern money'.[129] This case motivated Parliament to amend the existing Act, and the following year, in 1706, the Act was amended by another temporary act 'to explain and amend an Act of the last session of Parliament for Preventing Frauds frequently committed by Bankrupts'.[130]

During the years of the last two Stuarts, the sunset clause was developed into a useful mechanism entertaining mainly practical needs. In taxation, the use of sunset clauses was principally a mechanism to secure accountability on spending, and it is remarkable that the vague expression 'until the next Parliament' or 'until the next session of the Parliament' was omitted from the temporary legislation.[131]

124 Emily Kadens, 'The Pitkin Affair: A Study of Fraud in Early English Bankruptcy' (2010) 84 American Bankruptcy Law Journal 483, 485.
125 *Ex Parte Burton* 26 ER 163.
126 *Ex Parte Burton* 26 ER 163.
127 John C McCoid, 'Discharge: The Most Important Development in Bankruptcy History' (1996) 70 American Bankruptcy Law Journal 163, 182.
128 John C McCoid, 'Discharge: The Most Important Development in Bankruptcy History' (1996) 70 American Bankruptcy Law Journal 163, 168.
129 Emily Kadens, 'The Pitkin Affair: A Study of Fraud in Early English Bankruptcy' (2010) 84 American Bankruptcy Law Journal 483, 484.
130 Bankrupts Act 1706 (6 Anne c 22).
131 And when it is recorded, it is accompanied cumulatively by a specific number of years, for instance, Preventing Theft and Rapine upon the Northern Borders of England (12&13 Gul III c 6): '[. . .] thereby given and continue and are hereby continues in full force from and after the Expiration of the last mentioned Act for and during the Space and Term of Eleven Years and from thence to the End of the First Session of the next Parliament and no longer'.

Sunset clauses played a significant role in the transition period after the Interregnum, when the balance of powers was in a state of flux. Thus we have seen that the King used sunset clauses, albeit unsuccessfully, in an attempt to revive the royal prerogative to suspend laws. At the same time, the Commons applied short-term sunset clauses to taxation and mutinies because of the fact that frequent Parliaments were likely to occur, while they opposed the Lords' authority to amend the wording of such clauses pertaining to taxation.

Conclusions

In the first Stuart era, sunset clauses were used extensively, and this had interesting implications as regards first the co-operation between the King and the Commons and Lords. The main concern during this period was the allocation of sovereignty and the subsequent co-operation of institutions. Parliament steadily came to understand its role in government, with legislation becoming an indispensable tool for the implementation of policy.

During the first Stuart reign, the continuity of temporary legislation became a central political issue as the accidental expiration of the laws increased uncertainty, and during the reign of Charles I, the sunset clause in the Tonnage and Poundage Bill was a key part of the tension between the King and the Commons and was transformed as a tool in negotiating the conflicting relationship between Commons and the Crown.

After the Restoration, when Parliament steadily came to understand its role in government (having a decisive role in legislation, which was becoming an indispensable tool for the implementation of policy), sunset clauses were used as an instrument to shape the balance of powers in the legislative process. In the latter period of the Stuarts, sunset clauses were associated with two provisions of the Bill of Rights, the suspending powers of the Crown and the frequency of Parliaments. Furthermore, the consensual role of Parliament was enshrined in the use of sunset clauses, as they were used to facilitate the adoption of cutting-edge and innovative legislation.

This period witnessed the first law suspending habeas corpus, and the double sunset clause in the Act is an indication of the profound concern that was raised. Finally, the utility of such clauses was demonstrated in the field of legislative experimentation, as a series of new laws with sunset clauses were adopted, namely the new land tax and the first bankruptcy law.

4 Sunset clauses in the era of parliamentary sovereignty

> [Parliament] hath sovereign and controllable authority in the making, confirming, enlarging restraining, abrogating, repealing, reviving and expounding of laws, concerning matters of all possible denominations, ecclesiastical or temporal, civil, military maritime, or criminal.
>
> W Blackstone, *Commentaries*, Book 1, 17

Sunset clauses and parliamentary sovereignty

The era of parties

Queen Anne reigned for twelve years until her death in 1714. She was the last monarch to exercise the power of not giving assent to a bill. She was succeeded by George I according to the Act of Settlement, and he was the first monarch whose role in legislation was formal only.[1] During the same period, a new system of parliamentary government was established by legislation enacted in the years between 1689 and 1716,[2] which featured a system of cabinet government and, progressively, the development of party government.[3] As Kemp accurately remarks:

> if the years from 1689 to 1716 are the formative years for the relation between Kings and Commons, the years from 1716 to 1783 are the years of balance between them, and in the years from 1784 to 1832 this balance was slowly undermined.[4]

Stability in the constitutional order and the establishment of the doctrine of parliamentary sovereignty in the 18th century crystallised the use of the sunset clause in the internal matters of Parliament,[5] and despite the formation of political parties, the use of sunset clauses

1 See WI Jennings, *The Law of the Constitution* (5th edn, University of London Press 1959) 143.

2 Betty Kemp, *King and Commons 1660–1832* (MacMillan 1957) 32.

3 WS Holdsworth, *A History of English Law Vol X* (Methuen 1938) 55; Mark A Thomson, *A Constitutional History of England 1642 to 1801* (Methuen 1938) 305.

4 Betty Kemp, *King and Commons 1660–1832* (MacMillan 1957) 5.

5 The term of art 'sovereignty' was first recorded in 1776. See Pasi Ihalainen, *Agents of the People: Democracy ad Popular Sovereignty in British and Swedish Parliamentary and Public Debates, 1734–1800* (Brill, 2010) 254. For more analysis on parliamentary sovereignty, see Ch 6.

was more relevant to the ministerial–anti-ministerial controversy.[6] In addition, sunset clauses were associated with Parliament's effort to control the growth of the administration.

From the reign of William III onwards, the new mechanism for the promotion of governmental policies was the political parties, Whigs and Tories.[7] To a large extent the mechanism for the promotion of bills was mainly the ministers through which the Crown was expressing its will.[8] The House of Lords had the power to amend or even block a bill at least until 1911, when the Parliament Act was passed limiting the legislative authority of the Lords.[9] With the exception of acts forming the Constitution, the controversy surrounding the legislative process did not have an institutional dimension, for instance between the two Houses. The controversy during the 18th century was more on the ministerial and anti-ministerial front,[10] and less often at the front of party lines. With the institutionalisation of the political parties, conflict in the legislative process became located between the majority and the minority.

The Hanoverian succession hastened the transition from a Tory government to Whig dominance.[11] The Whig supremacy, though, ceased to provide a clash along party lines, and disputes were raised between groups of Whigs for the share of ministerial seats.[12] The most famous Whigs opposed to Walpole during his leadership were the 'Cobham's cubs' – among them, Grenville, Pitt and Lyttleton.[13] With reference to this balance of powers, in 1741 the ministry introduced a bill 'for the encouragement and increase of seamen, and for the better and speedier manning his majesty's fleet'.[14] This bill, which was rejected during the previous session of the Parliament, was a motion to revive and make perpetual a temporary act[15] adopted during the fourth year of the reign of Queen Anne.[16] The bill was hotly debated and was opposed strongly by many Whig members of the Parliament including Pitt, Lyttelton, Barnard, Sandys and Pulteney.[17] Eventually, the opposition managed to amend the bill, and, among other amendments, a three-month sunset clause limiting its duration was passed.[18]

6 Whereas the statute book has numerous temporary Acts, not all of them contain a sunset clause. An illustrative example is the series of indemnity Acts which were initiated in 1728 (1 Geo II c 23) and lasted for more than a century, until 1828. These Acts were relieving the Protestant Dissenters – office-holders from all penalties and consequences to which the Dissenters were liable according to the Test (25 Char II c 2) and Corporation (13 Char II Stat 2 c 1) Acts. What was commonly referred to as the 'Annual Indemnity Acts' were temporary and were renewed more or less annually; however, their temporal effect was retrospective, as Dicey remarks. See AV Dicey, *Introduction to the Study of the Law of the Constitution Vol I* (JWF Allison ed, OUP 2013) 135.

7 GR Elton, *Studies in Tudor and Stuart Politics and Government Vol II* (CUP 1974) 158. According to Hayton, the clear lines between the two parties were formed during the Exclusion Crisis: see David Hayton, 'Contested Kingdoms. 1688–1756', in Paul Langford (ed), *The Eighteenth Century* (OUP 2002) 47.

8 D Hume, *Essays, Moral, Political and Literary* (1862) 25.

9 The Parliament Act 1911 (1&2 Geo V c 13). With the exception of money bills, where Lords did not have the right to amend. See above text to n 18 in Ch III.

10 Sir David Lindsay Keir, *The Constitutional History of Modern Britain 1485–1937* (3rd edn, Adam and Chales Black, 1946) 317.

11 Brian Hill, 'Parliament, Parties and Elections 1688–1760', in HT Dickinson (ed), *A Companion to Eighteenth-Century Britain* (Blackwell Publishing 2002) 63.

12 HT Dickinson, *Liberty and Property: Political Ideology in Eighteenth-century Britain* (Weidenfeld and Nicolson, 1977) 121.

13 John Beckett, *The Rise and Fall of Grenvilles* (Manchester University Press 1994) 26.

14 *Cobbett's Parliamentary History of England Vol XII* (Hansard 1811) 27.

15 *Cobbett's Parliamentary History of England Vol XI* (Hansard 1810) 114.

16 Exportation Act 1705 (4&5 Anne c 19).

17 *Cobbett's Parliamentary History of England Vol XII* (Hansard 1811) 27.

18 *Cobbett's Parliamentary History of England Vol XII* (Hansard 1811) 53.

Furthermore, in 1756 William Pitt the Elder, from the opposition, advocated in favour of a 'militia bill' reconstituting the militia in order to meet imperial necessities.[19] The militia bill was quite popular, and as Yorke indicates, 'the zeal and eagerness shown in pressing on the measure was to embarrass the government by forcing ministers into opposition to a popular measure'.[20] Despite the approval of the bill at the House of Commons,[21] strong opposition was expected in the House of Lords, as the Earl of Temple[22] and William Lyttelton[23] confess. According to *Cobbett's Parliamentary History*, a fruitful debate took place in the House of Lords on the militia bill, and Lord Chancellor Hardwicke of the Newcastle administration opposed it and managed its rejection.[24] It is remarkable, though, that the Lords in favour of Pitt's bill were willing to compromise and put it in probation in order to have it approved by the government.[25]

Newcastle's administration was dismissed at the end of 1756, and on 15 November, King George offered the ministry to Pitt.[26] The militia bill was announced in the King's speech at the opening of the session of Parliament,[27] which was, according to Leadam,[28] a precondition of Pitt's acceptance of office. The militia bill was introduced once again in Parliament, and in the Committee of the whole House the bill was amended according to Hardwicke's objections.[29] Accordingly, a sunset clause was included and the duration of the act was restricted for five years,[30] for a trial period.[31]

Likewise, in 1770, during North's administration, Grenville introduced a bill to regulate the procedure of controverted elections.[32] Until that time, controverted elections were solved by an *ad hoc* committee which was not impartial and as a consequence was used by the ministerial party to increase its majority in the Commons.[33] The bill met ministerial opposition, which was expressed by Richard Rigby.[34] Several objections were raised but

19 Sir Charles Grant Robertson, *Select Statutes, Cases and Documents to Illustrate English Constitutional History* (4th edn, Methuen 1923) 194.

20 Yorke Philip, *The Life and Correspondence of Philip Yorke, Earl of Hardwicke, Lord High Chancellor of Great Britain Vol II* (CUP 1913) 262.

21 *Cobbett's Parliamentary History of England Vol XV* (Hansard 1813) 704.

22 *Cobbett's Parliamentary History of England Vol XV* (Hansard 1813) 759.

23 Robert Phillimore, *Memoirs and Correspondence of Lord Lyttelton Vol II* (James Ridgway 1845) 510.

24 *Cobbett's Parliamentary History of England Vol XV* (Hansard 1813) 725.

25 Lord Tablot stated, during the debate: 'now my lords, supposing that the law should upon trial be found not to answer all the good ends intended by it, we should from that trial be able to judge wherein it was deficient, and by what means those deficiencies might en supplied': see *Cobbett's Parliamentary History of England Vol XV* (Hansard 1813) 750.

26 Basil Williams, *The Whig Supremacy: 1714–1760* (Clarendon Press 1962) 354.

27 *Cobbett's Parliamentary History of England Vol XV* (Hansard 1813) 772.

28 IS Leadam, *History of England* (Longmans Green 1909) 1757.

29 Navy Act 1740 (14 Geo II c 38); *Cobbett's Parliamentary History of England Vol XV* (Hansard 1813) 739; Yorke Philip, *The Life and Correspondence of Philip Yorke, Earl of Hardwicke, Lord High Chancellor of Great Britain Vol II* (CUP 1913) 266.

30 See *Journal of the House of Lords 1756–1760 Vol XXIX* (1767–1830).

31 Yorke Philip, *The Life and Correspondence of Philip Yorke, Earl of Hardwicke, Lord High Chancellor of Great Britain Vol II* (CUP 1913) 266.

32 The political life of Britain at that time was influenced by the Wilkes case. For more discussion on this case see Pasi Ihalainen, *Agents of the People: Democracy ad Popular Sovereignty in British and Swedish Parliamentary and Public Debates, 1734–1800* (Brill, 2010) 136ff.

33 Philip Lawson, 'Grenville's Election Act: 1770' (1980) Historical Research 218.

34 *Cobbett's Parliamentary History of England Vol XVI* (Hansard 1813) 907.

subsequently dropped during the debate in the Commons.[35] Finally the act was adopted, though temporarily, and a seven-year sunset clause was added,[36] which was suggested to make the bill temporary by way of experiment.[37]

More revealing in so far as sunset clauses are concerned, in 1774 a bill was introduced to make the Grenville Act perpetual. Sir William Moleswoth, who seconded the motion, said that 'administration had been opposers of this bill',[38] and Aubrey added that:

> the fact is and I can appeal to some gentlemen now in the House to bear me witness in the assertion that Mr Grenville originally intended to make this a perpetual bill; but in compliance with the opinions and solicitations even of his friends, who feared, that, by attempting too much at once, as the subject was as new as it was important, they might lose the whole; and that there might be no complaint of its being hastily obtruded upon the house, he modestly recommended it only upon trial.[39]

From the examples mentioned above, it can be concluded that when a legislative initiative does not have widespread approval, a sunset clause is used in order to build a majority. Similarly, when the opposition opposed a bill, the motion for the inclusion of a duration clause was quite frequent. In *Hansard* there are several motions, opposing a bill that failed, to limit the duration of a proposed bill, for instance in the Technical Instruction Bill,[40] the Vexatious Actions Bill,[41] the Foreign Prison Made Goods Bill[42] and the Evidence in Criminal Cases Bill.[43] In particular, at the debate of the Licensing Bill in 1904, Lloyd George proposes the amendment of a sunset clause by arguing that '[i]f this Government had not the time, resource, or political courage to deal with a question of that magnitude in the way it should be treated, they ought not to stand in the way of future Governments dealing with it.'[44]

The use of sunset clauses, though, was not a unique mechanism to block legislation. The minority or the opposition quite often used procedural tactics such as the lack of quorum in order to block a voting procedure,[45] or the Lords would delay a bill until it had fallen asleep. The latter practice, which was abolished by the Parliament Acts of 1911 and 1949, was recorded when ministers and lords were in harmony and when the government did not want to openly oppose a legislative initiative.[46]

35 *Cobbett's Parliamentary History of England Vol XVI* (Hansard 1813) 916.
36 Parliamentary Elections Act 1770 (10 Geo III c 16).
37 *Cobbett's Parliamentary History of England Vol XVI* (Hansard 1813) 916.
38 *Cobbett's Parliamentary History of England Vol XVII* (Hansard 1813) 1063.
39 *Cobbett's Parliamentary History of England Vol XVII* (Hansard 1813) 1067. Nonetheless, Lord North argues the exact opposite, that Grenville did not intend to make this act perpetual, saying that 'he only meant it as a temporary and experimental act': cf *Cobbett's Parliamentary History of England Vol XVII* (Hansard 1813) 1063.
40 HC Deb 27 August 1889 vol 340 col 718.
41 HC Deb 10 August 1896 vol 44 col 456.
42 HC Deb 13 July 1897 vol 51 col 81.
43 HC Deb 30 June 1898 vol 60 col 748.
44 HC Deb 26 July 1904 vol 138 col 1234.
45 Peter David Gamer Thomas, *The House of Commons in the Eighteenth Century* (Clarendon Press 1971) 167.
46 E Neville Williams, *The Eighteenth Century Constitution 1688–1815* (CUP 1960) 136.

The practice of opposing a bill with a sunset clause amendment continued until recent years. The debates on the abolition of the death penalty illustrate this utility more clearly. In 1965, a bill abolishing the death penalty was introduced. It began as a private member's bill but was entirely endorsed by the government.[47] It was a controversial issue at the time, and thus the opposition managed to limit its duration with a five-year sunset clause.[48] Finally the bill passed,[49] and in 1969 it became permanent, in spite of the opposition who aimed at least to keep the act temporary.[50]

As long as the legislative process was concentrated in the House of Commons, the sunset clause lost its role as an interaction among the King, the Lords and the Commons. However, it kept its role between the executive and the legislative branches in expressing opposition to a bill. Maltzman and Shipan accurately remark that 'opponents of new policies can also advocate inclusion of sunset provisions, temporally limited reauthorisations, or other provisions that are likely to encourage public and organised interests to lobby against successful implementation'.[51] Furthermore, the motive of the opposition in adding a sunset clause to an act is empirically linked to the expectation that temporary laws are more likely to be amended than perpetual laws.[52]

Whereas the absence of strict party division in the House and the popular control over Members of Parliament was a main aspect of the 18th century,[53] increasingly in the following centuries the power was transferred from Parliament to the people.[54] According to Hayton, the active participation of the people in political life is explained on one hand through the rise in the importance of parliament and on the other hand through the expansion of state bureaucracy.[55] Thus, this evolution in the political system gives another role to the sunset clause – a link between representatives and constituents – especially when the expiration of the sunset clause occurs after an election. The prospect of a temporary law sunsetting, and the need for renewal, might be ground for debate between candidates opposing the renewal and those candidates in favour of renewal.

Indeed, this development was recorded in the debates. As Mr Lewis argued in favour of the inclusion of a sunset clause in the House of Commons Members' Fund Bill, he stated that:

> our constituents have not been consulted, nobody can say there is any popular mandate for this Bill, and I think many Members have very vague ideas as to how it will work in practice I submit it is reasonable to ask that within a period of years the matter should be bound to come up for Parliamentary attention by the expiry of the Act.[56]

47 HC Deb 13 July 1965 vol 716 col 358.
48 HC Deb 13 July 1965 vol 716 col 408.
49 Murder (Abolition of Death Penalty) Act 1965.
50 HL Deb 17 December 1969 vol 306 col 1138.
51 Forrest Maltzman, Charles R Shipan, 'Change, Continuity and the Evolution of the Law' (2008) 52 American Journal of Political Science 252, 254
52 Forrest Maltzman, Charles R Shipan, 'Change, Continuity and the Evolution of the Law' (2008) 52 American Journal of Political Science 252, 263.
53 Sir William R Anson, *The Law and Custom of the Constitution Vol I* (5th edn, Clarendon Press 1935) 369.
54 AF Pollard, *The Evolution of Parliament* (2nd edn, Longmans Green 1926) 340.
55 Paul Langford (ed), *Contested Kingdoms, 1688–1756: The Eighteenth Century 1688–1815* (OUP 2002) 43.
56 HC Deb 19 July 1939 vol 350 col 670.

The growth of the administration

The foundation of local organisations under the auspices of Parliament was one of the significant changes in public law and in the system of local government which took place in the 18th century and made the practice of delegated law making power more common.[57] From the Tudor period until the Restoration, local government was strictly controlled by the executive branch, while from the later Stuart Kings, Parliament progressively gained its management.[58] One remarkable example of delegation is the Mutiny Act of 1717, according to which Parliament delegated the power to the Crown to constitute and govern the army.[59] Indeed, as Vile remarks:

> [T]he demand for the establishment of 'harmony' between legislature and government, which characterized the theory of parliamentary government in Britain and France, and the Progressive movement in the United States, was accompanied by a new 'separation of powers' – that between the 'political' branches of government and the bureaucracy. The distinction between 'Regterung' and 'Verwaltung,' or between 'politics' and 'administration' was, paradoxically, to open a new chapter in the establishment of semi-autonomous branches of government in an age which stressed unity and cohesion.[60]

Thus, numerous statutes are recorded in the statute books regulating local issues. In 1711, we find the first temporary act introducing an *ad hoc* fiduciary body, the Turnpike Trustees. Initially the Turnpike Trustees was enacted through a private act entitled 'An act for repairing the Highway between Highgate Gatehouse in the Country of Middlesex and Barnet Blockhouse, in the Country of Hertford',[61] with a temporary duration of twenty-one years. Nonetheless, at the expiration of this act, the delegated authority of this body was renewed with successive public acts having a similar sunset clause.[62]

The use of sunset clauses in laws regulating local organisations pertains to the parliamentary control of local bodies. As Anderson points out, the inclusion of a sunset clause concerning the Turnpike Trustees is explained as the need for periodic renewal, thereby entrenching the local government's accountability to Parliament.[63] From another point of view, while examining the local organisations during 18th century, Holdsworth suggests that the Turnpike Trustees were far from being temporary, as they were always renewed, and his explanation for the sunset clause is that it prevented the growth of local opposition.[64]

57 The practice of delegating law making power is recorded from the 16th century. Regarding the history of delegated legislation see Paul Craig, *Administrative Law* (7th edn, Sweet and Maxwell 2008) [15–002].

58 WS Holdsworth, *A History of English Law Vol X* (Methuen 1938) 133.

59 As is shown in text to n 26 in Ch III, the first Mutiny Act passed in 1689, but the practice of delegating power to the Crown started only in 1717. See Mutiny Act 1716 (3 Geo I c 2). See also Committee on Ministers' Powers, *Report* (Cmd 4060 1932) [1].

60 MJC Vile, *Constitutionalism and the Separation of Powers* (2nd edn, Liberty Fund 1998) 6.

61 Militia, etc. Act 1711 (10 Anne c 33).

62 Highgate and Chipping Barnet Road Act 1720 (7 Geo I st 1 c 18); Northern Roads, London Act 1735 (9 Geo II c 39).

63 Stuart Anderson, 'Public Law', in William Cornish, J Stuart Anderson, Ray Cocks, Michael Lobban, Patrick Polden and Keith Smith (eds), *The Oxford History of the Laws of England Vol XI* (OUP 2010) 347.

64 WS Holdsworth, *A History of English Law Vol X* (Methuen 1938) 78.

Nevertheless, there is consensus on the fact that due to the profound social changes at the turn of the new century, difficult tasks were placed upon the central government, and the need for expertise and local focus with autonomy was inevitable and, indeed, necessary.[65] Thus, Parliament conferred upon these new institutions the power to legislate and regulate local and minor issues, with the aim of confronting the challenges of the new era. In total, Webbs estimates that during the 18th century, Parliament enacted legislation introducing 1100 turnpike trusts, 125 guardians of the poor and 300 improvement commissioners.[66] However, the control over the executive law making powers and the accountability of all these local and *ad hoc* bodies was achieved through a variety of mechanisms, such as consultation, publication, legislative scrutiny and judicial review.[67]

During the 19th century, Parliament introduced new local institutions such as the Poor Law Commission[68] and the Tithe Commission,[69] amending relevant *ad hoc* bodies. Even if Parliament aimed to introduce with these institutions a perpetual system of local administration seeking maximum independence from political influence,[70] its control over them was through the annual appropriation acts[71] that examined and approved their budget, and through the periodical appointment of commissioners.

In addition, Parliament sought control of bodies long-holding a privileged position in relation to the government. The East India Company was an early joint stock company holding trade monopolies[72] with sovereign powers.[73] The struggles between different members of the company to gain control and the criticism that the State would share in profits led the government to seek its control.[74] Thus a petition was submitted at the Commons, and according to the original proposal, the East India Company was required to pay annually a sum of £400,000 for three years in exchange for the territorial acquisitions and revenues lately obtained.[75] However, the proposal met opposition and the time limit was reduced to two years,[76] but in 1769 the statute was prolonged for five years.[77]

Moreover, another bill was introduced, the so-called dividend bill, which prevented the company from raising a dividend larger than 10 per cent.[78] This latter bill aroused more opposition. The East India Company unsuccessfully submitted a petition to limit the duration of the restriction to at least the duration of the agreement and to raise the dividend up to 12.5 per cent.[79] However, when the bill was sent up to the Lords, the anti-ministerial party was united

65 Committee on Ministers' Powers, *Report* (Cmd 4060 1932) 51; Paul Craig, *Administrative Law* (7th edn, Sweet and Maxwell 2008) [15–003].

66 See Sidney Webb, *The Manor and the Borough* (Longmans Green 1963)

67 Moreover, for a complete account of methods of central control to the local government see WI Jennings, *Principles of Local Government Law* (University of London Press 1931) 160.

68 Poor Law Amendment Act 1834.

69 Tithe Communication Act 1836.

70 Stuart Anderson, 'Public Law', in William Cornish, J Stuart Anderson, Ray Cocks, Michael Lobban, Patrick Polden and Keith Smith (eds), *The Oxford History of the Laws of England Vol XI* (OUP 2010) 348.

71 Appropriation Act 1849 (3&4 Vict c 112).

72 Bruce P Lenman, 'Britain and India', in HT Dickinson (ed), *A Companion to Eighteenth-Century Britain* (Blackwell Publishing 2002) 460.

73 Lucy S Sutherland, *The East India Company in Eighteenth Century Politics* (Clarendon Press 1952) 4.

74 WS Holdsworth, *A History of English Law Vol XI* (Methuen 1938) 342.

75 *Cobbett's Parliamentary History of England Vol XVI* (Hansard 1813) 342.

76 East India Company Act 1767 (7 Geo III c 57).

77 East India Company Act 1769 (9 Geo III c 24).

78 *Cobbett's Parliamentary History of England Vol XVI* (Hansard 1813) 343.

79 *Cobbett's Parliamentary History of England Vol XVI* (Hansard 1813) 343.

and blocked the bill at the third reading.[80] Eventually, during the following session of Parliament the bill passed with a one-year sunset clause,[81] which was renewed for another year.[82]

In the case of the East India Company, Parliament used alternative and more complicated methods to control it through temporary legislation, which temporarily regulated the financial status of the company. Moreover, when in 1772 the company could not comply with its financial obligations, a secret committee of enquiry was appointed. The committee proposed to suspend the power of the company and to appoint commissioners in order to regulate its affairs in its presidencies.[83] These proposals were passed as an act.[84] As regards this Act, it is noteworthy that the appointed supervisors of the East India Company were critical of the government's policy to use temporary enactments, speaking of:

> a misfortune which we are sorry to find greatly growing upon us by those temporary occasional and partial acts of parliament, which, without consideration of their conformity to the general principles of our law and constitution, are adopted rashly and hastily on every occasion.[85]

Progressively, it became customary for parliament to confer minor legislative authority to subordinate institutions, and this practice was recorded in numerous acts. Suffice to mention here the Land Drainage Act of 1914, section 4 of which provided that:

> The powers of making Provisional Orders under this Act shall not be exercised after the expiration of two years from the passing of this Act, except for the purpose of amending an existing Provisional Order made under this Act; but nothing in this subsection shall prejudice or affect any powers or provisions contained in any Provisional Order made before the expiration of that period.[86]

The autonomy of these institutions became a major concern of the UK Parliament, and in the 20th century a committee was tasked with investigating the issue and exploring solutions on implementing safeguards against the abuse of the delegated powers.[87] From the Donoughmore Report, and especially from the section on delegated legislation to administrative authorities and corporate organisations, it is possible to draw useful conclusions in relation to the use of sunset clauses in delegated legislation.[88]

The great concern of the committee was the autonomy of institutions exercising conferred law making power. Thus, one of the general principles laid down by this committee was that:

> the so called Henry VIII Clause, by which a dispensing power is given to a minister to modify the provisions of a statute, should never be employed except for the sole purpose

80 *Cobbett's Parliamentary History of England Vol XVI* (Hansard 1813) 343.
81 East India Company Act 1767 (7 Geo III c 49).
82 East India Company Act 1768 (8 Geo III c 11).
83 *Cobbett's Parliamentary History of England Vol XVII* (Hansard 1813) 559.
84 East India Company Act 1772 (13 Geo III c 9).
85 *Cobbett's Parliamentary History of England Vol XVII* (Hansard 1813) 662.
86 Land Drainage Act 1914, s 4(2). The same construction was used in the Fishery Harbours Act 1915, s 4(2).
87 Committee on Ministers' Powers, *Report* (Cmd 4060 1932) [4].
88 For more information regarding sunset clauses and delegation of power, see Ch 5.

of bringing an Act into operation, and should be subject to a time limit of one year for the period of its operation.[89]

The short sunset clause of one year that is proposed in the Donoughmore Report is related to the autonomy of the institution. The shorter the sunset clause, the more limited the autonomy vested in administrative authorities. As Tushnet observes,[90] and as Colonel Sibthorp had argued in favour of a shorter sunset clause, he 'would prefer the limitation to one year, to show that the House had no confidence [. . .]'.[91]

Nowadays, the use of time limits in delegated legislation to administrative authorities is a worldwide practice. Looking at the use of sunset clauses in legislation conferring legislative power to subordinate bodies and local organisations as a whole, it would be true to say that the sunset clause permits Parliament to monitor to an extent the subordinated bodies and reaffirm their actions.[92] On the one hand, the parliamentary authority to review from time to time the delegated power to subordinate bodies is an expression of the doctrine of parliamentary sovereignty.[93] On the other hand, the parliamentary review of delegated powers to the government is an expression of the doctrine of separation of powers.[94] Parliament limits the scope of the delegated authority, puts it in probation and gives more specific direction to the courts in case they review their actions.

Emerging elements of the rule of law and sunset clauses

Habeas Corpus Suspension Acts

The transition to the new Hanoverian regime was also turbulent and led to the suspension of habeas corpus. Following the establishment of George I in 1714, Tory Jacobites in England conspired against the new regime. The reaction of Parliament was to suspend habeas corpus for six months,[95] which was then extended for another six-month term during the same session of Parliament.[96] However, when in 1722 an annual Habeas Corpus Suspension Act was introduced in the House of Lords and was finally passed,[97] the Commons protested, raising concerns about the length of suspension. Revealing information is contained in Cobbett's reports regarding the Commons' protest about the length of the sunset clause. The main concern was that the sunset clause limiting the duration of the Habeas Corpus Suspension Acts was never above the term of six months, while the current Act included a one-year

89 Committee on Ministers' Powers, *Report* (Cmd 4060 1932) [15].
90 Mark V Tushnet, 'The Possibilities of Comparative Constitutional Law' (1999) 108 Yale Law Journal 1225, 1258.
91 HC Deb 17 June 1847 vol 93 col 696.
92 See Ch 6.
93 Regarding the nature of parliamentary sovereignty see AV Dicey, *Introduction to the Study of the Law of the Constitution Vol I* (JWF Allison ed, OUP 2013) 27.
94 See Ch 5.
95 Habeas Corpus Suspension, etc. Act 1714 (1 Geo I st 2 c 8): 'to impower his Majesty to secure and detain such persons as his Majesty shall suspect are conspiring against his person and government'.
96 Habeas Corpus Suspension, etc. Act 1714 (1 Geo I st 2 c 30): 'to impower his Majesty to secure and detain such persons as his Majesty shall suspect are conspiring against his person and government'.
97 Habeas Corpus Suspension Act 1722 (9 Geo I c 1).

sunset clause, which it was feared might set a precedent for the suspending habeas corpus on another occasion for a longer term.[98]

A series of successive Habeas Corpus Suspension Acts were passed, including at the turn of the 18th century under George III. The decade just before the 19th century was a period inspired by the French Revolution, and a radical movement against the constitutional order emerged, calling for constitutional reform.[99] The response of Pitt's government was the suspension of habeas corpus[100] from May 1794 until February 1795, which was further renewed until July 1795.[101] In 1795 the Seditious Permitting Act,[102] which forbade meetings of more than fifty people without prior permission from a magistrate, was introduced and had a three-year sunset clause. The Treasonable Practices Act[103] was set to expire upon the death of King George III, but it became perpetual in 1817.[104] Moreover, in 1798 another series of successive Habeas Corpus Suspension Acts were passed,[105] suspending habeas corpus until February 1799, which was then renewed until May 1799,[106] and which was further renewed until March 1800.[107]

The inclusion of sunset clauses in habeas corpus suspension acts was a parliamentary effort to impose an institutional restraint on the executive. In nature the writ of habeas corpus is a remedy, a procedural act which secures the effectiveness of a right.[108] In his chapter on the rule of law comparing the suspension of habeas corpus with the repeal of habeas corpus, Dicey states that the former is more effective than the latter, since the government can confront the emergency while the people are not deprived of their freedoms.[109] The reference by Dicey to the habeas corpus suspension acts contributes to the existing analysis, and useful conclusions can be drawn therefrom. The suspension of habeas corpus was 'the exclusive prerogative of Parliament',[110] as the legislature confers powers to the executive for a limited period, but retains control at the expiration of the sunset clause.[111] That said, this transfer of authority to the executive might lead to arbitrary powers in case a habeas corpus suspension act is coupled with an act of indemnity.[112] As an act of indemnity might *ex post facto* remove all liabilities of the executive, this empowers the executive with arbitrary powers and denies

98 *Cobbett's Parliamentary History of England Vol VIII* (Hansard 1813) 38.
99 J Steven Watson, *The Reign of George III 1760–1815* (Clarendon Press 1960) 360.
100 Suspension of Habeas Corpus Act 1794 (34 Geo III c 54).
101 Habeas Corpus Suspension Act 1795 (35 Geo III c 3).
102 The Treasonable Practices Act 1796 (36 Geo III c 8).
103 The Treasonable Practices Act 1796 (36 Geo III c 8).
104 Treason Act 1817 (57 Geo III c 6).
105 Habeas Corpus Suspension Act 1798 (38 Geo III c 36).
106 Habeas Corpus Suspension Act 1799 (39 Geo III c 15).
107 Habeas Corpus Suspension Act 1799 (39 Geo III c 44).
108 AV Dicey, *Introduction to the Study of the Law of the Constitution Vol I* (JWF Allison ed, OUP 2013) 129. For further analysis on Dicey's view about the nature of habeas corpus see JWF Allison, English Historical Constitution: Continuity, Change and European Effects (CUP 2007) 160.
109 AV Dicey, *Introduction to the Study of the Law of the Constitution Vol I* (JWF Allison ed, OUP 2013) 133.
110 David L Shapiro, 'Habeas Corpus, Suspension, and Detention: Another View' (2006) 82 Notre Dame Law Review 59, 71
111 For further analysis on the institutional impact of sunset clauses on the relationship between legislature and executive see Ch 5.
112 AV Dicey, *Introduction to the Study of the Law of the Constitution Vol I* (JWF Allison ed, OUP 2013) 135. For more analysis on Acts of Indemnity see Ch 1.

any relief to the people deprived from the writ of habeas corpus.[113] Nonetheless, this development depends on the spectrum of the indemnity act, whether it is construed widely or narrowly.[114]

The establishment of sunset clauses in emergencies

Temporary legislation was established at the turn of the 18th century as a legislative means to deal with emergencies and contingencies. Blackstone, when commenting on emergencies and the suspension of habeas corpus, affirms that 'this experiment ought only to be tried in cases of extreme emergency; and in these the nation parts with its liberty for a while, in order to preserve it for ever'.[115] Indeed, although the concept of the rule of law at that time was not as sophisticated as it is today,[116] criticism of the use of such clauses in emergencies is revealed.

In the late 18th century, a series of emergency legislation was enacted concerning the status of the US. Although Parliament had the power to legislate for the internal affairs of the colonies, it was mainly concerned with colonial trade and its organisation until at least 1765.[117] However, due to the inability of the executive branch to carry out its measures, Parliament was called to express its determination to tighten the economic and political control over the colonies.[118] It adopted a number of acts, including the Revenue Act,[119] the Currency Act,[120] the Stamp Act[121] and the Quartering Act.[122] These became a source of tension between the colonies and the British government, and were actively opposed by Colonial legislatures.[123] Among the aforementioned acts, only the Quartering Act, which aimed to ensure that the British soldiers would have housing and supplies in the US, was due to expire in March 1767. The sunset clause in this Act was in accordance with the annually renewed Mutiny Act, to which it was an amendment.

When the New York legislature refused to comply with the Quartering Act,[124] the Parliament responded with an 'Act for restraining and prohibiting the Governor, Council and House of Representatives of the Province of New York until provision shall have been made

113 AV Dicey, *Introduction to the Study of the Law of the Constitution Vol I* (JWF Allison ed, OUP 2013) 135.

114 AV Dicey, *Introduction to the Study of the Law of the Constitution Vol I* (JWF Allison ed, OUP 2013) 135.

115 Bl Comm, Book 1:136.

116 Galligan states: 'History gives little guidance, since it is only relatively recently that standards, such as the rule of law or due process, have been invoked to define the parameters of law's formal qualities': DJ Galligan, *Law in Modern Society* (OUP 2007) 258.

117 *Cobbett's Parliamentary History of England Vol XVI* (Hansard 1813) 69; WS Holdsworth, *A History of English Law Vol XI* (Methuen 1938) 159; cf WA Speck, 'Britain and the Atlantic World', in HT Dickinson (ed), *A companion to Eighteenth-Century Britain* (Blackwell Publishing 2002) 451. Speck sets the landmark at Parliament's focus on commerce with the US until the end of the Sir Walpole ministry in 1942.

118 *Cobbett's Parliamentary History of England Vol XVI* (Hansard 1813) 107, 1004; WS Holdsworth, *A History of English Law Vol XI* (Methuen 1938) 159; Merrill Jensen (ed), *English Historical Documents* (Eyre & Spottiswoode 1955) 659.

119 4 Geo III c 15.

120 Paper Bills of Credit Act 1763 (4 Geo III c 34).

121 Duties in American Colonies Act 1765 (5 Geo III c 12).

122 Mutiny, America Act 1765 (5 Geo III c 33).

123 Merrill Jensen (ed), *English Historical Documents* (Eyre & Spottiswoode 1955) 659.

124 *Cobbett's Parliamentary History of England Vol XVI* (Hansard 1813) 331.

for furnishing the King's Troops with all Necessaries required by Law from passing or assenting to any Act of Assembly'.[125] This Act included a sunset clause, with an imprecise sunsetting time; however, as soon as the Assembly complied with the Quartering Act, the Act would automatically sunset. In fact, it was the first time a sunset clause was used in order to suspend a local body of a province.

In 1774, however, the same practice was recorded as soon as Parliament passed an 'Act to Discontinue in such manner and for such time as are therein mentioned the Landing and Discharging, Lading or Shipping of Goods Wares and Merchandise at the Town and within the Harbour of Boston',[126] when the mob demonstrating against the Tea Act[127] dumped tea from Britain into the harbour.[128] This time the sunset clause was used in order to block a function of the city of Boston. In addition, Parliament passed a series of acts in order to reassert its authority in Massachusetts, changing its constitution with the Massachusetts Governments Act,[129] assuring the execution of the law with the Administration of Justice Act,[130] having a three-year sunset clause, and re-enacting the Quartering Act,[131] which was due to expire on March 1776.

Eventually, at the outbreak of the American War of Independence, Parliament passed an act prohibiting trade with the Colonies lasting for the period that the 'said colonies respectively shall remain in a state of rebellion'.[132] It was the first time that Parliament used an act with an uncertain expiration date. Thus the Committee upon Expired and Expiring Laws of 1796 had to clarify that the termination of temporary law occurs by the extinction of the subject matter of their operation.[133] In 1808 the same committee stated that temporary laws which depend on the duration of a war or other contingency are distinguished as laws of an uncertain duration.[134]

Likewise, during the Napoleonic Wars, Parliament passed a series of temporary legislation with similarly constructed sunset clauses with an uncertain duration.[135] For example, an act preventing correspondence with the French was enacted, lasting as long as the war was continuing.[136] Furthermore, an act regarding the manning of the navy was enacted, providing that 'this act shall continue in full force, until such matters and every thing dependent thereupon, shall be finally adjudged and determined'.[137]

In addition, another act was enacted which permitted French royalists to serve in the British Army, providing that 'this act shall be in force and have Continuance during the said War, and from the End thereof to the End of the then next session of Parliament'.[138]

125 Rebellion in America Act 1767 (7 Geo III c 59).
126 Trade Act (14 Geo III c 19).
127 Customs Act 1772 (13 Geo III c 44).
128 Merrill Jensen (ed), *English Historical Documents* (Eyre & Spottiswoode 1955) 778.
129 Massachusetts Governments Act 1774 (14 Geo III c 45).
130 Administration of Justice Act 1774 (14 Geo III c 39).
131 Quartering Act 1774 (14 Geo III c 54).
132 American Prohibitory Act 1776 (16 Geo III c 5).
133 Committee upon Temporary Laws, Expired or Expiring, *Report* (HC 13 May 1796) 831.
134 Committee upon Expired and Expiring Laws, *Report* (HC 25 January 1808).
135 However, temporary Acts were enacted with defined sunset clauses, such as the John Wilkinson's Estate Act 1794 (34 Geo III c 67) with a seven-year sunset clause, and the Negotiations of Notes and Bills Act 1797 (37 Geo III c 32) with a one-year sunset clause.
136 Correspondence with Enemies Act 1793 (33 Geo III c 27).
137 Manning of the Navy Act 1794 (34 Geo III c 66).
138 Enlistment Act 1794 (34 Geo III c 43).

However, in 1804, during the Napoleonic Wars, it was explicitly renewed.[139] Finally, an act of 1798, concerning the communication with people living in hostile territories, included in its title and in the preamble a sunset clause with a similar construction, namely as long as the war was continuing.[140] As Holdsworth points out, these were acts of 'temporary importance which were demanded by the exigencies of the war'.[141]

Interestingly, during the same period, in 1799 William Pitt introduced new duties as temporary measures because of the financial needs arising from the Napoleonic Wars. The innovation was that the new duties were imposed upon the assessed income. The Act was entitled 'An Act for granting to His Majesty an Aid and Contribution for the Prosecution of the War'[142] and incorporated a sunset clause conditional upon the end of the war in its title. These duties, which are also known as the 'Triple Assessment',[143] are, in essence, the origin of the income tax.

The same year, in 1799, the Act was repealed and replaced with an act imposing a 10 per cent tax on income, which was also limited to the duration of the war.[144] Irrespective of the existence of the sunset clause, the act was repealed following the Peace of Amiens in 1802.[145] However, as peace discussions with the French had failed,[146] the Act was revived by Pitt's successor Addington in 1803,[147] and it was amended in 1806.[148] The latter version, which was the foundation of the income tax as we know it in the modern era,[149] was to expire, according to the title, on 'the sixth day of April next after the ratification of a definitive treaty of peace',[150] even though the original proposal on the duration of the clause was six months after the restoration of peace.[151] Eventually, in 1816, the victory in Waterloo signalled the expiration of the act.[152] Nonetheless, in 1842, due to a £5 million deficit,[153] the defunct income tax was revived. According to the title, the initial duration was to last 'until the sixth day of April 1845'.[154]

The preceding paradigms show how sunset clauses in emergency legislation increasingly conformed to a 'pattern', although this raised concerns about the protection of civil liberties.[155] Suffice it to mention the reaction of the Members of Parliament enacting the Seditious Permitting Act and the Treasonable Practices Act who expressed their concern from a human rights perspective. Alderman Lushington in particular recognised that the former Act was a 'temporary sacrifice for the general good' and he proposed an annual restriction at most.[156] In the

139 Enlistment of Foreigners Act 1804 (44 Geo III c 75); Enlistment of Foreigners Act 1806 (46 Geo III c 23).
140 Residence in France During the War Act 1798 (38 Geo III c 79).
141 WS Holdsworth, *A History of English Law Vol XIII* (Methuen 1952) 175
142 Aid and Contribution for the Prosecution of the War 1798 (38 Geo III c 16).
143 Bertram Cox, 'Origin and Growth of Income Tax' (1919) 1 Journal Comparative Legislation and International Law 42.
144 Duties on Income Act 1799 (39 Geo III c 13).
145 Income Tax Repeal, etc. Act 1808 (42 Geo III c 42).
146 *Cobbett's Parliamentary History of England Vol XXXVI* (Hansard 1820) 1258.
147 Income Tax Act 1803 (43 Geo III c 122).
148 Income Tax Act 1806 (46 Geo III c 65).
149 See Albert Farnsworth, *Addington: Author of the Modern Income Tax* (Stevens & Sons 1951).
150 Income Tax Act 1806 (46 Geo III c 65).
151 *Cobbett's Parliamentary History of England Vol XXXVI* (Hansard 1820) 1596.
152 Stanley N. Katz (ed), *The Oxford International Encyclopaedia of Legal History Vol 5* (OUP 2009) 428.
153 Stanley N. Katz (ed), *The Oxford International Encyclopaedia of Legal History Vol 5* (OUP 2009) 428.
154 Income Tax Act 1842 (5&6 Vict c 35).
155 For further discussion see Ch 8.
156 *Cobbett's Parliamentary History of England Vol XXXII* (Hansard 1818) 303.

Duke of Bedford's speech, the first roots of the proportionality principle are identifiable, with the Duke stating that 'even allowing that some bill was necessary for the greater protection of his majesty, there was nothing in this bill that could tend to that purpose'.[157]

Difficulty from extensive use

At the turn of the 19th century, the expiration date of the sunset clause was even more precise. For instance the Molasses Act[158] prescribed that 'the same shall continue and be in force for the space of five years, to be computed from the twenty-fourth day of June one thousand seven hundred and thirty three, and to end of the then next session of parliament', while another expression was used regarding the punishment of mutiny, which prescribed that the 'act further continue until the expiration of six weeks after the commencement of the next session of parliament'.[159]

Both the precise expiration date of the temporary legislation and the extensive workload of the Parliament led to the expiration of several temporary acts without being renewed.[160] One example is the case of an important constitutional law, 16 Geo III c 107, which empowered the King to summon the Parliament in the case of a contingency but which was allowed to expire by mistake.[161] In fact, the Committee upon Temporary laws, Expired and Expiring remarked in 1796 that the volume of the statutes had at least doubled as compared with the previous six centuries.[162]

The responsibility over this omission was discussed in Parliament, as the responsibility was charged between ministers and MPs. The Chancellor of the Exchequer clarified that:

> the right hon. gent. seemed to think that it was the duty of ministers to attend to the acts that were likely to expire, but did not seem to be aware that a committee was appointed at the commencement of every session to inquire what bills were likely to expire, and if any neglect took place, it was the act of the house.[163]

Thus Parliament passed an act in 1808 prescribing that:

> Where any bill may have been or shall be introduced into this present or any future session of Parliament for the continuance of any Act which would expire in such sessions, and such Act shall have expired before the bill for continuing the same shall have received the royal assent, such continuing Act shall be deemed and taken to have effect from the date of the expiration of the Act intended to be continued as fully and effectually, to all intents and purposes, as if such continuing Act had actually passed before the expiration of such Act, except it shall be otherwise especially provided in such continuing Act.[164]

157 *Cobbett's Parliamentary History of England Vol XXXII* (Hansard 1818) 303 250.
158 Trade of Sugar Colonies Act 1732 (6 Geo II c 13).
159 Army and Navy Act 1798 (39 Geo III c 4).
160 A committee, annually appointed, was required to investigate the expiring laws, but its limited authority decreased its efficiency. See Committee upon Temporary Laws, Expired or Expiring, *Report* (HC 13 May 1796) 830.
161 Committee upon Temporary Laws, Expired or Expiring, *Report* (HC 13 May 1796) 832.
162 Committee upon Temporary Laws, Expired or Expiring, *Report* (HC 13 May 1796) 35.
163 HC Deb 16 June 1808 vol 11 col 912.
164 Acts of Parliament (Expiration) Act 1808 (48 Geo III c 106).

During the19th and 20th centuries, Parliament appointed several special committees with the task of improving the process of continuing the duration of temporary acts, and their records provide us with useful information. Until 1863, the duration of temporary laws was renewed by a separate act,[165] but since 1863 the temporary laws have been continued annually with the expiring continuance act, and since 1874 they more or less had one common expiration date.[166] However, the concern in 1922 was that until then, there was no systematic scrutiny upon the continuity as long as the continuance bills were introduced at a very late period of the parliamentary session, resulting in the renewal without adequate debate, infringing at the same time the rights of the MPs.[167]

In all respects, the committee's recommendation was that the expiring law continuity bill should be introduced at a much earlier stage of the session, while a triennial review of all temporary acts should be desirable in order to prevent the congestion.[168] Moreover, the argument that an act is controversial shall not be a reason for temporary regulation, while experimental legislation should after a reasonable period of trial either be made permanent or dropped.[169] Consequently, temporary laws were continued with the expiring continuance act. In fact, the expiring laws continuance bills were a permanent mechanism of renewing the duration of the temporary acts from 1928 to 1970,[170] and once an act was included in the list there was danger that it might became part of the permanent system of law.[171]

In the late 19th century, an act was passed for the further revision of the statute law repealing enactments that have ceased to be in force or have been unnecessary.[172] In the note attached to the proposed bill, it was prescribed that:

> for the purposes of the schedule six different classes of enactments are considered as having ceased to be in force although not expressly and specifically repealed; namely such enactments as are-expired- that is enactments which, having been originally limited to endure only for a specified period by a district provision, have not been either perpetuated or kept in force by continuance or which have merely had for their object the continuance of previous temporary enactments for periods now gone effluxion of time [. . .].[173]

With this Act, it is the first time that the basic principle of sunset clauses, *expressio unius, est exclusio alterious*, is adopted explicitly.

Hence, according to the above Act, a sunset clause was enacted in 1939 prescribing that:

> the act shall continue in force for a period of two years from the date of the passing thereof and no longer, so, however, that the provisions of the Interpretation Act 1889

165 Select Committee on the Expiring Laws Continuance Act, *Report* (HC 21 July 1922) [3].
166 Select Committee on the Expiring Laws Continuance Act, *Report* (HC 21 July 1922) [4].
167 Select Committee on the Expiring Laws Continuance Act, *Report* (HC 21 July 1922) [6].
168 Select Committee on the Expiring Laws Continuance Act, *Report* (HC 21 July 1922) [8–11].
169 Select Committee on the Expiring Laws Continuance Act, *Report* (HC 26 May 1925) [3].
170 Daniel Greenburg (ed), *Craies on Legislation* (8th edn, Sweet and Maxwell 2004) 385 (fn 9).
171 Select Committee on the Expiring Laws Continuance Act, *Report* (HC 21 July 1922).
172 Statute Law Revision Act 1894 (57&58 Vict c 56).
173 Explanatory Notes to the Statutory Revision Act 1894 [1].

> relating to the effect of repealing enactments shall apply upon the expiry of this Act in like manner as if this act had been repealed.[174]

Until recently, the drafting of a sunset clause was Parliament's concern, as it issued a series of Standing Orders from 1998 until 2012 regulating the way MPs are to conduct public business.[175]

Useful conclusions can be reached from the aforementioned examples which caused disruption to legislative work. The consolidated review of temporary acts proved to be inefficient. The Acts were not renewed on time, nor were proper evaluations taking place. The fact that a law is controversial does not excuse the temporary character of the law; as soon as the trial period expires, legislation should be evaluated and either be allowed to expire or made perpetual. While during the period of the first two Stuarts inconvenience was caused by the expiration of several Acts due to the lack of co-operation between the King and his Parliament, difficulty was also caused in a more modern period due to the extensive use of sunset clauses.

Conclusions

As the legislative process in the UK crystallised and the parties became the mechanism of legislative work, the use of sunset clauses became more limited as the opposition's role in influencing the adoption of bills diminished. Nevertheless, sunset clauses served to reinforce parliamentary sovereignty and were used as an expression of authority over subordinate bodies with delegated powers. Parliament can confer legislative functions, though if this delegation is perpetual, the Diceyan doctrine of sovereignty is challenged.

From another perspective, sunset clauses are a mechanism of interaction between previous and subsequent Parliaments. Sir Edward Grey accurately observed that by arguing in favour of a sunset clause amendment:

> the Solicitor-General had stated that another Parliament would be absolutely free to reverse legislation passed by the present Parliament. That, of course, was perfectly true, since every new Parliament had, in theory, a perfectly clear start, but what had been done in one Parliament might make it more or less difficult for another Parliament to feel itself free in the matter. Much of the Solicitor-General's speech was, in effect, an exemplification of the manner in which, if the Bill passed without a time limit, it would, year by year, become increasingly difficult for the House to adopt any alternative system of temperance reform.[176]

At the same time, the ordinary use of sunset clauses in specific types of legislation, such as the 'money bills' and the emergency acts, forms a pattern. Regarding the 'money bills', sunset clauses are taken for granted, as they are considered temporary.[177]

174 Prevention of Violence (Temporary Provisions) Act 1939. For more analysis on this interpretation rule, see Ch 1.

175 For the latest Standing Order, see Standing Orders of the House of Commons, *Public Business* (2012 HC 614).

176 HC Deb 26 July 1904 vol 138 col 1244.

177 KG Davies (ed), *Calendar of State Papers Colonial, America and West Indies Vol 45* (HM Stationery Office 1994, Digital version at British History Online) [67].

In addition, a new aspect of sunset clauses became apparent, with implications for the rule of law, as exemplified by the first emergency acts with sunset clauses. It would be inappropriate to elaborate in detail on the interaction of such clauses with the modern idea of rule of law. Nonetheless, the discussion revealed the interaction between sunset clauses and elements of the rule of law that were present in that period.

The use of a sunset clause in suspending habeas corpus for a certain period during the 18th century might be regarded as an institutional restraint on the executive. Nonetheless, the increasing concern of the MPs about the impact of temporary emergency legislation on civil liberties is worthy of note.

On the other hand, the difficulties caused by the extensive use of sunset clauses in legislation and the bureaucracy required to renew them led Parliament to more temperate usage. The recommendation of the Committee on Expiring Laws of 1922 is noteworthy. It set out the principle that the regulation of controversial issues cannot be a reason to 'preclude a recommendation of permanency'.[178]

178 Select Committee on the Expiring Laws Continuance Act, *Report* (HC 21 July 1922).

Part III

Institutional effect of sunset clauses

5 Sunset clauses and separation of powers

> Un peuple a toujours le droit de revoir, de réformer et de changer sa Constitution. Une génération ne peut assujettir à ses lois les générations futures. (People of a nation always have the right of examining, reviewing and amending their Constitution. A generation cannot force the forthcoming ones to follow its rules.)
>
> Constitution du 24 Juin 1793, Article 28

Defining separation of powers

The doctrine of separation of powers is a cornerstone in the foundation of modern democracies. Its roots, though, are drawn from the manuscripts of ancient philosophers, such as Aristotle.[1] Although several authors approached the idea of separation of powers, such as Locke[2] and Sir Humphrey Mackworth,[3] nowadays Montesquieu is considered the scholar who established its dogma, as Vile[4] and Casper[5] state. By laying out the theoretical framework of the doctrine, the main objective is to discover the potential interaction between sunset clauses and the separation of powers.

To begin with, Montesquieu does not mention the term 'separation of powers', but he clearly argues that 'in each state there are three sorts of powers: legislative power, executive power over the things depending on the right of nations, and the executive power over the things depending on civil rights [the power of judging]'.[6] Furthermore, he explains that

1 Aristotle, *Politics*, 1297b-1298a: 'All forms of constitution then have three factors in reference to which the good lawgiver has to consider what is expedient for each constitution; [. . .] Of these three factors one is, what is to be the body that deliberates about the common interests, second the one connected with the magistracies, that is, what there are to be and what matters they are to control, and what is to be the method of their election, and a third is, what is to be the judiciary.'

2 John Locke, *Two Treatises of Government* (J Whiston, W Strahan, J and F Rivington, L Davis, W Owen and 18 others1772) 293. Locke claimed that there should be a distinction between the body enacting legislation and the body executing it.

3 Sir Humphrey Mackworth, *A Vindication of the Rights of the Commons of England* (Printed and sold by the booksellers of London and Westminster 1701) 2. Mackworth explored his concept about a prudent distribution of power, particularly the legislative power that will safeguard the prerogatives of the king and the rights of the people.

4 MJC Vile, *Constitutionalism and the Separation of Powers* (2nd edn, Liberty Fund 1998) 83.

5 Gerhard Casper, 'An Essay in Separation of Powers: Some Early Versions and Practices' (1989) 30 William and Mary Law Review 213.

6 Montesquieu, *The Spirit of the Laws* (Anne Cohler and others trs, CUP 1989) 156. Regarding the criticism against this doctrine see JWF Allison, *English Historical Constitution: Continuity, Change and*

these powers should not be concentrated in the authority of the same person, or body, but they should be separate as 'all would be lost if the same man or the same body of principal men either of nobles, or of people, exercised these three powers: that of making the laws, that of executing public resolutions, and that of judging the crimes or the disputes of individuals'.[7]

In these words, jurists and political theorists have identified the 'pure' separation of powers according to which an evident distinction is drawn between institutions or persons holding and exercising unique functions.[8] There are three basic elements of the pure theory: first, government is constituted by three autonomous branches; second, each branch exercises exclusively specific function; finally, the three branches comprise distinct people or groups of people.[9]

The reference of Montesquieu to several forms of checks and balances, though, inspired some scholars to argue that Montesquieu implied a 'partial' separation of powers where a system of checks and balances among the institutions leads to a fusion of powers.[10] Montesquieu, focusing on the relations between the executive and the legislative, endorsed, to a degree, forms of checks and balances, mentioning that 'if the executive does not have the right to check the enterprises of the legislative body, the latter will be despotic, for it will wipe out all the other powers, since it will be able to give to itself all the power it can imagine'; and, 'but if, in a free state, legislative power should not have the right to check executive power, it has the right and should have the faculty to examine the manner in which the laws it has made have been executed'.[11]

Indeed, the latter interpretation was followed by Madison, who supported the interaction between the branches of the government and established the political theory of 'checks and balances'. His ideas are impressed in three federalist papers, numbers 47, 48 and 51.[12] Like Montesquieu, Madison advocated that the separation of powers doctrine is a critical principle for a democratic regime, as it would be an answer to tyranny.[13] Madison argued in favour of a limited sharing of power, as the real meaning of Montesquieu was that:

European Effects (CUP 2007) 83ff. Montesquieu conceptualised the doctrine of separation of powers inspired by the British Constitution, although he misrepresented it. See Roger Masterman, *The Separation of Powers in the Contemporary Constitution: Judicial Competence and Independence in the United Kingdom* (CUP 2011) 13.

7 Montesquieu, *The Spirit of the Laws* (Anne Cohler and others trs, CUP 1989) 157.

8 'The pure doctrine as we have described it embodies what might be called a "negative" approach to the checking of the power of the agencies of government. The mere existence of several autonomous decision-taking bodies with specific functions is considered to be a sufficient brake upon the concentration of power.' See MJC Vile, *Constitutionalism and the Separation of Powers* (2nd edn, Liberty Fund 1998) 19.

9 MJC Vile, *Constitutionalism and the Separation of Powers* (2nd edn, Liberty Fund 1998) 15.

10 Concerning the debate upon the real meaning of Montesquieu see MJC Vile, *Constitutionalism and the Separation of Powers* (2nd edn, Liberty Fund 1998) 94.

11 Montesquieu, *The Spirit of the Laws* (Anne Cohler and others trs, CUP 1989) 162.

12 The Federalist Papers are a series of eighty-five essays published anonymously in the New York newspapers with the aim to promote the ratification of the US Constitution. Although all of them are signed by an author named by the pseudonym 'Publius', these three papers are attributed to Madison. See Douglass Adair, 'The Authorship of the Disputed Federalist Papers' (1944) 1 William and Mary Quarterly 97.

13 Ralph Ketcham (ed), *Selected Writings of James Madison* (Hacket Publishing 2006) 109.

> [H]e did not mean that these departments ought to have no partial agency in, or no control over, the acts of each other. His meaning, as his own words import, and still more conclusively as illustrated by the example in his eye, can amount to no more than this, that where the whole power of one department is exercised by the same hands which possess the whole power of another department, the fundamental principles of a free constitution are subverted.[14]

Furthermore, he advocated the system of checks and balances, explaining that it:

> [D]oes not require that the legislative, executive, and judiciary departments should be wholly unconnected with each other. I shall undertake, in the next place, to show that unless these departments be so far connected and blended as to give to each a constitutional control over the others, the degree of separation which the maxim requires, as essential to a free government, can never in practice be duly maintained.[15]

Finally, Madison concluded in Federalist Paper number 51 that with the checks and balances system:

> [A] double security arises to the rights of the people. The different governments will control each other, at the same time that each will be controlled by itself. Second, it is of great importance in a republic not only to guard the society against the oppression of its rulers, but to guard one part of the society against the injustice of the other part.[16]

According to Madison's understanding, the negative status of checks between the institutions was not enough for good governance. Thus he also stressed the more positive side of separation of powers, where the three functions, and particularly the legislative function, are allocated and entrusted to more than one institution. As a result, he introduced a functional-based approach to the separation of powers, pursuant to which the three functions remain the same, the government is constituted by three branches, but nonetheless the governmental functions are exercised by more than one institution sharing powers – or, as Vile names it, as a system of 'partial separation of functions'.[17]

Madison himself expressed the view that there was no difference between his approach and that of Montesquieu, as he stated that 'from these facts, by which Montesquieu was guided, it may clearly be inferred that, [. . .] he did not mean that these departments ought to have no partial agency in, or no control over, the acts of each other'.[18] A closer examination of the two approaches reveals that both Montesquieu and Madison agreed on the independence of the judicial branch, while the competence of the legislative power and the extent of the checks and balances systems seems to be based on a different approach. From a more theoretical

14 Ralph Ketcham (ed), *Selected Writings of James Madison* (Hacket Publishing 2006) 111.

15 Ralph Ketcham (ed), *Selected Writings of James Madison* (Hacket Publishing 2006) 112.

16 Ralph Ketcham (ed), *Selected Writings of James Madison* (Hacket Publishing 2006) 123.

17 MJC Vile, *Constitutionalism and the Separation of Powers* (2nd edn, Liberty Fund 1998) 20. In practice, the exercise of these three functions among the institutions differs from case to case and depends mainly on necessity. Regarding the functionalist approach, see Daniel Farber, William Eskridge Jr., Philip Frickey, *Constitutional Law, Themes for the Constitution's Third Century* (2nd edn, West Group 1998) 909.

18 Ralph Ketcham (ed), *Selected Writings of James Madison* (Hacket Publishing 2006) 111.

approach, the normative starting points of Montesquieu and Madison are different. Montesquieu's approach is based on the institutions, expressing a more formal approach of the doctrine, while Madison emphasises the functional element of the separation of powers.

The perceived differences between the two doctrines of separation of powers are blunt or sharp depending on their practical application. Of great importance in the evaluation of each separation of powers system is the hierarchy between the separation of institutions, which is the formal approach, and the separation of functions, which is the functional approach. From the formal point of view, the extent of the institutional independence of the legislative branch from the executive and their interactions represents the first issue, which led to parliamentary, presidential and semi-presidential systems of government. From the functional point of view, legislative competence and institutional roles in the law making process are significant for the extent of the checks and balances.

Bearing in mind the separation of powers paradigm of the UK, according to which the boundaries between executive, legislative and judicial branch are volatile,[19] we shall consider the role of sunset clauses from a formal and functional perspective. The issue will be addressed by examining how the use of sunset clauses affects the separation of powers and how the separation of powers affects the use of sunset clauses.

How the use of sunset clauses affects the separation of powers

Until recently, the separation of powers principle was a neglected doctrine in UK constitutional theory.[20] Prior to the Human Rights Act 1998, the application of the separation of powers doctrine from a functional and formal perspective was weak.[21] The executive branch is incorporated in Parliament, and the executive function overlaps with the legislative.[22] This is captured by Bagehot, who remarked that 'the efficient secret of the English Constitution may be described as the close union, the nearly complete fusion of the executive and legislative powers'.[23]

Sunset clauses affect the Westminster conception of the separation of powers in the following ways. First, they permit legislators to introduce new institutions, new governmental functions and new mechanisms of checks and balances. Through the inclusion of a sunset clause, legislators are able to treat these innovations as experiments and check their compatibility with the constitutional status quo. Furthermore, sunset clauses can have another effect on the separation of powers, as they aid the review of executive regulations and enhance legislative oversight, limiting the impact of the centralisation of legislative initiative.

19 Roger Masterman, *The Separation of Powers in the Contemporary Constitution: Judicial Competence and Independence in the United Kingdom* (CUP 2011) 17.

20 For the reasons explaining this stance, see Eric Barendt, 'Separation of Powers and Constitutional Government' (1995) PL 599, 603.

21 The adoption of the HRA 1998 sharpened the separation of powers in the UK, particularly between the judiciary on the one hand and the executive and legislative branches on the other hand. See Adam Tomkins, 'The Rule of Law in Blair's Britain' (2007) 26 University of Queensland Law Journal 255, 290; cf JWF Allison, *English Historical Constitution: Continuity, Change and European Effects* (CUP 2007) 94–5.

22 Committee on Ministers' Powers, *Report* (Cmd 4060 1932) [1].

23 Walter Bagehot, *The English Constitution* (2nd edn, Chapman & Hall 1873) 48.

The initiation of constitutional experiments

The artificial connection between executive, legislative and judicial power in a specific institution, and the extent of checks and balances between the institutions, is dynamic, especially because a mere legislative act is capable of amending and reshaping the status quo. Therefore, sunset clauses permit legislators to apply the new order for a certain period of time and evaluate its efficiency and results before making permanent a new institution, or a mechanism of checks and balances. Thus the most significant use of sunset clauses in governmental functions is associated with the initiation of constitutional and institutional experiments.

In the long constitutional history of the UK, a plethora of constitutional developments took place prior to the current situation. Remarkably, during the early stage, as seen in the historical chapters of this book,[24] the House of Commons, as a condition of granting revenue to Henry IV, requested the list with the names of the Lords participating in the Council to be submitted beforehand to Parliament. This was, in effect, a form of parliamentary check over the executive and, consequently, a primitive expression of 'ministerial responsibility'. Henry IV complied with the Commons' request temporarily, because this practice was to last until the following parliament due to a sunset clause. Stubbs describes the whole bill as the 'trial and failure of a great constitutional experiment; a premature testing of the strength of the parliamentary system'.[25] This incident is marked in constitutional history as the 'Lancastrian experiment'. It was the first time that a mechanism of checks and balances between the Crown and the Commons was introduced, even though the experiment was not revived after the lapse of the sunset clause.

Unfortunately, in the UK this aspect of sunset clauses has limited use, and it is deployed mainly in relation to the status of Northern Ireland.[26] Indeed in 1972, the Northern Ireland (Temporary Provisions) Act was adopted, initiating the policy of direct rule from Westminster.[27] The Act contained a one-year sunset clause in combination with a Henry VIII clause.[28] Nonetheless, the following year, the expiration of the Act was set upon several conditions according to the Northern Ireland Constitution Act.[29] Eventually, in 1999, the Act imposing direct rule in Northern Ireland was repealed.[30]

Despite the fact that in the recent constitutional history of the UK sunset clauses were used scarcely in constitutional experiments, an act adopted in the US in 1978 as a response to the Nixon Scandal, also known as Watergate, exemplifies the impact that a temporary law may have on the separation of powers. Congress adopted the Ethics in Government

24 See Ch 3.

25 William Stubbs, *The Constitutional History of England in its Origin and Development Vol. III* (first published 1878, CUP 2011) 5.

26 As a Member of Parliament, Mark Dunkan remarked: '[S]unset clauses have been used in various bits of Northern Ireland legislation during the peace process, as institutions were established, different arrangements were put in place, and safeguards were introduced that it was hoped could later be disposed of. Sunset clauses were inserted in the hope that the circumstances and environment would change so the law would not have to remain permanently on the statute book, and there would not have to be a full Act of repeal.' See HC Deb 1 July 2009 Vol 495 col 403.

27 HL Deb 05 December 1972 vol 337 col 145.

28 Northern Ireland (Temporary Provisions) Act 1972, s 1(5).

29 Northern Ireland Constitution Act 1973, s 2 (among the conditions was the formation of the Northern Ireland Executive, and the adoption of several provisions by the Northern Ireland Assembly).

30 The Northern Ireland Act 1998 (Commencement No 5) Order 1999 SI 1999/3209.

Act 1978, according to which, an independent prosecutor was appointed to investigate abuse of executive power.[31] This Act was subject to a five-year sunset clause.[32]

According to Title VI of the Act, a new institution was founded, an independent prosecutor to exercise, with impartiality and integrity, control over the executive and to investigate abuse of executive power. The task of the new body was to ensure public confidence in criminal investigations of high-ranked governmental officials.[33] Through this legislation, part of the executive power, the authority to control the administration, was transferred to an independent body; in practice this was a judicial appointment.[34] The adoption of the independent prosecutor reshaped the separation of powers in the US. Suffice to say that President Reagan, while signing the Independent Counsel Reauthorization Act of 1987, stated that 'during the years leading up to the original enactment of this statute, and thereafter, the Department of Justice has repeatedly expressed profound concern over the serious departures authorized by the act from separation of powers principles'.[35]

A challenge to the independent counsel provisions of the Ethics in Government Act of 1978 was brought before the US Supreme Court. A principal question was whether 'the Act violates the separation of powers by reducing the President's ability to control the prosecutorial powers wielded by the independent counsel'.[36] Chief Justice Rehnquist delivered the opinion for the majority and concluded that 'we do not think that the Act works any judicial usurpation of properly executive functions'.[37] Justice Scalia, in his dissenting opinion, stressed that '[t]his is an open invitation for Congress to experiment', and he further pondered:

> What about a special Assistant Secretary of State, with responsibility for one very narrow area of foreign policy, who would not only have to be confirmed by the Senate but could also be removed only pursuant to certain carefully designed restrictions? Could this possibly render the President '[un]able to accomplish his constitutional role?' Or a special Assistant Secretary of Defense for Procurement?[38]

31 See Alexander I Tachmes, 'Independent Counsels under the Ethics in Government Act of 1978: A Violation of the Separation of Powers Doctrine or an Essential Check on Executive Power' (1988) 42 University of Miami Law Review, 735.

32 Pub L No 95-521, 92 Stat 1867 (1978).

33 See Alexander Tachmes, 'Independent Counsels under the Ethics in Government Act of 1978: A Violation of the Separation of Powers Doctrine or an Essential Check on Executive Power' (1987–1988) University Miami Law Review, 735; Public Papers of the Presidents, 'Statement on Signing the Independent Counsel Reauthorization Act of 1987' (US Government Printing Office 1989) 1524.

34 According to art II, para 2 of the US Constitution, the President 'shall nominate, and by and with the Advice and Consent of the Senate, shall appoint Ambassadors, other public Ministers and Consuls, Judges of the supreme Court, and all other Officers of the United States, whose Appointments are not herein otherwise provided for, and which shall be established by Law [. . .]', and according to para 3 the President is responsible to 'take care that the Laws be faithfully executed'. According to that obligation, the President appoints the Attorney General to head the Department of Justice to carry out this task. See Constance O'Keefe and Peter Safirstein, 'Fallen Angels, Separation of Powers, and the Saturday Night Massacre: An Examination of the Practical, Constitutional and Political Tensions in the Special Prosecutor Provisions of the Ethics in Government Act' (1982) 49 Brooklyn Law Review 113, 114.

35 Papers of the Presidents, 'Statement on Signing the Independent Counsel Reauthorization Act of 1987' (US Government Printing Office 1989) 1524.

36 *Morrison v Olson* (1988) 487 US 654, 694 (US SC).

37 *Morrison v Olson* (1988) 487 US 654, 696 (US SC).

38 *Morrison v Olson* (1988) 487 US 654, 727 (US SC).

As Ackerman pointed out:

> it [Congress] placed a five-year sunset on the statute in light of the risk that the new official might disrupt the traditional system of checks and balances between the legislature and the executive. After the tenure of independent counsel Kenneth W. Starr, few of us mourned the statute when it automatically expired and Congress refused to reauthorize the constitutional experiment.[39]

The Act was twice re-enacted with amendments[40] until it lapsed in 1992, as Congress refused to renew that piece of legislation and thus to re-authorise the authority of the independent prosecutor.[41] Although the Act expired, it was re-enacted by the Independent Counsel Reauthorization Act of 1994[42] and eventually lapsed in 1999.

All told, such clauses have a crucial utility in the hands of legislators when they promote institutional experimentation. In essence, sunset clauses in such legislation allow an in-depth estimation of the circumstances which led to the new institution first, coupled with a subsequent evaluation of its efficiency. New institutions are established, while the legislative branch evaluates their actions and monitors their expenditure, before then deciding upon the expiration date of the Act either to further renew the life span of these institutions and remove any deficiencies, or to terminate the experimentation. The introduction of new institutions and governmental functions inevitably affects the separation of powers and the checks and balances.

Reinforce the institutional role of the legislature

A principal challenge to separation powers theories, unforeseen by Montesquieu and Madison, is the centralisation of legislative initiative. In principle, legislative power was attributed to Parliaments. Nonetheless, as Craig points out:

> The orthodoxy among political scientists is that, over the last century, the executive has dominated the legislature. This view is reinforced by a whole series of select committee reports, which highlight deficiencies in the legislative process and in the accountability of the executive.[43]

The centralisation of legislative initiative resulted, nonetheless, in government control over law making power.[44] Montesquieu explicitly criticised the concentration of powers in a single body, saying that:

39 Bruce Ackerman, 'Sunset can put a Halt to Twilight of Liberty' September 20, 2001 <http://articles.latimes.com/2001/sep/20/local/me-47757> accessed January 16, 2015.

40 The act was renewed and amended in 1982 with the Ethics in Government Act Amendments, Pub L No 97–409, 96 Stat 2039 (1983), and it was reauthorized in 1987 by the Independent Counsel Reauthorization Act, Pub L No 100–191, 101 Stat 1293 (1987).

41 See Bruce Ackerman, 'Sunset can put a Halt to Twilight of Liberty' September 20, 2001 available at http://articles.latimes.com/2001/sep/20/local/me-47757 accessed February 16, 2014.

42 Pub L No 103–270, 108 Stat 732 (1994).

43 Paul Craig, 'Political Constitutionalism and the Judicial Role: A Response' (2011) 9 International Journal of Constitutional Law 112, 117.

44 Another reason for the increased power of the executive is the development of the party system. See below text to n 102 in Ch V.

> when legislative power is united with executive power in a single person or in a single body of the magistracy, there is no liberty, because one can fear that the same monarch or senate that makes tyrannical laws will execute them tyrannically.[45]

Craig identifies three main causes for the centralisation of legislative initiative: first, the development and the regular use of standing committees to consider legislation in the shortest possible length of time; second, legislative planning and drafting by cabinet committees; and finally, the delegation of law making to the executive.[46] Barendt concludes that 'the truth is that there is no effective separation of powers between legislative and executive in the United Kingdom in the sense of a system of check and balances'.[47]

The first two forms of centralisation were mechanisms to promote legislation adopted in the late-19th century and in the 20th century, respectively,[48] with the effect that Parliament was diminished from a deliberating body to a voting body with limited influence on the final draft of legislation. The delegation of law making powers has its roots in the 16th century.[49] The need to delegate power is an endemic feature of polities, but there are constitutional concerns when the delegated legislation covers broad issues of policy and general interest.[50]

In the historical chapters of this book it was shown that when Parliament gained control of the administration in the 18th century and legislation was enacted with delegation of powers, sunset clauses were used to retain the delegated authority and as an oversight mechanism.[51] Thus the legislative role is not restricted only to the adoption of legislation, but also encompasses legislative oversight of the executive.[52] Remarkably, Craig admits that 'little control is possible over the content of legislation, therefore the value of the Commons must lie elsewhere'.[53]

The need for legislative oversight over delegated power was stressed in numerous reports. Concerns were expressed in the Donoughmore Report, which stated that 'we have already expressed the view that the system of delegated legislation is both legitimate and constitutionally desirable for certain purposes, within certain limits, and under certain safeguards'.[54] The Donoughmore Report recommended a series of measures to prevent abuse of delegated powers, including the use of sunset clauses as a desirable mechanism to prevent abuse of power, especially in relation to Henry VIII clauses.[55]

45 Montesquieu, *The Spirit of the Laws* (Anne Cohler and others trs, CUP 1989) 157.
46 See Paul Craig, *Administrative Law* (7th edn, Sweet & Maxwell 2012) [3–004].
47 Erin Barendt, 'Separation of Powers and Constitutional Government' (1995) PL 599, 614.
48 Paul Craig, *Administrative Law* (7th edn, Sweet & Maxwell 2012) [3–005].
49 Regarding the birth and the growth of delegated legislation, see text to n 57ff in Ch III.
50 Paul Craig, *Administrative Law* (7th edn, Sweet & Maxwell 2012) [15–003]. 718. See also Gabriel Ganz, 'Delegated Legislation: A Necessary Evil or a Constitutional Outrage', in Peter Leyland and Terry Woods (eds), *Administrative Law Facing the Future: Old Constraints and New Horizons* (Blackwell 2003) Ch 3.
51 See Ch 4.
52 Regarding the role of the Legislature see Paul Craig, *Administrative Law* (7th edn, Sweet & Maxwell 2012) [3–006].
53 Paul Craig, *Administrative Law* (7th edn, Sweet & Maxwell 2012) [3–007].
54 Committee on Ministers' Powers, *Report* (Cmd 4060 1932) [11].
55 Committee on Ministers' Powers, *Report* (Cmd 4060 1932) [15].

The utility of sunsets in legislation as a mechanism to control the executive and the administration was popularised in the US after the Watergate Scandal.[56] Lowi, arguing in favour of sunsets at that time has said that:

> a termination date should not be considered a death sentence but an opportunity to learn from experience. This is why the notion of sunset is appropriate, because it implies a creative time during which the politics of the agency I likely to come unstuck and the opportunity for substantive reconsideration is most propitious.[57]

In theory, such clauses benefit the constitutional system as they increase the efficiency and effectiveness of agencies and their accountability to the legislature.

But, after a decade of implementation, a thorough evaluation was published by Kearney according to which twelve out of thirty-six states had implemented sunset clauses, repealed or suspended them, for a variety of reasons. The author concluded that legislators would rather repeal such clauses than make them more workable.[58]

Nowadays, sunset clauses are used extensively in legislation as a mechanism to have agencies controlled by Parliament; a series of acts delegating power to the administration set limits through the inclusion of a sunset clause. For example, in 2002 the government adopted the Education Act, delegating new powers to the Secretary of State for England and National Assembly of Wales to suspend by order several statutory requirements so as to enable innovative pilot projects.[59] However, the powers set out with this delegation were stated to last for a period of four years.[60]

In 2003 the government adopted the Fire Services Act, delegating a broad power to the Secretary of State to modify the conditions of service for fire brigade members and to give directions to fire authorities via an order.[61] This power was subject to a two-year sunset clause after the commencement of the Act.[62] However, the delegated power and its duration were the subject of discussion in the House of Lords. Specifically, the Lords were preoccupied with the effect of the sunset clause, namely whether the orders made before the expiration shall expire or not. Lord Rooker stated that:

> It is a general principle in English law that action taken before the repeal of legislation authorising that action is not affected by the repeal of the legislation. If an order were made, it would not fall under the terms of the sunset clause. The point about the sunset clause is that if an order is not made within two years there will be no power to make one as the relevant Act will no longer exist. The Act will be off the statute book.[63]

56 See Ch 1.

57 See Theodore J Lowi, *The End of Liberalism, The Second Republic of the United States* (2nd edn, WW Norton & Company 1979).

58 Richard C Kearney, 'A Survey and Analysis of the State Experience' (1990) 50 Public Administration Review 49.

59 Education Act 2002, s 2(1)

60 Education Act 2002, s 2(7)

61 Fire Services Act 2003, s 1(1).

62 Fire Services Act 2003, s 1(7).

63 HL Deb 19 June 2003 vol 649 col 1025.

In 2008 the government adopted the Children and Young Persons Act according to which the Secretary of State was enabled to establish a reviewing service, if the existing statutory framework did not prove to be effective.[64] However, if the delegated powers prove to be unnecessary, a seven-year sunset clause from the day the Act receives Royal Assent becomes operative.[65] In addition, in 2009 Parliament adopted the Parliamentary Standard Act as a response to the parliamentary expenses scandal. The main innovation of the Act was the creation of the Independent Parliamentary Standards Authority, with the principal task of monitoring the expenses of the Members of the Commons.[66] However, the provisions of the Act regarding the delegated powers dealing with the code of conduct on financial interest and the position of the independent commissioner for investigations were subject to a two-year sunset clause.[67] The sunset clause was an amendment set out in the House of Lords.[68] Eventually, the sunset clause was repealed with the Constitutional Reform and Governance Act, as the relevant provisions have been repealed as well.[69]

Furthermore, it is noteworthy that proposals to have secondary legislation subject to sunset clauses have been expressed. Indeed, the Chairman of the Delegated Powers and Regulatory Reform Select Committee, Lord Dahrendorf, raised the need for sunset clauses in relation to delegated powers, stating that:

> [I]n many, many cases, we should give much more serious consideration to the possibility, feasibility and usefulness of sunset clauses or, at any rate, of procedures which move in the direction of sunset clauses; that is, reviews in set periods and at particular times. That is by far the most effective way of deregulating and reducing the continuing burden of regulation. Those who gave evidence to the Constitution Committee – I believe that only one person gave evidence in support of sunset clauses – made an important point, certainly so far as secondary legislation is concerned. My personal preference would be for every piece of secondary legislation to contain a sunset clause or, at any rate, a severe review clause. In quite a few cases, it would be useful for primary legislation as well. It would offer our scrutiny process an additional weapon, as it were, to that of negative and affirmative resolution.[70]

Accordingly a report was issued addressing the advantages of making greater use of sunset clauses in statutory instruments and how it might enhance post-legislative scrutiny.[71] However, the report did not favour the idea of including a sunset clause in secondary legislation, since it was felt to be unrealistic.[72]

Thus not all proposals for the inclusion of sunset clauses are approved. In 2004 the Public Administration Select Committee issued a report concerning the prerogative powers of the ministers.[73] The main concern of the report was how to make these executive powers

64 Children and Young Persons Act 2008, s 11.
65 Children and Young Persons Act 2008, s 14.
66 Parliamentary Standard Act 2009.
67 Parliamentary Standard Act 2009, s 15 (1).
68 HL Deb 16 July 2009 vol 712 col 1324.
69 Constitutional Reform and Governance Act 2010, s 37.
70 HL Deb 6 June 2005 vol 672 col 754.
71 Law Commission, Post Legislative Scrutiny (Law Com No 302, 2006) [4.1].
72 Law Commission, Post Legislative Scrutiny (Law Com No 302, 2006) [4.9].
73 Public Administration Select Committee, Taming the Prerogative: Strengthening Ministerial Accountability to Parliament HC (HC 2003–4, 422) [8]. ('These executive powers were prerogatives of the Crown delegated to Ministers without parliamentary involvement.')

accountable and subject to parliamentary scrutiny. Among several approaches, a radical idea was proposed to include a sunset clause to outmoded powers specifying that the non-confirmed powers of the legislation would be abolished by a date specified.[74]

Having said that, a sunset clause can be used as a device for legislative oversight through which the legislature holds the executive to account. Moreover, authors have stressed that a sunset clause is a mechanism which enhances legislative oversight and have explored the rationale for their inclusion.[75] Some have, however, argued that sunset provisions are not the most efficient way of monitoring administrative rule making. Rockman draws a parallel, saying that:

> [S]unset provisions are more like an alarm clock. Nothing is required between the setting and the awakening. If one employs a strict definition of oversight, neither procedure fits, since one is a form of foresight and the other legislative afterthought. In a more general sense, though, each influences executive activity. Apparently, sunset provisions are popular, at least for their symbolic value, in legislatures that are otherwise under equipped to perform continuous oversight.[76]

On the flip side of the coin, it seems that the executive is not keen to accept an extensive use of sunset clauses in delegated legislation.[77] The executive has an interest to prevent the use of sunset clauses, as its powers are restricted by time limitation. Nonetheless, the government has issued a report according to which sunset clauses are encouraged in regulations for good reason, such as to keep effective regulations up to date and improve them when this is necessary.[78]

The essential question, therefore, is: are sunset clauses an efficient mechanism enhancing the legislative role? From a functional perspective, the expiration of sunset clauses automatically gives power back to the legislative branch. Moreover, sunset clauses have a symbolic role, since they act as a reminder that Parliament holds the original power, and that the delegated institution remains accountable to Parliament. Thus, at the expiration of the sunset clause the equilibrium of the original separation of powers is maintained. However, in practice, although the original separation of powers is ostensibly restored, the executive may still dominate the legislature and simply 'forcibly' renew the legislation. From a

74 Public Administration Select Committee, Taming the Prerogative: Strengthening Ministerial Accountability to Parliament HC (HC 2003–4, 422) Appendix 1 [28].

75 See Theodore J Lowi, *The End of Liberalism, The Second Republic of the United States* (2nd edn, WW Norton & Company 1979); Bruce Adams, 'Sunset: A Proposal for Accountable Government' (1976) 28 Administrative Law Review 511; Jacob K Javits, Gary J Klein, 'Congressional Oversight and the Legislative Veto: A Constitutional Analysis' (1977) 52 New York University Law Review 455; Lewis Anthony Davis, 'Review Procedures and Public Accountability in Sunset Legislation: An Analysis and Proposal for Reform' (1981) 33 Administrative Law Review 393; Mary K Marvel, 'Sunset: An early evaluation' (1984) 42 Public Choice 193; William Lyons, Patricia K Freeman, 'Legislation and the Legislative Process in Tennessee' (1984) 9 Legislative Studies Quarterly 151, 158; John D Huber, Charles R Shipan and Madeline Pfahler, 'Legislatures and Statutory Control of Bureaucracy' (2001) 45 American Journal of Political Science 330.

76 Bert A Rockman, 'Legislative-Executive Relations and Legislative Oversight' (1984) 9 Legislative Studies Quarterly 387, 426.

77 Law Commission, *Post Legislative Scrutiny* (Law Com No 302, 2006) [4.9]; HM Government, *Sunsetting Regulations: Guidance* (April 2011).

78 HM Government, *Sunsetting Regulations: Guidance* (March 2011) [6].

theoretical framework, sunset clauses are compatible with both perspectives of separation of powers that identified the need for checks and balances.

Delegated legislation is, on the one hand, the only way to regulate technical and minor issues,[79] but on the other hand it can bestow excessive powers to the executive. With the delegation of law making, we have the transfer of certain legislative powers to the executive, albeit with the possibility of some control by the legislature. The inclusion of a sunset clause means that the legislative branch, instead of enacting the legislation, exercises a monitoring authority. Thus, inclusion of sunset legislation in delegated power and in statutory instruments enacted by the executive changes the balance of power between the executive and the legislative branch. Parliament exercises its oversight role more actively and, at the same time, at least symbolically, retains its authority at the expiration of the sunset clause.

How the separation of powers affects the use of sunset clauses

More frequent utility in 'consensus democracies'

Lijphart, focusing on the law making process, distinguished between two patterns of democracy: 'A closely related difference is that the majoritarian model of democracy is exclusive, competitive, and adversarial, whereas the consensus model is characterised by inclusiveness, bargaining and compromise; for this reason, consensus democracy could also be termed "negotiation democracy".'[80] To be more specific, consensus is the mode of operation in a separation of powers system where the law making function is shared between different institutions. In contrast, there is less need for consensus when law making depends on a majority in the legislature.

With reference to this classification, the US is a 'negotiation democracy', as a bill must be approved by three different institutions: the House of Representatives, the Senate and the President. Each institution can block legislation,[81] thus sunset clauses may serve as a mechanism to reach a consensus between the different institutions.[82] When there is a disagreement, the branches may be willing to compromise and accept an agreement when the legislation is not permanent. This temporary character of legislation permits the branches to review their stance at the expiration of the law.

In parliamentarian systems, such as Westminster, although the legislative branch exercises the law making power, the executive holds a key role. The Prime Minister is the head of the government and at the same time leader of the majority party in Parliament. Moe and Caldwell explain this when they claim that 'the executive is the leadership of the majority

79 The Report on Ministers' Powers has stressed that 'if Parliament were not willing to delegate law-making power, Parliament would be unable to pass the kind and quantity of legislation which modern public opinion requires' Committee on Ministers' Powers, *Report* (Cmd 4060 1932) [4].

80 Arend Lijphart, *Patterns of Democracy, Government Forms and Performance in Thirty – Six Countries* (Yale University Press, 1999) 2. See also Klaus Armingeon, 'The Effects of Negotiation Democracy: A Comparative Analysis' (2002) 41 European Journal of Political Research 81.

81 Regarding the power to block legislation, its effect, and the distinction between majoritarian and negotiation democracies see Andre Kaiser, 'Types of Democracy: From Classical to New Institutionalism' (1997) 9 Journal of Theoretical Politics 419, 436.

82 On how sunset clauses can form a political compromise between proponents and opponents of regulation, see Tom Ginsburg, Jonathan S. Masur & Richard H. McAdams, *Libertarian Paternalism, Path Dependence, and Temporary Law* (2014) 81 Chicago Law Review 291.

party, and thus the leadership of the legislature itself. What the executive wants, it sets'.[83] Therefore, the winning party in an election forms the government, controls the majority in Parliament and aims to implement its policy.[84] In addition, even if Westminster maintains a bicameral system, House of Commons and House of Lords, the latter House does not have the power to veto legislation.[85]

Thus the government does not in general seek agreement with the opposition in order to pass legislation, and consensus is not a condition of the legislative process.[86] Consequently, the use of sunset clauses is expected to be more frequent in a separation of powers system where the legislative function is shared among different institutions. Nonetheless, under the majoritarian separation of powers regime, consensus might be an essential condition, either when no party controls a majority in the House of Commons, or when in spite of there being a single-party government, there is strong opposition from backbenchers.[87] Although single-party governments may have been the norm in Britain after the Second World War, coalition governments were a widespread phenomenon especially during the first half of the 20th century.[88] Where there is a coalition government, there is a need for consensus among the parties participating in government in order to pass legislation. Regarding the existence of opposition within the party in government, if there are enough backbenchers to block legislation, the government has to reach a consensus with them. Consequently, Ackerman accurately remarks that legislative obedience to the executive is in general due to party discipline, notwithstanding some instances in which backbenchers secure some changes in executive-driven legislation.[89]

The requirement of consensus is a decisive element to distinguish the respective separation of powers models. Thus, the use of sunset clauses is expected to be more common in separation of powers systems where there is a need to build consensus to pass legislation, such as the presidential system of the US. To the contrary, with the exception of coalition governments or in the event of strong opposition from backbenchers, it is not expected that sunset clauses will have widespread application in parliamentarian systems such as Westminster.

More frequent use when the legislature is autonomous

As was mentioned above, the presidential system of the US is a paradigm according to which the legislative function is shared between the Senate and the House of Representatives, while the President is vested with the power to veto legislation. However, as a body, Congress is

83 Terry M Moe, Michael Caldwell, 'The Institutional Foundations of Democratic Government: A Comparison of Presidential and Parliamentary Systems' (1994) 150 Journal of Institutional and Theoretical Economics 171, 178.

84 Lijphart explores in more detail nine reasons why the Westminster paradigm is not a system of governance based on consensus. Arend Lijphart, *Patterns of Democracy, Government Forms and Performance in Thirty – Six Countries* (Yale University Press 1999) 10.

85 See *Jackson and others v Attorney General* (2005) UKHL 56.

86 On the contrary, as it is shown in the historical chapters, consensus was prerequisite for passing legislation when the Lords had a decisive role in legislation. See Ch 2.

87 Regarding the tendency of MPs to vote against their own party see Philip Norton, 'Parliamentary Oversight', in Ian Holliday, Patrick Dunleavy, Andrew Gamble and Gillian Peele (eds), *Developments in British Politics 5* (MacMillan 1997) 161.

88 Regarding a full account of coalition governments in the UK see John Dearlove, Peter Saunders, *Introduction to British Politics* (2nd edn, Polity Press 1991) 55.

89 Bruce Ackerman, 'The New Separation of Powers' (2000) 113 Harvard Law Review 633, 643.

independent of and distinct from the separately elected executive, As has been precisely stated, 'the House of Representatives exists as a legislative and oversight forum whose policy preferences may or may not coincide with those of the separately elected government, that is, the presidency and the rest of the executive branch'.[90]

Although partisanship is the modus operandi in US politics, it is quite rare for a single party to dominate all three institutions – the Senate, the House of Representatives and the Presidency. A party has to win several biennial elections in a row in order to exercise plenary law making authority. Ackerman puts it correctly when he states that, 'even if party A wins big at time one, it may have to win n times more before it can gain plenary law making authority'.[91] In fact, in the recent political history of the US, only a few times has a party dominated all institutions. For instance in 1992 the Democrats gained control of Congress and the Presidency for two years, and in 2000 the Republicans did the same.[92]

Unlike the US, the Westminster system of governance is considered a parliamentary one which represents the minimum of separation between the executive and the legislative branch. The parliamentarian system, as it is known, has received criticism from a separation powers point of view.[93] Craig points out the role of political parties in the transfer of power to the executive, saying that 'the very existence of parties provided an avenue for the channelling of power from the legislature to the executive'.[94] As was shown in more detail above, with the exception of coalition governments or in the event of strong opposition from backbenchers, an endemic and enduring characteristic of the parliamentary system is the fact that the party in government exercises the law making power of the legislature. Consequently, instead of having the legislative branch controlling the executive, legislation becomes a prerogative of the executive.[95] In other words, government in parliament can implement its agenda and pass legislation according to its desired policy.

At first glance, the comparison between the US and the UK might not provide accurate results. The dominance of one party in the UK and the existence of divided government in the US do not create fertile ground for comparison, and this difference might explain the use of sunset clauses in the US. In the case of divided government in the US, it is plausible that sunset clauses create a common ground between the parties, as happened in England when the Lords and the Commons had an equal role in legislation or as happens when there is a coalition government. Attempting to draw parallels between the two legal systems, the scope of the comparison should be limited, first, to occasions where the presidential party dominates in Congress, so as to avoid the aforementioned 'divided government' explanation, and, second, where both legislative branches are discussing similar pieces of legislation under an equivalent state of conditions.

Remarkably, in the presidential election of 2000, a Republican candidate, George W Bush, won the presidency of the US at the same time the Republican Party controlled the

90 Congressional Research Service, 'Parliament and Congress: A Brief Comparison of the British House of Commons and the US House of Representatives' (Congress, 19 May 2005).

91 Bruce Ackerman, 'The New Separation of Powers' (2000) 113 Harvard Law Review 633, 644.

92 See Gary C Jacobson, 'A House and Senate Divided: The Clinton Legacy and the Congressional Elections of 2000' (2001) 116 Political Science Quarterly 5.

93 See Bruce Ackerman, 'The New Separation of Powers' (2000) 113 Harvard Law Review 633, 640

94 Regarding the development of the party system see Paul Craig, *Administrative Law* (7th edn, Sweet & Maxwell 2012) [3–005].

95 Paul Craig, *Administrative Law* (7th edn, Sweet & Maxwell 2012) [1–009]; Paul Craig, 'Public Law, Political Theory and Legal Theory' (2000) Public Law 222 fn 54.

legislative branch, holding a majority in both the House of Representatives and the Senate.[96] The 9/11 terrorist incident overshadowed the legislative work, and emergency law making was at the top of the agenda. Thus, in response to the terrorist actions, the USA Patriot Act[97] was adopted, which, among other things, provides the federal government with additional powers to combat terrorism.[98]

As Vermeule remarks, 'in the bargaining over the Patriot Act, a crucial moment occurred when President Bush's negotiators objected strenuously to the final version because it contained a sunset provision they found objectionable'.[99] Surprisingly, the sunset clause was an amendment in the original bill, which was proposed and supported by the Republican leader of the House, Dick Armey.[100] As Robert O'Harrow, a reporter for the Washington Post, affirms: 'a sunset provision would guarantee that some of the most troubling new powers would be revisited by Congress, giving law makers an important check on executive authority'.[101]

Likewise, 9/11 had an impact on the legislative agenda of Westminster. In the aftermath of these terrorist attacks, Parliament passed a series of emergency legislation.[102] Two statutes are particularly relevant for the purpose of this comparison: first, the Anti-terrorism, Crime and Security Act;[103] and second, the Civil Contingencies Act.[104] Although neither Act contained a sunset clause when introduced by the Labour Government, the inclusion of sunset clauses was proposed during parliamentary debate.

During the debate of the Anti-terrorism, Crime and Security Bill, several sunset clause amendments were proposed, and remarkably some of them had the support of Labour MPs. However, the Minister of Home Affairs agreed only with the inclusion of a five-year sunset clause referring specifically to sections 21 to 23,[105] and at the same time he rejected other sunset clause amendments, stating that:

> On sunset clauses, the Government have taken several measures in response to the Select Committee on Home Affairs and to the wishes of individual Members and to debates held earlier on Part 4. Those measures include a sunset clause after five years, review after a year and other provisions that reflect the will of the House. I want to make it clear – so that there is no doubt in the other place – that we strongly resist any further

96 Even if the Democrats were holding fifty seats and the Republicans fifty, respectively, the appointment of Dick Cheney as Vice President gave the control to Republicans with the tie-breaking vote. In the House of Representatives, the Republicans were the majority, controlling 221 seats out of 435.

97 Uniting and Strengthening America by Providing Appropriate Tools Required to Intercept and Obstruct Terrorism Act, Pub L No. 107–56, 115 Stat 272 (2001).

98 See Michael T McCarthy, 'Recents Developments: USA Patriot Act' (2002) 39 Harvard Journal on Legislation 435.

99 Adrian Vermeule, 'Emergency Lawmaking after 9/11 and 7/7' (2008) 75 University of Chicago Law Review 1155, 1165.

100 Robert O'Harrow Jr., 'Six Weeks in Autumn: A Year Ago, as a Nation Reeled from Attack, a Battle Was Joined for America's Future. Not in Afghanistan. In Washington. Washington Post W6 (October 27, 2002).

101 Robert O'Harrow Jr., Six Weeks in Autumn: A Year Ago, as a Nation Reeled from Attack, a Battle Was Joined for America's Future. Not in Afghanistan. In Washington. Washington Post W6 (October 27, 2002).

102 See Ch 8.

103 Anti-Terrorism, Crime and Security Act 2001.

104 Civil Contingencies Act 2004.

105 Anti-Terrorism, Crime and Security Act 2001, s 29(7).

move on sunset clauses. We shall not allow the Bill to be dismembered by the indiscriminate application of sunset clauses to different parts of it.[106]

Similarly, when the Civil Contingencies Bill was debated in the Joint Committee, a sunset clause was proposed[107] concerning the second part of the bill, and this was a recognition of the vested in the executive in cases of emergency.[108] Although the draft bill included a partial sunset clause regarding emergency regulations issued by the government,[109] the Lords proposed a three-year sunset clause amendment to limit the duration of the second part of the bill.[110] Opposition MPs supported this amendment and in doing so claimed that there is a precedent for emergency legislation to contain sunset clauses, mentioning examples such as 'it was agreed from the outset that the Anti-terrorism, Crime and Security Act 2001 should be subject to sunset provisions, as it contains some draconian powers'.[111] Eventually, the government opposed the inclusion of the sunset clause and the amendment was rejected.[112]

Although the evidence is relatively narrow in scope, it is suggested that the conclusions are based on sufficient grounds, due to the parallels drawn. First, both legislative branches, Congress and the House of Commons, elaborated on emergency legislation in the aftermath of 9/11. Second, at that time, the government comprised a single party, as there was no divided government in the US or coalition government in the UK. Accordingly, as Vermeule remarks, 'in Parliament – and in Congress when the president's party controls one or both houses – partisanship is the primary source of executive power over legislation'.[113] As a result, the executive role in legislation is significant in both parliamentarian and presidential systems.

Thus, focusing on the sunset clause amendment, it is remarkable that Congress imposed a sunset clause against the will of the executive, whereas Parliament in the UK failed and the executive's will prevailed. The words of Lord Dahrendorf, comparing the law making powers of Westminster and Congress, highlight the institutional competence of these bodies: 'We are not the United States Congress. In other words, we are not a Parliament in which legislation is created and where the Government are not in a position to create legislation.'[114] The essential question at this point is when and under which circumstances the legislature has the law making power to impose a sunset clause amendment.

According to the above, it is apparent that in parliamentary systems, where on the one hand the influence of the executive is more direct and significant, and on the other hand parliament is less distinct as an institution, a sunset clause amendment to render a

106 HC Deb 12 December 2001 vol 376 col 952.

107 Joint Committee on the Draft Civil Contingencies Bill, *Draft Civil Contingencies Bill* (2002–3, HL 184, HC 1074) [200].

108 Part B of the Bill allows the government to deploy the armed forces, restrict public assembly, force travel restrictions and limit public access to prescribed areas. See Civil Contingencies Act 2004, Part B.

109 See Civil Contingencies HC Bill (2003–04) 14 cl 26 (1) (a).

110 See Civil Contingencies HL Bill (2003–04) 77 cl 34.

111 HC Deb 17 November 2004 vol 426 col 1368.

112 The government's position was that it 'contains provision for detailed parliamentary scrutiny and amendment by Parliament of its provisions. It also contains in-built sunset clauses on the use of the regulations': HC Deb 17 November 2004 vol 426 col 1367.

113 Adrian Vermeule, 'Emergency Lawmaking after 9/11 and 7/7' (2008) 75 University of Chicago Law Review 1155, 1172.

114 HL Deb 6 June 2005 vol 672 col 754.

governmental bill temporary is less likely to succeed. In other words, although partisanship is the modus operandi of both political systems, the use of sunset clauses depends to an extent on the position of the legislative branch. The more independent the institution of the legislative branch is, the more possible it is to impose a sunset clause. On the contrary, the less independent the legislature, the more possible it is for the executive to reject a sunset clause amendment or to limit its effect with a Henry VIII clause.

Conclusions

The use of sunset clauses has a variety of normative implications in relation to the separation of powers. Although the pure theory of the separation of powers limits the institutional aspect of such clauses, since no interaction between the branches of government is prescribed, the partial separation of powers, depending on its application, reveals a variety of conclusions. The use of sunset clauses may affect the separation of powers, as sunset clauses, due to their temporary nature, may endorse constitutional experiments reshaping the separation of powers model. In addition, sunset clauses may have a role to play in safeguarding the separation of powers, as their effect of entrenching the role of the legislature and strengthening its oversight role in the end prevents the distortion of the separation of powers which occurs through the centralisation of the legislative initiative.

As regards the influence of the separation of powers model on the use of sunset clauses, it is apparent, first of all, that if a system of governance is based on consensus, such as the presidential system of the US, sunset clauses might have a more crucial role in legislation. Second, the institutional position of the legislature has a significant role on the inclusion of such clauses in legislation. As it was shown, the more independent the legislative branch, the more likely it is that sunset clauses will be included in legislation.

The analysis in this chapter has shown that sunset clauses serve different purposes and that separation of powers considerations influence the intent of legislators.

6 Parliamentary sovereignty, constitutional dialogues and sunset clauses

> Such is the natural and inevitable tendency of the best constituted governments. If Sparta and Rome perished, what State can hope to endure for ever?
>
> Jean-Jacques Rousseau, *On the Social Contract*, Book 3 XI

Defining parliamentary sovereignty

Besides separation of powers, parliamentary sovereignty is also a cornerstone of the UK constitution. The sovereignty of Parliament, or in other words the supremacy of Parliament (as it is also described),[1] is a doctrine well-respected in the UK, as all constitutional and political theorists agree.[2] Although these two doctrines are distinct from each other, their interaction is inevitable. Masterman asserts that 'the role and powers of Parliament are key to any understanding of the UK constitution, and therefore, to any understanding of the separation of power with the constitution'.[3]

Dicey crystallised the concept of parliamentary sovereignty, famously saying that:

> Parliament thus defined has, under the English constitution, the right to make or unmake any law whatever; and, further, that no person or body is recognised by the law of England as having the right to override or set aside the legislation of Parliament.[4]

The definition by Dicey provides us with the two elements of the doctrine; the positive aspect that Parliament – to be more precise, the Queen in Parliament – can legislate on whatever subject without limits, and the negative aspect that no court can set aside its legislation.[5]

Thus according to the above, on the one hand no Parliament can entrench legislation and, consequently, future Parliaments are equally autonomous to amend any law in an

1 See AW Bradley, KD Ewing, *Constitutional and Administrative Law* (14th edn, Pearson Education 2007) 55; WI Jennings, *The Law and the Constitution* (5th edn, University of London Press 1959) Ch 4.

2 AV Dicey, *Introduction to the Study of the Law of the Constitution Vol I* (JWF Allison ed, OUP 2013) 27; Jeffrey Goldsworthy, *The Sovereignty of Parliament, History and Philosophy* (Clarendon Press 1999) 1.

3 Roger Masterman, *The Separation of Powers in the Contemporary Constitution: Judicial Competence and Independence in the United Kingdom* (CUP 2011) 20.

4 AV Dicey, *Introduction to the Study of the Law of the Constitution Vol I* (JWF Allison ed, OUP 2013) 27.

5 See AW Bradley and KD Ewing, *Constitutional and Administrative Law* (14th edn, Pearson Education Limited 2007) 55; WI Jennings, *The Law and the Constitution* (5th edn, University of London Press 1959) 55; and Alison L Young, *Parliamentary Sovereignty and the Human Rights Act* (Hart Publishing 2009) 2.

express or implied way,[6] and on the other hand no court can review acts of Parliament. In other words, parliamentary sovereignty does not permit past and present Parliaments to impose constraints on future Parliaments, and it limits the space for interaction between the legislature and the judiciary.[7]

But the doctrine of parliamentary sovereignty has suffered a series of incursions. Relevant to the possibility to have laws entrenched are the following: one of the first limitations may have been realised after the entry of the UK into the European Union, in the *Factortame* litigation.[8] Subsequently the adoption of the Human Rights Act in 1998 had great influence, given that this act created another exception to the doctrine of implied repeal,[9] as did the Supreme Court's decision in the *HS2* case,[10] more recently, according to which a number of statutes with constitutional value are not subject to the doctrine of implied repeal.[11]

Moreover, the adoption of the Human Rights Act has equally affected the negative aspect of the doctrine of parliamentary sovereignty. Although courts cannot strike down an act of Parliament, they can declare it incompatible with the European Convention of Human Rights.[12] Tomkins admits that the incorporation of the European Convention of Human Rights into the law of the UK contributed to the strengthening of the judges' role,[13] and Lord Hope, in his 2005 decision in *Jackson v Attorney General*, remarked that 'our constitution is dominated by the sovereignty of Parliament. But Parliamentary sovereignty is no longer, if it ever was, absolute'.[14]

Dialogue between Parliament and the courts

The emergence of the courts

The weakening of the doctrine of parliamentary sovereignty has opened up room in the constitutional order for new constitutional phenomena, in particular that of constitutional dialogue between the courts and Parliament. In principle, this dialogue depends mainly on

6 This is the so-called doctrine of implied repeal which was developed with judge-made law. See *Vauxhall Estates Ltd. v Liverpool Corporation* (1932) 1 KB 733; and *Ellen Street Estates Ltd. v Minister of Health* (1934) 1 KB 590.

7 In theory, the interaction between the institutions, or alternatively, between the branches of the government, in constitutional law matters or in ordinary law matters is often paralleled as a 'dialogue'. On the 'dialogic' character of separation of powers and judicial review, there is thorough analysis about the US: see Barry Friedman, 'Dialogue and Judicial Review' (1993) 91 Michigan Law Review 577; Louis Fisher, *Constitutional Dialogues: Interpretation as Political Process* (Princeton University Press, 1988); Robert Post and Reva Siegel, 'Popular Constitutionalism, Departmentalism, and Judicial Supremacy' (2004) 92 California Law Review 1027.

8 *Factortame Ltd v Secretary of State for Transport (No 2)* (1991) 1 All ER 70 (HL). Concerning the influence of EU law on the doctrine of parliamentary sovereignty, see JWF Allison, *English Historical Constitution: Continuity, Change and European Effects* (CUP 2007) 103ff.

9 Human Rights Act 1998, s 3.

10 *R (on the application of HS2 Action Alliance Ltd) v Secretary of State for Transport* (2014) UKSC 3.

11 Thus confirming the precedent from Thoburn. See *Thoburn v Sunderland City Council* (2003) QB 151.

12 Human Rights Act 1998, s 4.

13 See Adam Tomkins, 'The Rule of Law in Blair's Britain' (2007) 26 University of Queensland Law Journal 255, 277. In addition, the independence of the courts was further advanced, and the separation of powers was enhanced, with the adoption of the Constitutional Reform Act 2005. See JWF Allison, *English Historical Constitution: Continuity, Change and European Effects* (CUP 2007) 94–5.

14 *Jackson and others v Attorney General* (2005) UKHL 56 [104].

the structure of the separation of powers and the constitutional framework, given that it permits a degree of interaction between the institutions.

The normative discussion on the concept of constitutional dialogue in the UK, and in a number of commonwealth countries that adopted a bill of rights, was spurred by the enactment of the Human Rights Act in 1998.[15] Nowadays, it is commonly accepted that according to section 4 of the Human Rights Act 1998, a distinct dialogue between Parliament and the courts occurs, as the courts declare that a specific provision is not compatible with Convention Rights and subsequently Parliament may debate whether it will amend or replace the relevant provision taking into account the court's decision.[16]

Furthermore, while Masterman states that the 'separation of powers in the UK is both defined and delimited by the doctrine of parliamentary sovereignty and the decisions it takes over where governmental competence may lie at a given time',[17] he goes on to admit that 'separation of powers is increasingly used as a tool of judicial reasoning capable of lending coercive support to limitations placed on the executive and possibly Parliament'.[18]

On the other hand, Ewing remarks that:

> although it is purported to reconcile in 'subtle' form the protection of human rights with the sovereignty of Parliament (a claim even more credible after an important but unsung Commons amendment), the Act also represents an unprecedented transfer of political power from the executive and legislature to the judiciary, and a fundamental re-structuring of our 'political constitution'.[19]

More controversial is the stance of Bogdanor, who argues that:

> The constitutional reforms implemented since 1997 have fundamentally altered the balance between the main institutions of government – the legislature, the executive and the judiciary. [. . .] The consequence may be summarised by saying that the idea of the sovereignty of parliament has been replaced by that of the separation of powers, so putting Britain on the path to becoming a genuine constitutional democracy.[20]

Irrespective of the divergent views on the impact of the developments in the constitutional framework of the UK, it is undeniable that the recent developments strengthen the judiciary, underpin further the separation of powers and affect at least contemporarily the doctrine of parliamentary sovereignty to a greater or lesser extent.

15 Stephen Gardbaum, 'The New Commonwealth Model of Constitutionalism' (2001) 49 American Journal of Comparative Law 707;

16 TRS Allan, 'Constitutional Dialogue and the Justification of Judicial Review' (2003) 23 Oxford Journal of Legal Studies 563, 566; R Clayton, 'Judicial Deference and "Democratic Dialogue", the Legitimacy of Judicial Intervention under the Human Rights Act 1998' (2004) PL 33; Tom R Hickman, 'Constitutional Dialogue, Constitutional Theories and the Human Rights Act 1998' (2005) Public Law 306; Alison L Young, *Parliamentary Sovereignty and the Human Rights Act* (Hart Publishing 2009) 10.

17 Roger Masterman, *The Separation of Powers in the Contemporary Constitution: Judicial Competence and Independence in the United Kingdom* (CUP 2011) 23.

18 Roger Masterman, *The Separation of Powers in the Contemporary Constitution: Judicial Competence and Independence in the United Kingdom* (CUP 2011) 244.

19 KD Ewing, 'The Human Rights Act and Parliamentary Democracy' (1999) Modern Law Review 79.

20 Vernon Bogdanov, *The New British Constitution* (Hart Publishing 2009) 285.

Sunset clauses in defence of parliamentary sovereignty

A main feature in the aforementioned, vigorous debate is the expansion of the role of the judiciary through the adoption of the Human Rights Act and the Constitutional Reform Act, and the judiciary's responsibility to evaluate the compatibility of acts of Parliament with Convention Rights. But, the way Parliament reacts to a declaration of incompatibility is meaningful in the preservation of its sovereignty, and sunset clauses may have a crucial role to play.

Parliament's reaction to a declaration of incompatibility was discussed during the adoption of the HRA, and was a central issue relating to parliamentary sovereignty.[21] Gardbaum, comparing the approach of the US (which gives the authority to courts to strike down legislative acts) with the Commonwealth model of interaction between the courts and Parliament, remarks that:

> Between 1982 and 1998, each of the Commonwealth countries of Canada, New Zealand, and the United Kingdom – countries that were previously among the very last democratic bastions of traditional legislative supremacy – adopted a bill of rights in a form that self-consciously departed from the American model by seeking to reconcile and balance the rival claims, to create a middle ground between them rather than adopt a wholesale transfer from one pole to the other. Most noticeably, while granting courts the power to protect rights, they decouple judicial review from judicial supremacy by empowering legislatures to have the final word.[22]

Nonetheless, sunset clauses might be a useful mechanism to permit Parliament to respond promptly to courts' decisions, thereby reversing their effect. Hence a dialogue flourishes between Parliament and the courts. Interestingly, following the first decision of the Supreme Court that found a piece of legislation incompatible with the Convention Rights, Parliament responded immediately, adopting legislation with a sunset clause. To be more specific, the court (at that time the House of Lords) held on 16 December 2004 that the measure of indefinite detention of foreign suspects for terrorism without trial, introduced with the Anti-Terrorism, Crime and Security Act in 2001,[23] was incompatible with the Human Rights Act.[24]

21 The original proposal was to give ministers the power to enact legislation replacing the incompatible piece of legislation with the Convention Rights. However, this approach was rejected for ebing inconsistent with parliamentary sovereignty. Ewing confesses that 'the power which it was proposed to confer on ministers was extraordinary, in the sense that it would not be confined to a power to amend legislation to the extent necessary to deal with the incompatibility, but could include "such incidental, supplemental, consequential and transitional provision as the person making [the order] considers appropriate". Although these proposals were warmly supported in some quarters, they were strongly criticised as "unnecessary and unconstitutional" in others, with concern being expressed about "Henry VIII trampling through the statute book". The offending clause (10) was amended at the committee stage in the Commons, in perhaps the most significant victory in the parliamentary history of this particular Bill. The result is to restore the principle that primary legislation should be amended or repealed only by primary legislation, and to this extent the Act gives rather greater weight to the government's commitment to parliamentary sovereignty than had originally been proposed, by restoring Parliament's authority in the legislative process.' See KD Ewing, 'The Human Rights Act and Parliamentary Democracy' (1999) 62 Modern Law Review 79, 93.

22 Stephen Gardbaum, 'The New Commonwealth Model of Constitutionalism' (2001) 49 American Journal of Comparative Law 707, 709.

23 S 23.

24 *A v Secretary of State for the Home Department* (2004) UKHL 56.

Parliament had limited time to enact new legislation replacing the indefinite detention measure with a substitution, as on 14 March the detention orders were about to expire.[25] The Secretary of State introduced the Prevention of Terrorism Bill in Parliament for a first reading on 22 February 2005,[26] proposing the measure of control orders.[27] Due to the fast track procedure, the bill was fiercely debated, and the sunset clause amendment proposed by the Lords was a point of disagreement between the Commons and the Lords, and indeed caused delay.[28] As the government did not have the privilege of time, it eventually compromised in order to replace the 'indefinite detention' measure with the new piece of legislation.[29]

In addition, in 2010 the UK Government passed the Terrorist Asset-Freezing (Temporary Provisions) Act, which was limited in duration through a sunset clause in section 1.[30] This Act was a parliamentary response to the Supreme Court decision in *Ahmed v HM Treasury*, which invalidated terrorist orders, and according to which the funds of suspects supporting terrorism were frozen.[31] In this case the sunset clause was introduced by the government with the aim of maintaining the invalidated terrorism orders until a new and permanent framework was adopted.[32]

The temporary nature of the law permits Parliament to adopt new legislation without delay, reversing the effect of judicial decisions, and therefore reasserting the power to initiate legislation. It is remarkable, though, that sunset clauses were used in the US as a mechanism to respond to a US Supreme Court decision and reverse its effect. In 1990 the US Supreme Court held as unconstitutional the Indian tribal jurisdiction over non-members of the tribe.[33] Thereafter, Congress amended the Indian Civil Rights Act to include the power to 'exercise criminal jurisdiction to all Indians'[34] and consequently reversed the US Supreme Court Decision *Duro v Reina*.[35]

Parliamentary sovereignty is the doctrine which epitomises the constitutional law of the UK. Recent developments in the constitutional framework have strengthened the role of the courts. However, the inclusion of sunset clauses defends the doctrine of parliamentary sovereignty against the increasingly prevalent role of the judiciary. Parliament may use sunset clauses in

25 The Anti-terrorism, Crime and Security Act 2001 (Continuance in force of sections 21 to 23) Order 2004 SI 2004/751, art 2. For further discussion on the political environment at that time see Aileen Kavanagh, 'Constitutionalism, Counterterrorism, and the Courts: Changes in the British Constitutional Landscape' (2011) 9 International Journal of Constitutional Law 172, 185.

26 HC Deb 22 February 2005 vol 431 col 186.

27 Prevention of Terrorism HC Bill (2004–2005) [61].

28 See Ch 8.

29 Lord Owen stated: 'And so you come to the sunset clause. It seems to me that the sunset clause is purely and simply a delaying mechanism in circumstances where we are ready not to exercise our delaying power on this legislation. It is a way of effectively retaining the power of delay. I do not feel very strongly about whether it is a nine months' delay, a year's delay, 18 months' delay or even, at the uppermost limit, two years' delay; however, I cannot understand the argument of the Lord Chancellor that we are in some way challenging the House of Commons in an unconstitutional way by voting for a sunset clause.' See HL Deb 10 March 2005 vol 670 col 1040.

30 Terrorist Asset-Freezing (Temporary Provisions) Act 2010, s 1.

31 (2010) UKSC 2 [83].

32 Terrorist Asset – Freezing (Temporary Provisions) HC Bill (2009–10) Explanatory Notes [19].

33 *Duro v Reina* (1990) 495 US 676 (US SC).

34 Indian Civil Rights Act, 25 USC para 1301.

35 L Scott Gould, 'The Congressional Response to Duro v. Reina: Compromising Sovereignty and the Constitution' (1994) 28 University of California Davis 53, 63; Mark D Rosen, 'Multiple Authoritative Interpreters of Quasi – Constitutional Federal Law: Of Tribal Courts and the Indian Civil Rights Act' (2000) 69 Fordham Law Review 479, 571.

order to react promptly to a court's decision finding legislation incompatible with Convention Rights, and consequently sunset clauses might be used as a mechanism to preserve Parliament's legislative initiative. Having said that, the use of sunset clauses facilitates the dialogue between the courts and Parliament and enhances the dialogic aspect of the separation of powers.

Dialogue between present and future Parliaments

Parliamentary sovereignty over the manner and form

The relationship between present and future Parliaments and the possibility of present Parliaments to entrench legislation is also examined from the perspective of possible restrictions on the manner and form set by past Parliaments. Restrictions in form or manners are, for instance, the prerequisite of a referendum[36] or the imposition of a supermajority.[37]

Craig sketches out the two antithetical views on parliamentary sovereignty, on the issue, between the upholders of the traditional approach and the proponents of the new view.[38] Suffice to mention here, the upholders of the traditional approach support that Parliament by no means can entrench legislation, while the proponents of the modern approach support that Parliament can impose legal restrains upon itself.

In particular, Wade, one of the principal upholders of the traditional view on parliamentary sovereignty, remarks that:[39]

> [A]n orthodox English lawyer, brought up consciously or unconsciously on the doctrine of parliamentary sovereignty stated by Coke and Blackstone, and enlarged upon by Dicey, could explain it in simple terms. He would say that [. . .] no Parliament could bind its successors; and that the legislature had only one process for enacting sovereign legislation, whereby it was declared to be the joint Act of the Crown, Lords and Commons in Parliament assembled. [. . .] If he were then asked whether it would be possible for the United Kingdom to 'entrench' legislation – for example, if it should wish to adopt a Bill of Rights which would be repealable only by some specially safeguarded process – he would answer that under English law this is a legal impossibility: it is easy enough to pass such legislation, but since that legislation, like all other legislation, would be repealable by any ordinary Act of Parliament the special safeguards would be legally futile. This is merely an illustration of the rule that one Parliament cannot bind its successors.

While Jennings, one of the main proponents of the new view, admits that 'the "legal sovereignty" may impose legal limitations upon itself, because its power to change the law includes the power to change the law affecting itself'.[40]

36 For instance, Constitution Act 1902, s 7A provides that a bill to abolish the Legislative Council has to be approved by the electors in a referendum. See *Attorney-General (New South Wales) v Trethowan* (1932) UKPC 1 [PC].

37 For instance, South Africa Act, ss 63 and 152 provide for a two-thirds majority in order to remove the voting rights of Cape Coloured voters. See *Harris v Minister of the Interior* (1952) 4 SA 769 (South Africa Appellate Division).

38 PP Craig, 'Sovereignty of the United Kingdom, Parliament after Factortame' (1991) Yearbook of European Law 221 and, regarding the nature of the arguments, see Paul Craig, 'Public Law, Political Theory and Legal Theory' (2000) Public Law 211, 222.

39 See HWR Wade, 'The Basis of Legal Sovereignty' (1955) 13 The Cambridge Law Journal 172, 174.

40 WI Jennings, *The Law and the Constitution* (5th edn, University of London Press 1959) Ch 4.

In practice, though, the position that present Parliaments can impose on future Parliaments restrictions to the form and the manner of future legislation is weakened so long as the courts consider the manner and the form of legislation as *interna corporis*, and thus courts do not review whether the legislation passed by Parliament was in accordance with an exceptional manner or form. This approach from the courts is based on the article 9 of the Bill of Rights.[41] For instance the courts cannot review irregularities in the conduct of parliamentary business,[42] and, more recently, the Supreme Court held that it does not have the authority to review the process by which legislation is enacted in Parliament.[43]

However, the use of sunset clause may, as an exception and under specific conditions, impose constraints on future parliaments by setting their legislative agenda, and thus a distinct dialogue between present and future Parliaments is formed.

The effect of sunset clauses on future Parliaments

In exploring the whole history of sunset clauses in the UK, it was shown that such clauses have an effect on future Parliaments if such clauses expire during the session of a following Parliament. The impact of such clauses is twofold. On the one hand, a clause may be seen as a burden on future Parliaments. Yet, on the other hand, the expiration of a clause may remove a burden. This part concerns the situation when an election takes place between the adoption of a sunset clause and its expiration. The Parliament which is formed after the election has the option either to renew the Act before the expiration of the sunset clause or to let it expire.

More specifically, if the present Parliament includes sunset clauses that will lapse during the session of a future Parliament, the future Parliament has two options – either to leave the legislation to expire or to renew it. Accordingly, an inherent limit or entrenchment of legislation occurs, as the sunset clause restricts the possible movements of subsequent Parliaments and limits their discretion.

Two opposing choices faced by subsequent Parliaments were recorded in the debates on the European Union Bill, which was later adopted as the European Union Act, requiring a referendum to take place before the ratification of any European treaty.[44] Before the adoption of the European Union Act, a fruitful debate took place in the House on whether a sunset clause would be approved. The expiration date was set to arise on the dissolution of Parliament in order to have the statute lapse before the convening of a new Parliament.[45]

An MP stated that:

> The sunset clause puts the onus on a Government after an election to reintroduce the legislation, and no doubt a sensible Government would do that, but if there is no sunset clause, the onus is on the new Government to get rid of the legislation. They could do that by

41 'That the freedom of speech and debates or proceedings in Parliament ought not to be impeached or questioned in any court or place out of Parliament'.

42 Lord Campbell said: 'All that a Court of Justice can do is look to the Parliament Roll; if from that it should appear that a bill has passed both Houses and received the Royal Assent, no Court of Justice can inquire into the mode in which it was introduced into Parliament, nor into what was done previous to its introduction, or what passed in Parliament, during its progress in its various stages through both Houses.' See *Edinburgh and Dalkeith Railway Co v Wauchope* (1842) UKHL 710.

43 *R (on the application of HS2 Action Alliance Ltd) v Secretary of State for Transport* (2014) UKSC 3 [79].

44 European Union Act 2011, s 1.

45 European Union HL Bill (2010–2012) [55] s 15 'Part 1 and Schedule 1 shall expire on the day on which the Parliament in which this Act is passed dissolves'.

> repealing it, but they would then face the anger of the British people for having taken away their referendum rights. A sunset clause is very different from the possibility of repeal after election. The House can repeal any legislation – even, I suspect, treaty obligations.[46]

In the House of Lords, Lord Kerr of Kinlochard remarked that:

> I begin with the constitutional argument. I see two of them. First, the provisions of this Bill are all otiose in this Parliament. The coalition has made it clear that there will in this Parliament be no treaty changes, no transfers of power and no extensions of qualified majority voting. Therefore, there will be no referenda and none of the matters which have engaged us through all these days and nights are of any relevance to this Parliament; they apply only in the next Parliament. I cannot think of any previous constitutional Bill which has had that effect. I can think of no precedent for a Bill that is designed solely to influence future Parliaments. Of course, the letter of the doctrine that one Parliament cannot bind its successor will remain the case, because a new Government could repeal the Act. In my contention, however, the spirit of the doctrine would be much better honoured if there were a requirement for an affirmative decision as a first act of each new Parliament that the provisions of this Act should continue. My second constitutional argument concerns the fact that the referenda called for in the Bill would in every case be asking – whatever the substance of the issue – the question, 'Do you wish to overrule your Government and your Parliament?'. Before the referendum stage was reached the Government must by definition be in favour of the measure, because they all require unanimity in Brussels and both Houses of Parliament would have voted for the measure before the referendum question. The result of the referendum, if it was no, would be that an Act of Parliament was thereby revoked. I can think of no precedent for that. It has not applied to any past referendum in this country. In my contention, a referendum called for in this Bill is a direct undercutting of parliamentary sovereignty. I believe it entirely right that each successive Parliament should be asked whether it wished its sovereignty to be undercut in the way provided for in this Bill, and that is why I favour a sunrise clause.[47]

Indeed, both MPs highlighted the influence of the present Parliament on those that would follow. Having said that, sunset clauses reveal an interesting interaction between present and subsequent Parliaments. As a result, sunset clauses reveal the inter-temporal dimension of the separation of powers.

In fact, Posner and Vermeule remark that:

> sunset clauses are the mirror image of entrenching clauses and might also be said to control the authority of later legislatures: An entrenching clause forbids the later legislature to prevent a statute from remaining in force by an affirmative repeal, while the sunset clause forbids the later legislature to allow a statute to remain in force by declining to repeal.[48]

Consequently, the use of sunset clauses might be regarded as a limit to the way the future Parliament would exercise its power. From a different perspective, Calabresi recognises the

46 HC Deb 11 July 2011 vol 531 col 85.
47 HL Deb 15 June 2011 vol 529 col 809.
48 Eric A Posner and Adrian Vermeule, 'Legislative Entrenchment: A Reappraisal' (2002) 111 Yale Law Journal 1665, 1676.

implication of such clauses to future Parliaments, as he claims that a sunset clause 'only deprives a past majority of the benefit of inertia and gives it to those who object to the laws'.[49]

If a later Parliament wishes to re-enact the specific legislation, it is evident that the legislative agenda is not formed by that Parliament but by the earlier Parliament. The time pressure and the loss of control over the agenda are critical elements in understanding the burden imposed, as the later Parliament has to comply with the deadline set by its ancestor and is obliged to form its agenda according to the sunset clause.[50]

In contrast, and on the assumption that ordinary legislation imposes a burden on successive Parliaments, the expiration of a sunset clause may have the exact opposite effect, removing the burden. An example of legislation imposing a burden on subsequent Parliaments is the requirement of a referendum before a bill becomes statute.[51] Indeed, Roberts and Chemerinsky argue that 'sunset clauses are the antibook of entrenching legislation. A sunset clause frees future legislatures from being constrained even by the existence of a law.'[52]

Several scholars have approached this phenomenon from different perspectives. For instance, Dixon and Ginsburg argue that a sunset clause, among other mechanisms, is a form of delegation to future legislators:

> Delegating to legislatures also makes sense in thinking about error costs. If the issue is one on which the consequences of the policy will not be immediately apparent, then delegating to a future legislature shifts the decision to a body that will have superior information.[53]

Among other mechanisms, such as constitutional vagueness, flexible constitutional amendment rules and mandatory review periods, 'sunset clauses are all potentially valuable mechanisms of reducing error costs'.[54]

The prospective effect of sunset clauses on future Parliaments depends on the nature of the law. To the extent that sunset clauses set the agenda for subsequent Parliaments, such clauses impose a burden on the latter. On the other hand, on the assumption that ordinary legislation imposes a limit on future Parliaments, sunset clauses might have the exact opposite effect. Instead of imposing a limit, their expiration might remove it.

49 Guido Calabresi, *A Common Law for the Age of Statutes* (Lowboy Exchange 1999) 61.

50 Regarding the importance of agenda control see Richard D McKelvey, 'Intransitivities in Multidimensional Voting Models and Some Implications for Agenda Control' (1976) 12 Journal of Economic Theory 472.

51 Nonetheless, according to the traditional view on parliamentary sovereignty, subsequent Parliaments can repeal the requirement of referendum and consequently there is no burden. See HWR Wade, 'The Basis of Legal Sovereignty' (1955) 13 Cambridge Law Journal 172, 176. However, this point of view undermines the effect of path dependence and legislative inertia. Posner and Vermeule remark that some policies might be entrenched due to path dependence and inertia. See Eric A Posner, Adrian Vermeule, 'Legislative Entrenchment: A Reappraisal' (2002) 111 Yale Law Journal 1665, 1676.

52 John C Roberts, Erwin Chemerinsky, 'Entrenchment of Ordinary Legislation: A reply to Professors Posner and Vermeule' (2003) 91 California Law Review 1773, 1784. They endorse as well that sunset clauses may be a burden to future legislators, as they admit that '[i]t is quite true that a sunset provision makes life harder for legislators who continue to support the legislation because they have to recreate their legislative majority and overcome practical obstacles to legislative action all over again when sunset looms'. See John C Roberts, Erwin Chemerinsky, 'Entrenchment of Ordinary Legislation: A reply to Professors Posner and Vermeule' (2003) 91 California Law Review 1773 ct 39.

53 Rosalind Dixon and Tom Ginsburg, 'Deciding Not to Decide: Deferral in Constitutional Design' (2011) 9 International Journal of Constitutional Law 636, 646.

54 Rosalind Dixon and Tom Ginsburg, 'Deciding Not to Decide: Deferral in Constitutional Design' (2011) 9 International Journal of Constitutional Law 636, 652.

The role of the electorate

The dialogical setting between present and future Parliaments due to a sunset clause is relevant to the idea of participatory and deliberative democracy. More specifically, if the present Parliament enacts temporary laws that will lapse during the session of a future Parliament, the elections that take place in between the past and the future Parliament give the opportunity to the voters to participate indirectly in the law making process and influence the stance of the political parties regarding the renewal of the sunset.

People's participation in the political and the decision making process complies with the ideal of deliberative democracy, which is a concept coined by Besset[55] in the 1980. The 'theoretical principles underlying deliberative democracy' have attracted the interest of scholars such as Ackerman,[56] Cohen,[57] Elster,[58] Habermas,[59] Rawls[60] and Sunstein,[61] and given that temporary legislation may enable 'the people' to participate in the parliamentary law making procedure, the concept of deliberative democracy finds a working model in which the electorate evaluates the temporary legislation and with its vote supports the political party in favour or against the continuance of the particular law.

But the activation of the electorate to participate in the law making process is more probable on issues that in general attract the interest of the voters, such as temporary tax laws or temporary tax cuts. This is exemplified with the tax cuts subject to sunset clauses introduced in the US under the Bush administration in 2001 and 2003.

In fact, the Bush administration proposed two major tax cuts, in 2001 and 2003, and it was the first time in recent US legal history that a clause was used to sunset tax legislation as a whole:[62] the Economic Growth and Tax Relief Reconciliation Act 2001 was stated to expire on 31 December 2010,[63] and the Jobs and Growth Tax Relief Reconciliation Act 2003 was set to expire on 31 December 2008.[64]

Before the expiration of the Economic Growth and Tax Relief Reconciliation Act 2001 and during the 2012 US presidential election, such clause imposed a burden on the Obama administration concerning the renewal or expiration of the tax cuts.

55 Joseph M Bessette, 'Deliberative Democracy: The Majority Principle in Republican Government', in Robert A Goldwin and William A Schambra (eds), *How Democratic is the Constitution?* (American Enterprise Institute for Public Policy Research 1980) 102, 102–16.

56 Bruce Ackerman, *We the People: Foundations* (Harvard University Press, 1991); Bruce Ackerman, *We the People: Transformations* (Harvard University Press, 1998).

57 Joshua Cohen, 'Deliberation and Democratic Legitimacy', in James Bohman and William Rehg (eds), *Deliberative Democracy: Essays on Reason and Politics* (MIT Press 1997) 67.

58 Jon Elster, 'Deliberation and Constitution Making' 97 in Jon Elster (ed), *Deliberative Democracy* (CUP 1998).

59 Jurgen Habermas, 'Popular Sovereignty as Procedure', in James Bohman and William Rehg (eds), *Deliberative Democracy: Essays on Reason and Politics* (MIT Press 1997) 35.

60 John Rawls, *The Law of Peoples* (Harvard University Press 1999).

61 Cass R Sunstein, 'Deliberative Democracy in the Trenches' November 2, 2015, forthcoming, Daedalus, symposium on deliberative democracy, available at SSRN http://ssrn.com/abstract=2685195 or http://dx.doi.org/10.2139/ssrn.2685195.

62 In practice, sunset clauses were used in minor tax provisions, and such tax provisions are commonly referred as the 'extenders', since they are constantly renewed with the exception of a single occasion. See Elizabeth Garrett, 'Accounting for the Federal Budget and Its Reform' (2004) 41 Harvard Journal on Legislation 187, 194; Rebecca M Kysar, 'The Sun Also Rises: the Political Economy of Sunset Provisions in the Tax Code' (2006) 40 Georgia Law Review 335, 359.

63 Pub L No 107–16, 115 Stat 38, (2001) 901.

64 Pub L No. 108–27, 117 Stat 752 (2003) 303.

In particular, upon the expiration of the Economic Growth and Tax Relief Reconciliation Act in 2010, the Obama administration and the Democrats who held the majority in Congress faced the dilemma of whether to let the tax cuts expire or to renew them. The Democrats were against policies favouring tax cuts,[65] but the expiration of the Act was seen as an 'unwise' action in raising taxes.[66] Eventually, the Obama administration reached a compromise with Republicans and renewed most of the tax cuts for a couple of years.[67]

Thus, even if the sunset clause was meant to be a mechanism to bypass the budget rule,[68] it ended up becoming a political burden to the new administration. But most importantly, it gave the opportunity to the electorate to express its views on the issue and influence the policy decision of the law makers.

Conclusions

Interestingly, the use of sunset clauses enhances the dialogue between different institutions, and in particular the recent constitutional developments in the UK provide us with useful insights.

Due to their temporary nature, sunset clauses allow a dialogue between Parliament and the courts to evolve. Parliament may use such clauses to respond promptly to judicial decisions finding legislative acts incompatible with the Convention Rights, and therefore to preserve the legislative initiative. This was the case in respect of the adoption of the control orders in 2005, as soon as the Supreme Court found that the indefinite detention measure was incompatible with the Human Rights Act.

In addition, while the main analysis of the institutional dialogues focuses on the interaction between different institutions, the use of sunset clauses reveals another dimension to the dialogue – the inter-temporal interaction between the same institution, the Parliament. This is relevant to the discussion over agenda setting.

Sunset clauses, as a method of entrenching legislation, may impose a procedural burden on future Parliaments, while they might also have the exact opposite effect, as the expiration date may free future Parliaments from procedural burdens. As a consequence, the use of sunset clauses highlights both the interaction between successive Parliaments and the inter-temporal dimension of the constitutional dialogue.

Finally, the interaction between present and future Parliament forms a working model of participatory and deliberative democracy. In the artificial dialogue between present and future Parliament, the voters have the opportunity to participate actively in the law making process and influence the political parties about the renewal or the sunset of the temporary law.

65 Jennifer Steinhauer, 'Some Democrats Count on 'Millionaires' Strategy on Tax Cuts' New York Times (New York, 2 December 2010) <http://www.nytimes.com/2010/12/03/us/politics/03million.html> accessed February, 1 2016.

66 David M. Herszenhorn, 'Next Big Battle in Washington: Bush's Tax Cuts' New York Times (25 July 2010) <http://query.nytimes.com/gst/fullpage.html?res=9B01E0D71239F936A15754C0A9669D8B63> accessed February, 1 2016.

67 Tax Relief, Unemployment Insurance Reauthorisation, and Job Creation Act of 2010, Pub L 111–312, 124 Stat 101 (2010) 101.

68 For further details about the budget rule, see Ch 7.

Part IV

Rule of law and sunset clauses

7 Sunset clauses and formal rule of law

We suggested that it [the Supplies and Services (Transitional Powers) Bill] should be put in the Expiring Laws Continuance Act, which would enable it to be judged every year.
W Churchill, House of Commons, 08 August 1947

Formal conceptions of the rule of law

Defining rule of law

The concept of the 'rule of law' is rooted in early Western philosophy with the scripts of Aristotle.[1] The term was later popularised by Dicey, as Lord Bingham accurately stresses.[2] Since its crystallisation, the rule of law has inspired thinkers such as Allan,[3] Lord Bingham,[4] Craig,[5] Dworkin,[6] Raz[7] and Unger,[8] all of whom have expounded upon different facets of the notion. Indeed, this array of divergent views confirms that the rule of law is an 'essentially contested concept'.[9] Waldron first approached the rule of law from this perspective in 2002 during the legal controversy surrounding the recounting of votes in Florida in the 2000 presidential elections.[10]

1 Aristotle, *Politics* 3.16: 'Wherefore it is thought to be just that among equals every one be ruled as well as rule, and therefore that an should have their turn. We thus arrive at law; for an order of succession implies law. And the rule of the law, it is argued, is preferable to that of any individual. On the same principle, even if it be better for certain individuals to govern, they should be made only guardians and ministers of the law.' Regarding the rule of law in Ancient Greece see Edward M Harris, *The Rule of Law in Action in Democratic Athens* (OUP 2013).

2 See Tom Bingham, *The Rule of Law* (Allen Lane 2010) 3.

3 TRS Allan, *Law, Liberty and Justice: The Legal Foundations of British Constitutionalism* (OUP 1995).

4 Tom Bingham, *The Rule of Law* (Allen Lane 2010) 3.

5 Paul Craig, 'Formal and Substantive Conceptions of the Rule of Law: An Analytical Framework' (1997) PL 467.

6 Ronald Dworkin, *A Matter of Principles* (OUP 1985).

7 Joseph Raz, 'The Rule of Law and its Virtue' (1977) 93 LQR 195.

8 Roberto Mangabeira Unger, *Law in Modern Society: Towards a Criticism of Social Theory* (Free Press 1976).

9 Gallie, who introduced the term 'essential contested concept' to the Aristotelian Society on 12 March 1956, defines it as 'concepts the proper use of which inevitably involves endless disputes about their proper uses on the part of their users': see WB Gallie, 'Essentially Contested Concepts' (1956) 56 Proceedings of the Aristotelian Society 167, 169.

10 Jeremy Waldron, 'Is the Rule of Law an Essentially Contested Concept (In Florida)' (2002) 21 Law and Philosophy 137, 148. For further elaboration on the idea that the rule of law is an 'essential

Although a great deal of literature elaborates on the concept from almost every conceivable dimension, as Paul Craig notes,[11] there is relatively little discussion of its application to temporary legislation, despite its widespread contemporary prominence. Given that there are divergent views on the 'rule of law', the analysis is not restricted the to only one meaning of the rule of law, nor to formulate a new one. However, our understanding of sunset clauses and their constitutional value will be improved by focusing on specific aspects of the rule of law relevant to such clauses, such as the construction of the clause and the type of the legislation into which such clauses are incorporated.

This chapter seeks to locate temporary legislation within an overarching theoretical framework of the rule of law; to clarify whether the sunsetting of a law has an impact on the guiding of conduct; to consider such clauses from the perspective of ambiguity; and, finally, to identify the normative implications of the use of temporary legislation with regard to the promulgation of laws. This chapter, therefore, fits broadly within the discussion started by Craig and Tamanaha on the rule of law and will evaluate the utility and constitutional legitimacy of sunset clauses, with regard to the formal conceptions of the rule of law (while the substantive conceptions of the rule of law is the subject matter of the next chapter).[12]

Rule of law and the construction of the clause

The various constructions of sunset clauses have different impacts on the formal conception of the rule of law.[13] In particular, as regards sunset clauses, formal conceptions of the rule of law address (1) the temporary quality of legislation, (2) the clarity of the clause's construction, specifically concerning expiration and (3) the legislative process of enacting and renewing them. What is the impact of these features on the standards of legal stability, certainty and proper procedure?

The analysis from the perspective of the formal conceptions of the rule of law has three principal aims. First, it will argue that although temporary legislation does not promote stability and continuity of laws, it complies with the rule of law to a certain extent because temporary legislation prevents laws becoming obsolete and because in some legal areas there is need for flexibility. Also it will clarify that vague expiration dates and ambiguous legal effects of the expiration do not meet the standards of the rule of law.

---

contested concept' see David Collier, Fernando Daniel Hidalgo and Andra Olivia Maciuceanu, 'Essentially Contested Concepts: Debates and Applications' (2006) 11 Journal of Political Ideologies 211.

11 Paul Craig, 'Formal and Substantive Conceptions of the Rule of Law: An Analytical Framework' (1997) PL 467. Alternatively, this distinction is framed as thick and thin rule of law. See Brian Z, *Tamanaha On the Rule of Law: History, Politics, Theory* (CUP) Chrs 7–8.

12 With regard to the former, Craig includes concerns about the enactment of laws and their procedural effects, and with regard to the latter, he includes concerns about fundamental rights which form core features of our legal system. See also Brian Z, *Tamanaha On the Rule of Law: History, Politics, Theory* (CUP) 91. Besides Craig and Tamanaha, Dyzenhaus follows the same dichotomy between substantive and procedural conceptions on the rule of law. See David Dyzenhaus, *The Constitution of Law: Legality in a Time of Emergency* (CUP 2006) 2.

13 Craig notes that 'formal conceptions of the rule of law address the manner in which the law was promulgated (was it by a properly authorised person, in a properly authorised manner etc.); the clarity of the ensuing norm (was it sufficiently clear to guide an individual's conduct so as to enable a person to plan his or her life etc.); and the temporal dimension of the enacted norm (was it prospective or retrospective etc.)': Paul Craig, 'Formal and Substantive Conceptions of the Rule of Law: An Analytical Framework' (1997) PL 467.

Second, it will discuss the problem of the transaction cost from the use of temporary legislation. Finally, it notes that the renewal of sunset legislation without parliamentary participation due to Henry VIII clauses is problematic. Consequently, it urges that the construction of the clauses should reinforce the requirement for parliamentary intervention in the renewal process.

The rule of law and the temporary nature of laws

The petrification of laws

Generally, the rule of law demands that the law should guarantee stability and continuity. Raz mentions that 'stability is essential if people are to be guided by law in their long term decisions',[14] and that 'uncertainty generated by instability of law also affects people's planning and action'.[15] Prima facie, the sunset of a law is not in accordance with this requirement and has a plethora of practical implications.[16] However, it is counter-argued that the absolute and eternal force of specific laws is not always desirable and, to an extent, the flexibility is acceptable. In light of this counterargument, this section suggests that sunset clauses comply to an extent with the rule of law, because they enrich the law with desirable flexibility.

Ashford v Thornton highlights this age-old legal issue. In 1818, Abraham Thornton was accused of raping and murdering Mary Ashford. Although the jury found him not guilty during the trial at first instance, the elder brother of Mary Ashford, William, filed a writ of appeal before the Court of King's Bench. In response to the appeal, Thornton pleaded not guilty and invoked his right to trial by battle or wager of battle. His counterclaim was approved by the court despite the fact that the right to trial by battle had been inactive for centuries. The Lord Chief Justice stated that 'the general law of the land is in favour of the wager of battle and it is our duty to pronounce the law as it is, and not as we may wish it to be'.[17]

This decision highlights the fact that the doctrine of desuetude is not applicable in England. Desuetude (desuetudo), unenforced in common law countries, originates in Roman law, and in its early incarnation was a method of repealing inactive custom.[18] The contemporary version of the doctrine is yet broader and prescribes that even statutory legislation

14 Joseph Raz, *The Authority of Law: Essays on Law and Morality* (2nd edn, OUP 2009) 215.

15 Joseph Raz, *The Authority of Law: Essays on Law and Morality* (2nd edn, OUP 2009) 215 ct 5.

16 Madison namely argues that 'all the rights depending on positive laws, that is, most of the rights of property would become absolutely defunct; and the most violent struggles be generated between those interested in reviving and those interested in new-modelling the former State of property' and he adds that 'the uncertainty incident to such a state of things would on one side discourage the steady exertions of industry produced by permanent laws, and on the other, give a disproportionate advantage to the more, over the less, sagacious and interprizing part of the Society': see Letter from James Madison to Thomas Jefferson (February 4, 1790) in JCA Stagg (ed), *The Papers of James Madison* (Digital edn, University of Virginia Press 2010) 20. In addition, this deficiency is acknowledged by the Mandelkern report as 'in some circumstances, sunset [. . .] clauses would increase uncertainty and thus have an adverse effect on the investment climate and on individuals' confidence in the protection afforded them by regulation. This would be particularly the case where the regulation required investment in new equipment or facilities or dealt with the rights of individuals or businesses': Mandelkern Group on Better Regulation, *Final Report* (13 November 2001) 18.

17 *Ashford v Thornton* (1818) 106 ER 149, 169 (KB).

18 William Warwick Buckland, *Roman Law & Common Law: A Comparison in Outline* (2nd edn, CUP 1952) 17. See *Black's Law Dictionary* (Bryan A Garner ed, 8th edn, Thomson West 2004) 'desuetude'.

unused for a long time becomes obsolete and does not have legal effect.[19] As a result, the right to trial by battle in England, though unused for centuries,[20] was held to be in force at that time and thus was a binding law regardless of its compatibility with the contemporary notion of legality and justice.

In the same year, Lord Hamilton, in reference to this case, stated that:

> in England, the old law of appeal of murder had lately occupied the public's attention. The judges had declared that trial by battle was the law of the land. There was no one who heard him who did not regret that this was the law; but no one would therefore say that the judges had the power of annulling the law.[21]

The application of such outdated law prompted the legislature to put forward a bill abolishing the right in Parliament[22] via an expedited process, with three readings in the same night.[23] In this respect, one cannot deny the need for the regulation of outdated legislation which would complement parliamentary process.

English law has never incorporated the doctrine of desuetude, and the difficulty of changing an entire aspect of our legal heritage cannot be overstated. Yet, sunset clauses achieve the same purpose without drastically altering the nature of a well-established legal tradition, and form a more efficient alternative to parliamentary intervention in each problematic case. Scholarly opinion is inclined to agree – among them, Raz,[24] Fuller[25] and Hart.[26] Hence, constitutional experts recognise the undesirability of the absolute, and the need for 'relativism', in law. The question then turns to where the line is to be drawn between the absolute and the absolutely uncertain.[27] Are sunset clauses a constitutionally legitimate mechanism of policing this boundary and ensuring justice for citizens? Or do they cause more injustice than they remedy? In addition, are we to justify them on precarious theoretical grounds?

The creation of temporary legislation by a sunset clause gives legislators flexibility, which is occasionally more important than the stability of permanent laws. Posner and Vermeule point out that:

19 Appleton Morgan, 'American Law and the Desuetudo' (1916) 50 American Law Review 815.

20 Regarding the origin and the application of the right to battle, see MJ Russell, 'I Trial by Battle and the Writ of Right' (1980) 1 Journal of Legal History 111.

21 HC Deb 20 May 1818 vol 38 col 840.

22 Appeal of Murder, etc. Act 1819 (59 Geo III c 46).

23 MJ Russell, 'II Trial by Battle and the Writ of Right' (1980) 1 Journal of Legal History 135, 157.

24 Raz, although he considers the stability of the laws to be a main tenet of the rule of law, explicitly refers to 'relatively stable' laws, and furthermore notes that the laws 'should not be changed too often': Joseph Raz, *The Authority of Law Essays on Law and Morality* (2nd edn, OUP 2009) 214.

25 Fuller admits that 'it is difficult to imagine for example, a constitutional convention unwise enough to resolve that no law should be changed more often than, say, once a year': Lon L Fuller, *The Morality of Law* (Yale University Press 1969) 79.

26 Hart also identifies that the 'acceptance of a rule by a society at one moment does not guarantee its continued existence. There may be a revolution: society may cease to accept the rule. This may happen either during the lifetime of one legislator': HLA Hart, *The Concept of Law* (Paul Craig ed, 3rd edn, OUP) 59.

27 Allison accurately points out that the balance between change and continuity is a key constitutional principle. See JWF Allison, *English Historical Constitution: Continuity, Change and European Effects* (CUP 2007) 205ff.

the 'default' – that statutes persist until repealed – creates a compromise between stability and flexibility, but this balance is more appropriate for some policy areas than others.[28] Indeed, Congress recognizes as much when it provides certain statutes with sunset provisions, reflecting the view that greater flexibility than the norm is needed in that policy area.[29]

In conclusion, it is evident that the stability and continuity of laws is not always in accordance with the rule of law. But the impact of unseating a law is twofold. On the one hand it does not entrench the stability and continuity of laws, but on the other it prevents the distortion of outdated laws since the automatic expiration date removes them from the statute books. Under the latter condition, the sunset clause is desirable and accords with the rule of law. A fortiori, in specific areas, such as economic policies and state of art regulations, where conditions are constantly subject to rapid development, such clauses are highly recommended.

Legal certainty and the expiration date

Nowadays, the concept of legal certainty is recognised as a central normative modality of the rule of law.[30] Arbitrary legislation infringes the rule of law because law is unable to provide sufficient guidance to individuals, who then cannot rely on its terms.[31] Laws must provide a predictable guide to behaviour. As a consequence, the law should be clear in order to guide people in planning their lives.[32] In fact, certainty was one of the main principles of the epistemology of Auguste Comte when he described his perspective of positivism in 'The Course

28 About policies where flexibility is a substantial value, such as taxation and emergency laws, see Ch 8.

29 Eric A Posner, Adrian Vermeule, 'Legislative Entrenchment: A Reappraisal' (2002) 111 Yale Law Journal 1665, 1672.

30 Sir John Laws, 'The constitution: morals and rights' (1996) PL 622, 630; Danilo Zolo, 'The Rule of Law: A Critical Reappraisal', in Pietro Costa and Danilo Zolo (eds), *The Rule of Law: History Theory and Criticism* (Springer 2007) 24.

31 Hayek, in his definition on the rule of law, suggested the notion of predictability, stating that '[. . .] stripped of all technicalities, this means that government in all its actions is bound by rules fixed and announced beforehand-rules which make it possible to foresee with fair certainty how the authority will use its coercive powers in given circumstances and to plan one's individual affairs on the basis of this knowledge': FA Hayek, *The Road of Selfdom* (George Routledge & Sons 1944) 54. This definition soon became an issue of controversy. In 1977 Raz wrote an article, later included in his book *The Morality of Law*, where he disputed the primacy of the rule of law as opposed to the different values that law serves. Nonetheless, Raz agreed on the conceptual account of the rule of law in that the law should be such that people are able to be guided by it. Furthermore, he agreed that one of the main principles was that 'if it [the law] is to guide people they must be able to find out what it is. For the same reason its meaning must be clear. An ambiguous, vague, obscure, or imprecise law is likely to mislead or confuse at least some of those who desire to be guided by it': Joseph Raz, *The Authority of Law Essays on Law and Morality* (2nd edn, OUP 2009) 214–28.

32 Fuller explores the need for clarity explicitly, stating that 'the desideratum of clarity represents one of the most essential ingredients of legality'; nonetheless, he accurately remarks that there is little discussion: see Lon L Fuller, *The Morality of Law* (Yale University Press 1969) 63. Walker, focusing on anti-terrorism legislation, remarks that 'Perhaps the most important lesson which can be learnt from the considerable experience of anti-terrorism legislation is that the rule of law demands as much clarity in the law before the crisis or emergency arises'. See Appendix 5: Note by Professor Clive Walker Specialist Adviser to the Committee in Joint Committee on the Draft Civil Contingencies Bill, Draft Civil Contingencies Bill (2002–3, HL 184, HC 1074) 96.

in the Positive Philosophy'.[33] Nonetheless, the concept of the legal certainty and its affiliation to the rule of law was first explored by the German lawyer Gustav Radbruch. It was one of the three precepts that defined law, along with purposive construction and justice.

> '[. . .] we are confronted with a third postulate concerning law, ranking with the other two [justice and expediency], a third element of the idea of the law: legal certainty. The certainty of the law requires law to be positive: if what is just cannot be settled, then what ought to be right must be laid down; and this must be done by an agency able to carry though what it lays down. So, most oddly, the positivity of the law itself becomes a prerequisite of its rightness: to be positive is implicit in the concept of right law just as much as rightness of content is a task of positive law.[34]

The construction of the sunset clause in relation to expiration has a twofold impact on the legal expectations of the subjects. On the one hand, it is self-evident that the prospect of the expiration does not promote certainty, and a fortiori a vague or conditional expiration date increases the level of uncertainty. On the other hand, inasmuch as the certain expiration date makes the law predictable, the subject can plan accordingly and be guided.

Currently, any construction with a vague and ambiguous expiration date based on a future condition, such as 'that this statute shall continue in force until the end of the crisis', would be incompatible with contemporary standards of the rule of law.[35] However, expiration dates were not always definite and legal effects were not always clear. Thus the development of the construction of expiration dates in sunset clauses and their effect on parliamentary history occurred at the same time as the development of the rule of law.

In the early parliamentarian period of the 15th century, the cardinal constitutional principle of the legal order was based on the king's personal rule.[36] The rule of law as we understand it today did not exist, and legal certainty was a quality far less closely affiliated to legislation. As a consequence, the vast majority of the sunset clauses, as originally worded, prescribed an indefinite expiration date, since the expression 'to expire until the next Parliament' was quite common. Over time, though, the expiration date became more precise. From the late 16th century onwards, no temporary law encompassed an indefinite sunset clause. This development arose for a number of reasons, such as the establishment of parliamentary sessions, as well as the need for certainty and clarity in the law.

Nevertheless, the use of conditional sunset clauses with an indefinite duration occurred in the 20th century under states of emergency, during a series of acts recorded during First World War. The Local Government Act, for instance, provided that:

33 Harriet Martineau (trs), *The Positive Philosophy of Auguste Comte Vol I* (Calvin Blanchard 1858) 47: 'There is one liability to be guarded against which may mention here. We must be aware of confounding the degree of precision which we are able to attain in regard to any science, with the certainty of the science itself. The certainty of science, and our precision in the knowledge of it, are two very different things, which have been too often confounded; and are so still, though less than formerly.'

34 Kurt Wilk (trs), *The Legal Philosophies of Lask, Radbruch and Dabin* (Harvard University Press 1950) 108.

35 Nonetheless, in 2011 a sunset clause with a vague expiration date was recorded, namely the Sovereign Grant Act, s 16, which provides: 'The Sovereign Grant provisions cease to have effect 6 months after the end of the present reign unless continued under subsection 3.' On this occasion the vague expiration date was justified using the substance and the content of the law, which is quite topical. See The Sovereign Grant Act 2011, s 16(1).

36 Elizabeth Wicks, *The Evolution of a Constitution* (Hart Publishing 2006) 7.

> This Act, except the provisions of sections two, three, sixteen, seventeen, eighteen and paragraph (4) of section twenty three thereof, shall have effect only during the continuance, of the present war and afterwards for such period or periods (if any) not exceeding one year as the Local Government Board may fix; and the Board may fix different periods for different provisions of the Act.[37]

Finally, it is worth mentioning the National Registration Act of 1915, because although Parliament included a sunset clause with an uncertain expiration date, at the same time, the clause explicitly states the effects of the expiration.[38] In fact, the National Registration Act prescribes that 'this Act shall continue in force during the continuance of the present war and no longer, without prejudice, however to the taking or prosecution for any offence committed before the expiration of this Act'.[39]

In addition to the use of indefinite expiration dates, interpretational difficulties and uncertainty surround the use of a sunset clause coupled with the Henry VIII clause. The combination of a sunset clause with a Henry VIII clause results in the neutralisation of the sunset clause. In practice, the minister might renew the law indefinitely, and as a consequence there is no foreseeable expiration date. In fact, the Home Secretary, comparing two proposals (the former having a sunset clause and the second having a sunset clause coupled with a Henry VIII clause), said that:

> there is a choice with the legislation. One can take the approach, suggested by the Opposition parties, that [with a sunset clause] there is a defined moment at which anti-terrorist legislation simply disappears. The other approach, which I think is better, is to say that we need to have a system that improves the operation of our counter-terrorism legislation, learns from experience and decides how, if necessary, we make amendments.[40]

The constant renewal of temporary legislation with a Henry VIII clause was a core issue in the 1951 case *Willcock v Muckle*.[41] The novel question before the court was whether the National Registration Act of 1939, which had both a sunset clause and a Henry VIII clause, was still in force.[42]

Section 12 of the Act provided that:

> This Act shall continue in force until such date as His Majesty may by Order in Council declare to be the date on which the emergency that was the occasion of the passing of

37 Local Government (Emergency Provisions) Act 1916, s 24(2). A similar construction of the sunset is recorded in the Price of Coal (Limitation) Act 1915. Another construction of an uncertain expiration date is recorded in the Munitions of War Act, which prescribes in section 20 that 'this Act shall have effect only so long as the office of Minister of Munitions and the Ministry of Munitions exist: Provided that Part I of this Act shall continue to apply for a period of twelve months after the conclusion of the present war to any difference arising in relation to the performance by the owner of any establishment of his undertaking to carry out the provisions set out in the Second Schedule to this Act notwithstanding that the office of Minister of Munitions and the Ministry of Munitions have ceased to exist': Munitions of War Act 1915, s 20(2).

38 The same construction is found in Coastguard Act 1925, s 2.

39 S 16(2). Same construction as the Maintenance of Live Stock Act 1915, s 4(3).

40 HC Deb 10 March 2005 vol 431 col 1859.

41 (1951) 2 KB 844 (KB).

42 (1951) 2 KB 850 (KB).

> this Act came to an end, and shall then expire expect as respect things previously done or omitted to be done.[43]

Despite the fact that the emergency had been terminated, and that several other temporary Acts with similar construction, such as the Regional Commissioner Act 1939, had expired,[44] no specific order was issued terminating the present Act.

The Court eventually resolved the issue, holding that the Act was still in force. Interestingly, Lord Doddard CJ confessed that:

> this Act was passed for security purposes; it was never passed for the purposes for which it is now apparently being used. To use Acts of Parliament passed for particular purposes in wartime when the war is a thing of the past – except for the technicality that a state of war exists – tends to turn law-abiding subjects into lawbreakers, which is a most undesirable state of affairs.[45]

In addition, uncertainty surrounds the legal effect of the expiration, which is of equal importance. Concerning the legal effect of the expiration, it is worth mentioning the seminal case *Steavenson v Oliver* from 1841.[46] The plaintiff claimed for debt on account of the work he had done as a surgeon and apothecary for certain surgical operations. The defendant's argument was that the plaintiff did not have the right to practice as an apothecary since the statute had expired due to a sunset clause. Consequently, the plaintiff argued that 'though the act itself may have expired, persons who have acquired rights under it are not to be deprived of those rights because the act has ceased to be in force as a law'.[47]

Although the Apothecaries Act in 1815 first regulated the medical profession in the UK by setting several conditions,[48] in 1825 an amendment was enacted that entitled several persons to practice as an apothecary.[49] Nonetheless, the latter statute was of a limited duration due to a sunset clause in section 11 prescribing that 'this act shall take effect from and

43 National Registration Act 1939, s 12.

44 Article 2 of the Regional Commissioners Act (Expiry) Order in 1946 prescribed that 'it is hereby declared that the leventh day of June, nineteen hundred and forty five, is the date on which the emergency that was the occasion of the passing of the Regional Commissioners Act 1939 came to an end'. See Regional Commissioners Act (Expiry) Order 1946 SR & O 1946/164, s 2.

45 *Willcock v Muckle* (1951) 2 KB 844, 851 (KB).

46 (1841) 151 ER 1024.

47 (1841) 151 ER 1026.

48 For a detailed analysis of the Act, see SWF Holloway, 'The Apothecaries' Act, 1815: A Reinterpretation Part 1 The Origin of the Act' (1966) 10 Medical History 107.

49 Apothecaries Amendment Act 1825, s 4: 'That every person who heretofore has held, or who now holds, or hereafter shall hold a commission or warrant as surgeon or assistant – surgeon in his Majesty's navy, or as surgeon or assistant – surgeon or apothecary in his Majesty's army, or a surgeon or assistant-surgeon in the service of the Honourable the East India Company, shall be entitled to practise as an apothecary in any part of England or Wales, without having undergone any such examination, or received any such certificate, as by the said recited act of the 55th year of the reign of his Majesty King George the Third is directed, and without being liable to any penalty or disability whatsoever imposed by the said recited act on persons who, not having been in practice as apothecaries on the said 1st day of August, 1815, without having been examined and received certificates in the manner directed by the said recited act, commenced practice as apothecaries in any part of England or Wales; and no such person shall be obliged, in order to recover in a court of law any charges claimed by him as an apothecary, to prove that he was in practice as an apothecary on the said 1st day of August, 1815, otherwise than as holding a commission or warrant as surgeon or assistant-surgeon in his Majesty's navy, or as surgeon or

after the passing thereof, and shall continue until the 1st day of August next, in the year 1826'.[50]

The Court unanimously decided for the plaintiff. Lord Abinger stated: 'It is by no means a consequence of an act of Parliament's expiring, that rights acquired under it should likewise expire.'[51] Parke further elaborated:

> Then comes the question, whether the privilege of practising given by the stat. 6 Geo. 4, referred to in the replication, is one which continues notwithstanding the expiration of that statute. That depends on the construction of the temporary enactment. There is a difference between temporary statutes and statutes which are repealed; the latter (except so far as they relate to transactions already completed under them) become as if they had never existed; but with respect to the former, the extent of the restrictions imposed, and the duration of the provisions, are matters of construction. We must therefore look at this act, and see whether the restriction in the 11th clause, that the provisions of the statute are only to last for a limited time, is applicable to this privilege.[52]

In light of the court's decision, a public act clarifying the effect of its expiration was subsequently recorded. In 1873, Parliament adopted the Regulation of Railways Act. Section 37 prescribes that:

> This Act shall continue in force for five years next after, the passing of this Act, and thenceforth until the end of the then next session of Parliament, but the expiration of this Act shall not affect the validity of anything done before such expiration.[53]

Similar constructions are recorded in the 20th century as well, for instance the Coastguard Act 1925.[54]

Thus, the compatibility of sunset clauses with the concept of predictability is questioned given that the expiration of the laws diminishes the level of legal certainty. Yet while an uncertain expiration date reinforces uncertainty, it is crucial to mention that such clauses might also promote predictability. The recent example of the Holocaust Act 2009 is remarkable.[55] Parliament enacted a private member's bill stipulating the return to the lawful owners of items stolen between 1933 and 1945, including those from museums and collections.[56]

In section 4(7), a sunset clause limits the duration of the Act to ten years,[57] and as the MP who presented the bill emphasised:

---

assistant-surgeon or apothecary in his Majesty's army, or as surgeon or assistant-surgeon in the service of the Honourable the East India Company.'

50 Apothecaries Amendment Act 1825, s 11.

51 *Steavenson v Oliver* 151 ER 1024, 1026 (CE).

52 *Steavenson v Oliver* 151 ER 1024, 1027 (CE).

53 Regulation of Railways Act (Short title) 1873.

54 Coastguard Act 1925.

55 Holocaust (Return of Cultural Objects) Act 2009.

56 HC Deb 26 January 2009 vol 487 col 22.

57 Holocaust (Return of Cultural Objects) Act 2009, s 4(7).

> a sunset clause is important in the particular circumstances of the Bill. We need to give sufficient time to ensure that any outstanding claims can be dealt with, but we also want to be able to give long-term certainty to the institutions concerned. A 10-year period achieves the best of both worlds.[58]

Indeed, without the inclusion of a sunset clause, this particular act would leave museums, art collectors and owners of artefacts perpetually uncertain as to whether they would retain uncontested possession of their items. Hence, on this occasion, the time limitation of the sunset clause ensures predictability and certainty of the parties' rights to ownership.

Unger also views predictability as one of the defining notions of the rule of law.[59] The expiration of laws increases uncertainty since people cannot predict whether the law would be renewed or be replaced with a different regulation. But uncertainty also surrounds permanent laws to an extent as well, because nobody can guarantee that an ordinary law will not be amended or repealed in the future.

All is all, it is widely accepted that expiration of laws does not increase the level of legal certainty. However, under certain circumstances, sunset clauses may in fact enhance legal certainty. An exact expiration date promotes certainty, as it provides a degree of guidance concerning the development of the law.

This issue is relevant to the construction of sunset clauses, and specifically to the expiration date and the legal effect of the expiration given that the construction of the clause is clear and precise in order to enhance predictability and minimise legal uncertainty. A provision that exemplifies an ideal contraction of a sunset clause provision is section 4 of the Murder (Abolition of Death Penalty) Act 1965 which provides:

> This Act shall continue in force until the thirty-first day of July nineteen hundred and seventy, and shall then expire unless Parliament by affirmative resolutions of both Houses otherwise determines: and upon the expiration of this Act the law existing immediately prior to the passing of this Act shall, so far as it is repealed or amended by this Act, again operate as though this Act had not been passed, and the said repeals and amendments had not been enacted: Provided that this Act shall continue to have effect in relation to any murder not shown to have been committed after the expiration of this Act, and for this purpose a murder shall be taken to be committed at the time of the act which causes the death.[60]

On the contrary, certain constructions of the clause maximise legal uncertainty such as expiration dates dependent upon a condition (also known as conditional sunset clauses)[61] and sunset clauses coupled with a Henry VIII clause. Finally, as the legal effect of the expiration is not always clear, this should be explicit in the formulation and construction of the relevant clause.

58 Holocaust (Return of Cultural Objects) (formerly known as Holocaust (Stolen Art) Restitution) Bill Deb 10 June 2009 col 10.
59 Roberto Mangabeira Unger, *Law in Modern Society; Towards a Criticism of Social Theory* (Free Press 1976) 176.
60 Murder (Abolition of Death Penalty) Act 1965, s 4.
61 Regarding the typology of sunset clauses as conditional and unconditional, see Ch 1.

Sunset clauses for flexible legislation

The pragmatic application of sunset clauses has shown that their time limitation can be the means to regulate occasional and temporary issues. Without doubt, this is not in accordance with the needs of certainty and stability in specific legal areas where the priority is the long-term planning.

However, that flexibility of laws is the norm in some legal areas. Given the utility of sunset clauses and, in particular, their potential impact on adapting and implementing different aspects of policy, such clauses are highly desirable and their inclusion in laws does not contravene the need for legal certainty and stability. Having said that, the use of sunset clauses in order to regulate policies that require flexibility, experimentation and constant review, and the convenience caused by the need for frequent recourse to new legislation, is recorded in areas such as taxation, financial and economic policies and international relations.

In taxation

As seen in the historical chapters of this book, sunset clauses are extensively used in public finance, from taxation to economic policies. Taxation in late medieval England and up to the early 18th century was occasional, and thus sunset clauses in taxation were accorded with the temporal character of the occasion. In contrast to the exceptional character of taxation in the early period, taxation is now considered an ordinary part of the statute books in the UK and throughout the world. Consequently, the use of sunset clauses is quite a rare phenomenon in tax laws.

For instance, a commentator on the Finance Act 2008 urged for inclusion of a sunset clause and stated that 'the so-called "sunset clauses" is a technique neglected in this country, yet in a situation such as this it would have afforded both certainty and timetabled opportunity to review progress'.[62] Nonetheless, the reality is that Parliament has adopted the Finance Act annually since 1894.[63]

The Finance Acts provide the authority to collect taxes until 5 April of the following calendar year.[64] As the new Finance Bill might not have received Royal Assent, the Provisional Collection of Taxes Act 1968 gives interim statutory force to resolutions of the House of Commons, which provide the renewal of taxes in force with or without modifications for a further period of four or five months.[65] The practical purpose of a law imposing a short-term sunset clause is that it allows the government to collect taxes at the declaration of the budget, before the Financial Bill receives Royal Assent.[66]

The aforementioned support for the inclusion of a sunset clause in tax legislation in the UK was inspired by the paradigm shift in the US in recent tax legislation adopted during the George W Bush administration. In general, sunset clauses were used in minor tax provisions, and such tax provisions are commonly referred as the 'extenders', since they are constantly renewed with the exception of a single occasion.[67]

62 Andrew Harper, 'Finance Act notes: annual investment allowance etc – sections 74–76 and Schedule 24' (2008) British Tax Review 480, 485.

63 Finance Act 1894 (57&58 Vict c 30).

64 Hilaire Barnett, *Constitutional and Administrative Law* (5th edn, Cavendish Publishing 2004) 411.

65 Provisional Collection of Taxes Act 1968, s 1(3).

66 HM Treasury, *Overview of Tax Legislation and Rates* (HM Revenue & Customs 2011) A153.

67 See Elizabeth Garrett, 'Accounting for the Federal Budget and Its Reform' (2004) 41 Harvard Journal on Legislation 187, 194; Rebecca M Kysar, 'The Sun Also Rises: the Political Economy of Sunset Provisions in the Tax Code' (2006) 40 Georgia Law Review 335, 359.

Interestingly, the inclusion of a sunset clause in the Economic Growth and Tax Relief Reconciliation Act 2001[68] revealed new aspects of temporary legislation. It is claimed that the sunset clause was originally used in order to overrule a budget voting procedure,[69] which raised concerns, however, from a substantive perspective of the rule of law.[70]

As the Economic Growth and Tax Relief Reconciliation Act was considered as a reconciliation act, a fast track procedure applied and a filibuster was not permitted, so in order to pass, the bill had to be voted by a simple majority in the Senate. However, this rule was not without exceptions. According to the Byrd Rule, if the spending increased or the tax cut exceeded the window budget, then it must be voted into law by a super majority of three-fifths.[71] Consequently, as the Republicans held a one-seat majority in the Senate, they decided to use the reconciliation process in order to pass tax cuts. By adding the sunset clause, they managed to pass the tax cut with a simple majority and thereby circumvent the Byrd Rule.[72]

By way of contrast, in the UK sunset clauses are not evident in recent tax cut legislation. Nonetheless, taxation seems to be a fertile field for sunset clauses. Indeed, a series of governmental reports refer to them and support their inclusion in a series of tax bills. In June 2010, HM Treasury issued a discussion document to improve its tax policies and restore the system's reputation, proposing to make more use of sunset clauses for post-implementation evaluation.[73] The feedback on the initiative to use sunset clauses in tax legislation was controversial,[74] thus HM Treasury stated that the government:

> in light of the mixed response to the proposed use of sunset clauses, considers that the case has not yet been made for their regular use in relation to tax policy. It will consider the appropriateness of a sunset clause, or alternative trigger for formal evaluation, in a case by case basis. This may be something that the Government will explore during consultation on individual tax policies.[75]

The government intended to add a sunset clause to the Finance Bill 2012 in relation to a series of reliefs, so as to implement its strategy to simplify tax codes.[76]

68 Pub L No 107–16, 115 Stat 38, (2001).

69 Elizabeth Garrett, Elizabeth Graddy and Howell E Jackson (eds), *Fiscal Challenges: An Interdisciplinary Approach to Budget Policy* (CUP 2008) 65; Rebecca M Kysar, 'The Sun Also Rises: the Political Economy of Sunset Provisions in the Tax Code' (2006) 40 Georgia Law Review 335, 375.

70 See Ch 8.

71 Michael W Evans, 'The Budget Process and the Sunset Provision of the 2001 Tax Law' (2003) 99 Tax Notes 405, 410.

72 Michael W Evans, 'The Budget Process and the Sunset Provision of the 2001 Tax Law' (2003) 99 Tax Notes 405, 414.

73 HM Treasury, *Tax Policy Making: A New Approach* (HM Revenue & Customs 2010) [2.20].

74 HM Treasury, *The New Approach to Tax Policy Making: A Response to the Consultation* (HM Revenue & Customs 2010) [2.75]: 'Some of those who responded were wholly positive; one citing the current economic circumstances as a pretext for temporary policy. Another suggested that sunset clauses would be useful in identifying which tax policies are temporary and which policies are permanent. Many respondents were in favour of the principle of committing to target dates for post-implementation policy reviews and the automatic triggering of policy reviews, though they cited as a concern the uncertainty that sunset clauses would introduce in the tax system.'

75 HM Treasury, *The New Approach to Tax Policy Making: a Response to the Consultation* (HM Revenue & Customs 2010) [2.77].

76 HM Treasury, *Consultation on the Abolition of 36 Tax Reliefs* (HM Revenue & Customs 2011) see Table A.15: [Relief 17] and Table A.31: [Relief 33]. Nonetheless, the Financial Act 2012, which was adopted accordingly, does not contain any sunset clauses.

The preceding analysis indicates the current uses of sunset clauses in taxation and their potential impact on forthcoming legislation. Sunset clauses act as a fulcrum, supporting the implementation of financial policies and providing flexibility while allowing for post-implementation evaluation. Interestingly, alongside the proposal for the inclusion of new sunset clauses, criticism has been raised concerning sunset clauses in financial Acts. The complexity and length of the bills, along with the strict process of voting, led to support for the reform of the financial bill regime. It was proposed to extend the sunset clause from an annual to biennial lapse,[77] or even to adopt a permanent tax system with a multi-annual review process.[78]

In financial and economic policies

In relation to other economic policies, sunset clauses are a widespread tool in market regulation. Historically, such clauses were a useful tool for the prevailing early 18th-century economic theory, 'mercantilism'. According to that theory, the prosperity of the nation is dependent upon the supply of capital, as one of its founders, Thomas Mun, stated that 'the ordinary means therefore to encease our wealth and treasure us by Foreign Trade, wherein wee must ever observe this rule: to sell more to strangers yearly than wee consume of theirs value'.[79] Thus the 'mercantile system' required a series of acts following the economic conditions and to adjust and readjust the policy.[80] Accordingly, trade and commerce was one major concern of the Westminster Parliament which was steadily rising, and as Rule points out, by 1688, 27.7 per cent of the population was engaged in industry and commerce, and by 1759 that figure had increased to 35.8 per cent.[81]

Numerous Acts are recorded in the statute book regulating the supply and demand of products, such as the Act 'to discontinue, for a limited time the duties upon wheat and wheat flour imported; and also the bounty payable on the exportation of wheat and wheat flour'[82] and the Act 'to enable his Majesty with the Advice of his Privy Council to prohibit the exportation of wheat, wheatean meal, flour, bread, biscuit and starch, during the next recess of Parliament as such time, and in such manner, as the necessity of the time may require and he in this wisdom shall think convenient and needful'.[83] Both statutes are in accordance with mercantilism, although the whole piece of the Act is excised from the statute book, having just a note stating that it is expired.

In addition, such clauses were used in the colonial policy. The expansion of England overseas through the development of the colonies was one major factor influencing public law during

77 HC Deb 04 July 2002 vol 388 col 487; Mr Edward Davey has stated that 'we should move to a system in which a full Finance Bill is introduced every other year'.

78 HC Deb 05 February 2002 vol 379 col 217WH. (Mr Edward Davey has furthermore proposed: 'Lord Howe and others have suggested that we should get rid of the annual Finance Bill. I agree. The right hon. Member for Fylde talked about the need to protect the revenue yield to the Treasury. That is right. Nevertheless, we have an annual Finance Bill only because income tax and corporation tax are not permanent taxes on the statute book. If we reformed the Provisional Collection of Taxes Act 1968 and made income tax permanent, we could think about tax policy in a longer term way.')

79 Thomas Mun, *Englands Treasure by Forraign Trade or the Balance of our Forraign Trade is the Rule of our Treasure* (Printed by John Grismond 1664) 11.

80 Sir Charles Grant Robertson, *Select Statutes, Cases and Documents to Illustrate English Constitutional History* (4th edn, Methuen 1923) 194.

81 John Rule, 'Manufacturing and Commerce', in HT Dickinson (ed), *A Companion to Eighteenth-Century Britain* (Blackwell Publishing, 2002) 127.

82 Indemnity Act 1763 (4 Geo III c 31).

83 Court of Chancery Act 1763 (4 Geo III c 32).

the 18th century.[84] The British Empire was a statehood with a flexible structure and a 'palimpsest' constitution. Broad policies were laid down by the Westminster Parliament, if legislation dealt with a matter expressly.[85] Several navigation Acts were introduced during the whole colonial period;[86] however, only one of them, the so-called Molasses Act in 1733, entitled 'an act for the better securing and encouraging the trade of his Majesty's sugar colonies in America',[87] was temporary, having a five-year sunset clause. It was renewed with successive acts,[88] and it became perpetual in 1764 with the introduction of the Sugar Act.[89]

This Act, which is considered not to fall within the general principles outlined by the navigations Acts, was a direct result of the political pressure of a group favouring the trade from the West Indies as against the mainland colonies.[90] In practice, the Molasses Act was among the least effective of the navigation Acts,[91] and one main reason it became perpetual was the intuition that if it is perpetual it will be more effective.[92] The structure of the later Act of 1764 brings a novelty in the use of the sunset clause, because in section IV the Molasses Act is further continued until 30 September 1764, and in section V it is prescribed that the said Act with all the amendments contained at the following sections will be perpetual. Consequently, the sunset clause is used in order to accommodate the need for a transitional period.

Currently, sunset clauses are also used in the EU and at an international level. HM Treasury recently issued the Budget Report, and in relation to market regulations proposed the inclusion of a seven-year sunset clause to create a more competitive corporate tax system.[93] Consequently, the government decided to include such a clause as a mandatory component in domestic regulations that impose a net burden on business and the civil society organisations,[94] while for other organisations the precise type of sunset clause will depend on their nature.[95] The benefit of sunsetting the regulations is that unnecessary regulations will expire, the overall volume of regulations will be reduced, the quality and design of the

84 WS Holdsworth, *A History of English Law Vol X* (Methuen 1938) 26.

85 William Cornish, 'Empire's Law', in William Cornish, J Stuart Anderson, Ray Cocks, Michael Lobban, Patrick Polden and Keith Smith (eds), *The Oxford History of the Laws of England Vol XI* (OUP 2010) 240.

86 Car II c 18; 15 Car II c 7; 25 Car II c 7; Plantation Trade Act 1695 (7&8 Gul III c 22).

87 Trade of Sugar Colonies Act 1732 (6 Geo II c 13).

88 Continuance of Acts 1737 (11 Geo II c 18); Growth of Coffee Act 1745 (19 Geo II c 23); Continuance of Acts, etc. 1753 (26 Geo II c 32); Sugar Colonies, etc. Act 1756 (29 Geo II c 26); Continuance of Acts, etc. 1757 (31 Geo II c 35); Colonial Trade Act 1760 (1 Geo III c 9).

89 Custom, Duties, etc. Act 1763 (4 Geo III c 15).

90 Merrill Jensen (ed), *English Historical Documents* (Eyre & Spottiswoode, 1955) 354.

91 As its application was not successful in the North American colonies see Richard B Sheridan, 'The Molasses Act and the Market Strategy of et British Sugar Planters' (1957) 17 Journal of Economic History 63, 83; Albert B Southwick, 'The Source of Molasses Act' (1951) 8 William and Mary Quarterly 389, 404.

92 Gersen and Posner confess that 'timing rules can have both desirable and unfortunate effects on new law': Jacob E Gersen, Eric Posner, 'Timing Rules and Legal Institutions' (2007) 121 Harvard Law Review 543, 546

93 HM Treasury, *Budget Report* (HM Revenue & Customs 2010) 61 [1.65].

94 HM Government, *Sunsetting Regulations: Guidance* (Department for Business, Innovation and Skills 2011) [6].

95 HM Government, *Sunsetting Regulations: Guidance* (Department for Business, Innovation and Skills 2011) [8].

existing regulations will improve, and the cost to business and civil society organisations will be reduced.[96]

The combination of a sunset clause with a Henry VIII clause was used in the Debt Relief (Developing Countries) Act 2010.[97] The limited duration of the Act was a last-minute compromise.[98] The Act then became permanent, with a Treasury's order,[99] since the impact of the legislation was evaluated and negative effects were not found.[100] Nevertheless, the criticism over the practice of combining sunset clauses with Henry VIII clauses was expressed by the Chairman of the Public Accounts Committee, who stressed the contradiction of using a sunset clause with a Henry VIII clause. The MP stated:

> At first sight, that (the sunset provision) would appear a perfectly sensible provision, because one presumes it would give time for the House and the Government to consider whether a more permanent Government Act should be placed on the statute book. I think that sunset clauses, as they are described, might often perform a perfectly useful purpose, especially when we are dealing in areas such as this, which have not been tested sufficiently by the Government and by courts in the past. [. . .] Subsection (1) states: 'This Act expires at the end of the period of one year beginning with commencement", which is fair enough. However, subsection (3) states that "The Treasury may by order provide that this Act has permanent effect.' That is what I am slightly worried about. If this Act is to have permanent effect-after all, we are talking in terms of the wash-up of Parliament, and this is a private Member's Bill involving the Government in difficult areas – I would prefer to have more protection for Parliament. Why can the Government just decide that the Act should have permanent effect?[101]

Another unique use of a sunset clause was recorded in the Superannuation Act 2010,[102] which amended the Superannuation Act 1972 by limiting the redundancy payouts of civil servants which are prescribed according to the Civil Service Compensation Scheme (CSCS). In practice, the CSCS can be revised either with an agreement between the government and the civil service unions by virtue of the Superannuation Act of 1972,[103] or with a legislative act amending the existing framework.

The previous government reached an agreement with five out six civil service unions in order to revise the CSCS.[104] However, the new scheme was invalidated by a High Court decision brought by the sixth union.[105] The new government was committed to reform the CSCS, and thus it passed an amendment to the Superannuation Act 1972, imposing limits

96 HM Government, *Sunsetting Regulations: Guidance* (Department for Business, Innovation and Skills 2011) [4].
97 Debt Relief (Developing Countries) Act, 2010, s 9.
98 See Michael Waibel, 'Debt relief to poor countries: rules v discretion' (2010) Butterworths Journal of International Banking and Financial Law 295, 296.
99 The Debt Relief (Developing Countries) Act 2010 (Permanent Effect) Order 2011 SI 2011/1336.
100 HC Deb 28 March 2011 vol 526 col 34W.
101 HC Deb 7 April 2010 vol 508 col 1044.
102 Superannuation Act 2010, s 4(4).
103 Superannuation Act 1972, s 2(3).
104 Explanatory Memorandum to the Superannuation Act 2010 (Repeal of Limits on Compensation) Order 2010 SI 2010/ 2996.
105 *Public & Commercial Services Union, R (on the application of) v Minister for the Civil Service* (2010) EWHC 1027 (Admin).

to the benefits. However, these limits were under the scope of a one-year sunset clause. The Minister for the Cabinet Office and Paymaster General, explaining the inclusion of the sunset clauses, stated:

> We are seeking to negotiate a new scheme, which would effectively make the terms in the Bill redundant. [. . .] I stress again that we have no desire to see this legislation continue any longer than is absolutely necessary. The inclusion of a sunset provision prevents the legislation from continuing ever onwards. [. . .] there is also the option to bring forward the termination date. As I have already said, my intention is absolutely to resolve the issue by discussion and negotiation rather than by legislation, and I look forward to making the order that will repeal section 1 (as it then was) of the Act.[106]

Interestingly, after the Act received royal assent, a consensus was reached revising the CSCS, and the minister issued the Superannuation Act 2010 (Repeal of Limits on Compensation) Order[107] repealing the limits before the activation of the sunset clause. Two main conclusions can be drawn from this use of the sunset clause. On the one hand, the clause in the Act was a parliamentary response to a judicial decision invalidating the revised CSCS. On the other hand, it was an interim measure pushing the unions to a consensus.

Proposals for inclusion of sunset clauses in financial legislation, however, have not always been successful. For example, in the Regulatory Enforcement and Sanctions Bill, the Lords proposed an amendment sunsetting the bill after five years. Mr Prisk stated:

> As we have discussed, the scope of the Bill is quite significant – technical, yes, but significant none the less. It creates an entirely new local regulatory system and an entirely new non-departmental public body, albeit there is a company in shadow at present. It provides extensive powers of sanction and enforcement, involving not one single regulator but 27; and not one piece of legislation but over 140 different laws. The Bill permits the Secretary of State to make, by order, important changes to both the current and the proposed system of local regulation. That means, I hope, that in all local authority areas we, as Members of this House, will see the potential for improvement in the regulatory environment. However, those changes will affect all our constituents. In the other place, my noble Friends were able to secure some important concessions, not least that of a three-year review under clause 17 that covers only the LBRO. Given that the LBRO is not, as we have debated, directly accountable to this House, it was right to seek that review. However, clause 17 and the review contained therein does not apply to the whole Bill and that is why it is important to insert the means to debate whether this legislation should persist after a five-year period. New clause 2 offers a number of important advantages to us as a House. It enables us to assess the whole Act and look at how it has worked in practice.[108]

As mentioned above, EU law has a significant role in the regulation of the market.[109] EU policies have revealed new perspectives on the use of sunset clauses. In 2007 the European

106 HC Deb 7 September 2010 vol 515 col 218.

107 The Superannuation Act 2010 (Repeal of Limits on Compensation) Order 2010 SI 2010/2996.

108 Public Bill Committee, 'Regulatory Enforcement and Sanctions Bill [Lords]' 4th sitting (19 June 2008) cols 117–8.

109 Regarding the 'Single Market', see Paul Craig and Grainne de Burca, *EU Law: Text, Cases, and Materials* (5th edn, OUP 2011) 605.

Parliament and the Council adopted a regulation on roaming charges and mobile networks in Europe.[110] The regulation, according to article 13, was subject to a sunset clause due to expire on 30 June 2010. Interestingly, the primary aim of the sunset clause was to establish normal market conditions, eliminating the difference between roaming and national prices.[111] Thus the inclusion of the sunset clause regulates the market, but through its expiration the principal aim is revealed, namely to deregulate the market. However, as the market conditions were not met, the European Commission decided on the renewal of the regulation until 2012,[112] and in 2012 a new regulation was adopted with a sunset clauses until 2017.[113]

Moreover, with regard to international trade policies that fall in the EU's commercial policy competence,[114] dumping and anti-dumping duties are regulated at a European level. In general, dumping measures are classified by duration into sporadic, intermittent and continuous categories.[115] Thus, a Council regulation was adopted in 2009 prescribing a five-year sunset clause on anti-dumping measures.[116] The regulation is in accordance with the equivalent framework in the World Trade Organization and the Anti-dumping Agreement of the Uruguay Round.[117]

Through the above examples, it is evident that legislators have relied on sunset clauses in order to implement a financial policy. Time limitations permit legislators to implement short-term policies and to reconsider and evaluate them afterwards. Therefore this clause is quite useful, especially in the financial field where flexibility is required but long-term planning is not always effective. The use of sunset clauses aims to improve existing regulation and therefore advances the rule of law. As regards the separation of powers, such clauses were used in the US in order to bypass procedures that enhance the checks and balances system, and this raises concerns and diminishes their constitutional value.

In international relations

In the past, sunset clauses were used effectively in order to implement policies in the international arena. Currently, sunset clauses are used in EU policies. The legal history of sunset

110 Regulation (EC) No 717/2007 of the European Parliament and of the Council of 27 June 2007 on roaming on public mobile telephone networks within the Community and amending Directive 2002/21/EC OJ L 171/32.

111 European Commission, Digital Agenda for Europe: What would it do for me? (19 May 2010, MEMO/10/199).

112 European Union Committee, Mobile Phone Charges in the EU: Follow – up Report (HL 2008–9, 42) [14]; Regulation (EC) No 544/2009 of the European Parliament and of the Council of 18 June 2009 amending Regulation (EC) No 717/2007 on roaming on public mobile telephone networks within the Community and Directive 2002/21/EC on a common regulatory framework for electronic communications networks and services OJ L167/12, art 14.

113 Regulation (EU) No 531/2012 of the European Parliament and of the Council of 13 June 2012 on roaming on public mobile communications networks within the Union OJ L172/10, art 8 (2).

114 Regarding the EU's competence on the issue see Paul Craig and Grainne de Burca, *EU Law: Text, Cases, and Materials* (5th edn, OUP 2011) 319.

115 Mitsuo Matsushita, Thomas Schoenbaum and Petros Mavroidis, *The World Trade Organisation: Law, Practice and Policy* (2nd edn, OUP 2006) 399. Moreover, sunset clauses are used extensively in safeguard measures under the WTO regime. Mitsuo Matsushita, Thomas Schoenbaum and Petros Mavroidis, *The World Trade Organisation: Law, Practice and Policy* (2nd edn, OUP 2006) 457.

116 Council Regulation (EC) No 1225/2009 of 30 November 2009 on Protection against Dumped Imports from Countries not Members of the European Community OJ L343/51, art 11(2).

117 Agreement on Implementation of Article VI of the General Agreement on Tariffs And Trade of April 12, 1979, BISD 26 S/171 art 11(3).

clauses provides us with two further examples. The first is the example of the unification of the Kingdom of England with the Kingdom of Scotland, and the other is the Constitution of South Wales.

Remarkably, a sunset clause was used in order to promote the unification between the Kingdom of England with the Kingdom of Scotland. In particular, in 1701 the Parliament of England passed the Act of Settlement,[118] regulating the issue of the Hanoverian succession. In response to this legislation, the Parliament of Scotland passed the Security Act,[119] which provided that the Kingdom of Scotland has the power to choose a monarch who might not be the same person as the monarch of the English throne. As a consequence, the Parliament of England responded with the Act 'for the Effectual Securing the Kingdom of England from the apparent Dangers that may arise from several Acts lately passed in the Parliament of Scotland', which was passed in 1704 and provided that:

> from and after the Five and twentieth Day of December One thousand seven hundred and five no Person or Persons being a Native or Natives of the Kingdom of Scotland (except such as are now settled Inhabitants within the Kingdom of England or the Dominions thereunto (Exception) belonging and shall continue Inhabitants thereof and such as are now in Service in Her Majesties Fleet or Army) shall be capable to inherit any Lands Tenements or Hereditaments within this Kingdom of England or the Dominions thereunto belonging or to enjoy any Benefit or Advantage of a Natural born Subject of England but every such Person shall be from thenceforth adjudged and taken as an Alien born out of the Allegiance of the Queen of England until such Time as the Succession to the Crown of Scotland be declared and settled by an Act of Parliament in Scotland in the same Manner the Succession to the Crown of England is now settled by Act of Parliament in England in case of Her Majesties Demise without Issue of Her Body.[120]

The aforementioned Act thus prescribed a set of economic sanctions against the Scottish, who were regarded as aliens. However, these sanctions would automatically expire if the Parliament of Scotland repealed the Security Act and approved the Union with England.[121] Eventually, delegates from both Parliaments negotiated and concluded the Treaty of Union, and the aforementioned law expired.

With reference to British colonial policy, a sunset clause introduced in 1823 justified the conclusion that there exists a connection between the use of sunset clauses and the separation of powers. In particular, Parliament adopted the New South Wales Act. Among other things, in section 8 it authorises the king, with the advice of the Privy Council, to introduce trial by jury; section 19 authorises the establishment of Courts of Quarter Sessions with

118 Act of Settlement 1701 (12&13 Gul III c 2).

119 Regarding The Security Act see PWJ Riley, 'The Union of 1707 as an Episode in English Politics' (1969) 84 English Historical Review 498.

120 Union of England and Scotland Act 1704 (3&4 Anne c 6).

121 The Parliament of Scotland approved the Union, and although the sanctions expired automatically, the Parliament of England explicitly repealed them: Union of England and Scotland Act (4&5 Anne c 15) [An Act to repeal several Clauses in the Statute made in the Third and Fourth Years of Her present Majesty's Reign for securing the Kingdom of England from several Acts lately passed in the Parliament of Scotland].

jurisdiction for crimes not punishable by capital punishment; and section 24 authorises the creation of a legislative assembly with appointed members.[122]

This Act was of limited duration due to a sunset clause which provided that 'this act shall be and continue in force until the first day of July in the year of our Lord one thousand eight hundred and twenty seven and from thence until the end of the next session of parliament', and it is considered to be the first step towards representative democracy in Australia.[123]

In 1828 the Secretary of State for War and the Colonies, William Huskisson, was authorised to bring a bill in order to renew the New South Wales Act, which was about to expire, and to provide 'for future alterations in the administration of justice'.[124] However, when the bill was presented before the commons, it did not contain a sunset clause. Thus Mr Bright complained that:

> the bill threw too much power into the hands of the Crown and of the privy council, and needlessly limited the other branches of the legislature in their power of interference [. . .] and would be better pleased that it should be passed for a limited period than be made perpetual.[125]

Eventually the bill passed with an eight-year sunset clause, due to expire in December 1936.[126]

More recently and in relation to the EU, the Financial Services and Markets Act 2000, which among other things sets the framework for market abuse penalties, contains a three-year sunset clause for specific clauses.[127] This reveals the interaction between the UK and EU legal orders. The original Act did not contain such a clause,[128] but its amendment with the inclusion of a sunset clause was decided while adopting the regulation[129] giving effect to the EC's Market Abuse Directive.[130] Since the existing UK framework provided a broader scope of market abuse prohibitions than the Market Abuse Directive, it was decided to limit the duration of the areas going beyond the scope of the directive.[131]

Nevertheless, such clauses were used selectively in the international arena, in order to safeguard the interest of UK in the broader international environment. As shown above, such clauses were used in order to spur on the unification between the Kingdoms of England and Scotland, in order to preserve the colonial interest of the UK over South Wales and, finally, in order to preserve the internal markets regime over the European common market policies.

122 The New South Wales Act 1823 (4 Geo IV c 96).

123 Alex C Castles, 'The Judiciary and Political Questions: The First Australian Experience, 1824–1825' (1975) 5 Adelaide Law Review, 294, 298.

124 HC Deb 01 April 1828 vol 18 col 1430.

125 HC Deb 18 April 1828 vol 18 col 1565.

126 Australian Courts Act 1828 (9 Geo IV c 83).

127 S 118 (9).

128 Financial Services and Markets Act 2000.

129 The Financial Services and Markets Act 2000 (Market Abuse) Regulations 2005 SI 2005/381 Sch 2 (1).

130 Council and European Parliament Directive (EC) 2003/6 of 28 January 2003 on insider dealing and market manipulation (market abuse) (2003) OJ L96/16.

131 Explanatory Memorandum to the Financial Services and Markets Act 2000 (Market Abuse) Regulations 2005 SI 2005/381 [7.6]. The three yeas sunset clause was renewed accordingly with the Financial Services and Markets Act 2000 (Market Abuse) Regulations 2009 SI 2009/3128.

The transaction cost of good law making with temporary legislation

In theory, the inclusion of a sunset clause permits legislators to review their past enactments and to evaluate them according to their practice, as well as to experiment on innovative policies and new institutions. In practice, though, the making of better regulation has a transaction cost in the sense that temporary legislation is a burden in terms of the legislature's time.

For the purposes of this discussion, good law[132] is the need to ensure that the technical quality of all legislation is sustained and improved; bad laws are those that, due to inefficient regulation, create loopholes or produce unreasonable and unfair results.

In relation to sunset clauses, Gersen demonstrates that:

> from an informational perspective, temporary legislation provides concrete advantages over its permanent cousin by specifying windows of opportunity for policy makers to incorporate a greater quantity and quality of information into legislative judgments. By redistributing the decision costs of producing legislation, temporary measures also facilitate experimentation and adjustment in public policy.[133]

Remarkable are the words of Lord Cobbold, who said:

> [M]y Lords, as a humble Back – Bencher from the Cross Benches who has listened to the debate in both this House and looking down from the Gallery in the other, I am amazed that there is still such a political battle on issues on which we all agree. The only issue that could solve the problem is the sunset clause. Whatever the faults, benefits or good qualities of the legislation, all the sunset clause asks is the chance to have a look at it again in a year's time.[134]

In addition, during the discussion of the Football Disorder Bill, an MP stated that:

> [B]y and large, hon. Members on both sides of the House recognise the need to be broadly reasonable and they recognise that the Government has a right, with a democratic majority, to pass their legislation. However, they also recognise the right and duty, to which Madam Speaker referred yesterday, to challenge legislation if we believe it to be bad. Nothing that has happened today or in another place alters the fact that this is a bad Bill, which has been introduced in haste and which we shall repent at leisure. The only fundamental difference between the Bill and the Dangerous Dogs Act 1989 is that, sadly, the Act did not contain the sunset clause that the Minister has now said the Government intends to accept. The Bill is about tokenism; it is a bad Bill.[135]

Thus we see that there is a wealth of evidence in favour of the ability of sunset clauses to empower the legislature to review Acts of Parliament and consequently ameliorate the legal position. While the temporary nature of the laws permits legislators to evaluate the practical implementation of the laws and to consider how to improve them, the legislative body,

132 About the discussion on the substance of the law, see Ch 8.

133 Jacob E Gersen, 'Temporary Legislation' (2007) 74 Chicago Law Review 247, 263.

134 HL Deb 10 March 2005 vol 670 col 1024.

135 HC Deb 27 July 2000 vol 354 col 1290.

instead of making new laws, spends its time reviewing pre-enacted laws. As the legislature has limited time, the extensive use of sunset clauses can overburden the legislative process with the review of temporary laws.

Calabresi refutes this, asserting that 'the most obvious response to the problems caused by the ageing of statutes would be seen to be freeing up of the legislatures so that they would find it as easy to revise laws as they do to pass them'.[136] Nevertheless, he points out that adding sunset clauses to all statutes is unsatisfactory, as it becomes time-consuming and ineffective.[137] This procedural deficiency of sunset clauses was noted in the Mandelkern report.[138]

To illustrate this point further, the dialogue between Sir Philip Holland and Prime Minister Margaret Thatcher provides us with information about the procedural deficiency caused by the coexistence of a review clause and a sunset clause. In response to the question of Sir Philip Holland regarding the introduction of sunset legislation for all advisory non-departmental bodies, Prime Minister Margaret Thatcher remarked, in 1984, that:

> Current arrangements provide for the continued justification for all advisory non-departmental public bodies to be reviewed on a three-yearly cycle. In the circumstances, I do not consider that to require legislation to provide for a finite life span for all advisory non-departmental public bodies, subject to renewal by Parliament, would provide sufficient additional benefit to justify the use of parliamentary time.[139]

Theoretically, it is correct to identify the need to retain efficacy of law making by eschewing sunset clauses in the vast majority of legislation. Indeed, Gersen acknowledges that there is neither theoretical nor empirical evidence that temporary legislation burdens the legislative procedure more than permanent legislation in specific cases.[140] In practice, the inclusion of sunset clauses in a small amount of legislation does not overburden the legislature.

That said, both proponents and adversaries of sunset clauses share the common concern that such clauses permit legislators to reconsider their enactment at the expiration of the law. This is particularly significant, given the past experience from the regular use of sunset clauses in the US after the Watergate Scandal, according to which it was shown that legislators are more keen to let a law expire than to spend time and review it.[141]

Consequently, sunset clauses promote good drafting of laws and can be a useful tool in ameliorating the quality of the content of the law.[142] Some argue that while the temporary nature of laws is theoretically compatible with the rule of law, in practice constant re-enactment of legislation overwhelms the legislative process. Therefore, it is recommended that sunset clauses be used in a selective, circumspect and discrete manner.

136 Guido Calabresi, *A Common Law for the Age of Statutes* (Lowboy Exchange 1999) 59.

137 Guido Calabresi, *A Common Law for the Age of Statutes* (Lowboy Exchange 1999) 62.

138 Mandelkern Group on Better Regulation, *Final Report* (13 November 2001) 18.

139 HC Deb 21 March 1985 vol 75 col 568W.

140 Jacob E Gersen, 'Temporary Legislation' (2007) 74 Chicago Law Review 247, 263.

141 Richard C Kearney, 'A Survey and Analysis of the State Experience' (1990) 50 Public Administration Review 49. See Chapter 5 for further discussion on the issue.

142 However, this category – the aim for better regulation – has substantive implications, for instance when legislation fulfils these procedural requirements but is not in accordance with fundamental rights. See text to n 97 in Ch VI.

Proper authority to renew the sunsets

Several commentators mentioned that the rule of law encompasses the proper manner of promulgation of laws.[143] Hence the third aspect of the formal conceptions on the rule of law is the process of the renewal of the temporary legislation. In practice, Parliament either holds the power to review and re-enact the temporary legislation or it empowers a minister of the government with a Henry VIII clause. The latter option consistently raises concerns, though, from a rule of law perspective.

In principle, upon the sunset of a law, Parliament debates whether to renew it or let it expire, and accordingly, MPs vote on the matter. However, as is evident in a series of Acts, such as the Anti-terrorism Crime and Security Act, the sunset clause was renewed due to a Henry VIII clause in secondary legislation. Hence, Parliament, which in principle has the foremost authority to legislate, ends up with a passive or limited role in the renewal procedure. Strictly speaking, as long as secondary legislation renewing the temporary law has its foundation in the sunset clause, it is properly renewed.

That having been said, the process of renewing temporary legislation is achieved via two models. Using the first, temporary legislation is renewed by Parliament due to a simple sunset clause, and according to the second, the legislation is renewed with secondary legislation as the sunset clause is coupled with a Henry VIII clause. It is noteworthy that MPs, during parliamentary debates, and academics define both clauses as sunset clauses, for the sake of simplicity.[144] However, this is inaccurate.

The distinction between the two clauses was, however, drawn by the House of Lords in their debate on the Anti-terrorism, Crime and Security Bill. Two alternative sunset clauses were proposed, the first clause in combination with a Henry VIII clause, and the second as a pure sunset clause. Lord Bledisloe proposed the sunset clauses in the Anti-terrorism Crime and Security Bill as amendment 105, according to which, in paragraph 1, the expiration dates were set, with the more objectionable measures to expire after two years, and the rest after five years;[145]while in paragraphs 2 and 3, according to a Henry VIII clause, the Secretary of State was empowered to renew the force of the law with statutory instruments after independent consultation.[146] Finally, the order renewing the force of the law had to be approved by resolution of each House of Parliament.[147]

143 Dicey has said that 'the rule of law is contrasted with every system of government based on the exercise by persons in authority of wide, arbitrary or discretionary powers of constraint': AV Dicey, *Introduction to the Study of the Law of the Constitution Vol I* (JWF Allison ed, OUP 2013) 97.

144 John Ip, 'Sunset Clauses and Counterterrorism Legislation' (2013) PL 74, 93.

145 '(1) Subject to subsections (2) to (5), and without prejudice to any other provisions of this Act – (a) Parts 3, 4, 5, 10, 11 and 13 of this Act shall cease to have effect at the expiry of two years from the date on which the Act is passed; and (b) Parts 1, 2, 6, 7, 8 and 9 of this Act shall cease to have effect at the expiry of five years from the date on which the Act is passed': HL Deb 10 December 2001 vol 629 col 1198.

146 '(2) If the Secretary of State considers that it may be appropriate that any Part of this Act should continue in force without amendment beyond the expiry of its specified period, he may consult such persons as seem to him appropriate to obtain their views as to whether that Part can safely and properly continue in force without amendment. (3) If, following such consultation, the Secretary of State certifies that no substantial grounds have been advanced as to why that Part should not continue in force, he may by order provide that that Part of the Act shall continue in force for a specified period not exceeding five years': HL Deb 10 December 2001 vol 629 col 1198.

147 '(5) An order made by the Secretary of State under subsection (3) or (4) must be made by statutory instrument and may not be made unless a draft has been laid before and approved by resolution of each House of Parliament': HL Deb 10 December 2001 vol 629 col 1198.

On the other hand, Lord Dixon-Smith, together with Lord Goodhart, proposed another type of sunset clause, amendment 106,[148] according to which the bill 'should continue in force through the full parliamentary process'.[149] Lord Goodhart added:

> [W]e believe that it will be much better to take the simple and direct course and to have proper reconsideration of this legislation in Parliament, where we will have a proper opportunity to consider the parts that are contentious and the parts that turn out not to have worked well. We should do that in due course and in proper time.[150]

Lord Rooker, comparing the two amendments, noted:

> [A]mendment No. 105 [the sunset clause in combination with the Henry VIII clause] may not fit parliamentary niceties but it is more intelligent than Amendment No. 106. That is not to disparage the Conservative Opposition – far from it. However, Amendment No. 105 is more practicable because implicit in it is that a good part of the Bill should remain permanently in force.[151]

Eventually, however, amendment 106, containing the pure sunset clause, prevailed in the House of Lords.[152] Yet despite the fact that some MPs argued in favour of the Lords' amendment in the Commons, the Lords' amendment was rejected,[153] as the government supported the inclusion of a sunset clause coupled with a Henry VIII clause.[154] In fact, the structure of the latter clause was similar to the amendment proposed by Lord Bledisloe, since in section 29 of the Act, there is a one-year sunset clause in paragraph 1, and in paragraph 2 the minister is empowered to renew the Act according to the Henry VIII clause.[155]

148 '(1) This Act, apart from Part 12, shall (subject to subsections (2) to (5)) cease to have effect at the end of the period of one year beginning with the day on which the Act receives Royal Assent. (2) 1 he Secretary of State may, subject to subsections (3) to (5), by order provide – (a) that a provision of the Act which is in force (whether or not by virtue of this subsection) shall continue in force for a specified period not exceeding twelve months; (b) that a provision of this Act shall cease to have effect; (c) that a provision of this Act which is not in force (whether or not by virtue of this subsection) shall come into force and remain in force for a specified period not exceeding twelve months. (3) Parts 1, 2, 6, 7, 8, 9 and 14 of this Act shall, by virtue of this subsection, cease to have effect at the end of the period of five years beginning with the day on which this Act is passed. (4) Parts 3, 5, 10, 11 and 13 of this Act shall, by virtue of this subsection, cease to have effect at the end of the period of two years beginning with the day on which this Act is passed. (5) Part 4 of this Act shall, by virtue of this subsection, cease to have effect at the end of the period of one year beginning with the day on which this Act is passed. (6) Any order made by the Secretary of State under subsection (2) must be made by statutory instrument and may not be made unless a draft has been laid before and approved by resolution of each House of Parliament': HL Deb 10 December 2001 vol 629 col 1205.

149 HL Deb 10 December 2001 vol 629 col 1199.

150 HL Deb 10 December 2001 vol 629 col 1201.

151 HL Deb 10 December 2001 vol 629 col 1202.

152 Anti – terrorism, Crime and Security HL Bill (2001–2) 33.

153 HC Deb 12 December 2001 vol 376 col 959: 'That this House disagrees Lords amendment No 66: Ayes 322, Noes 215'.

154 HC Deb 12 December 2001 vol 376 col 952.

155 '(1) Sections 21 to 23 shall, subject to the following provisions of this section, expire at the end of the period of 15 months beginning with the day on which this Act is passed. (2) The Secretary of State may by order – (a) repeal sections 21 to 23; (b) revive those sections for a period not exceeding one year; (c) provide that those sections shall not expire in accordance with subsection (1) or an order under

The government's proposal was criticised on the grounds that it diminished the role of Parliament. One MP stated:

> I am not quite clear what the Home Secretary is saying, but if it is that whatever the recommendations made by the review body, the Government will automatically accept them, that is not what was said in the House of Lords. If that is what he is saying, it is welcome, but it is not a substitute for a proper sunset clause that limits emergency, far-reaching and draconian legislation.[156]

Indeed, a sunset clause, when it is not coupled with a Henry VIII clause, or if it is a pure sunset clause, permits MPs to debate reasonably and to ask the government to justify their proposal and, ultimately, to carefully scrutinise the bill. However, when the sunset clause is coupled with a Henry VIII clause, the outcome is that the parliamentary procedures are circumvented. Having said that, it is remarkable that without parliamentary intervention, a report issued by the Home Affairs Select Committee provided that '[u]nless the Bill provided for a final expiry date – or "sunset" provision – beyond which no further renewal could be made, it would be possible for the provisions to continue in force for many years, or even decades'.[157]

Although combining sunset clauses with Henry VIII clauses was extensively used before the Second World War, concerns were raised regarding the extent of review and the lack of parliamentary intervention in the renewal process.[158] Indeed, it makes a significant difference in relation to the parliamentary role. In order to renew an act that expires by virtue of a sunset clause, new legislation, and therefore strong parliamentary scrutiny, is required. The converse occurs with the combination of sunset clauses and Henry VIII clauses, since Parliament might not have a role at all, and thus parliamentary scrutiny is weakened.

Even if the minister who renews the legislation is an authorised person according to an Act of Parliament, this delegation of power seems to test the rule of law, as the process of renewal from a body other than Parliament infringes the legal maxim *cujus est dare ejus est disponere*, which means 'he who has the power to give, has the right to designate the mode of its application'.[159]

In light of these remarks on the distinction between the two alternative sunset clauses, Justice Devlin in *Willcock v Muckle* criticised the prolongation of legislation with Henry VIII clauses, even if such legislation would expire due to a sunset clause. He held that:

---

paragraph (b) or this paragraph, but shall continue in force for a period not exceeding one year. (3) An order under subsection (2)—(a)must be made by statutory instrument, and(b)may not be made unless a draft has been laid before and approved by resolution of each House of Parliament': Anti – terrorism, Crime and Security Act, s 29.

156 HC Deb 12 December 2001 vol 376 col 956.

157 Home Affairs Select Committee, The Anti-Terrorism, Crime and Security Bill 2001 (HC 2001–2, 351) [41].

158 For instance, the Import, Export and Customs Powers (Defence) Act 1939 in section 9, paragraph 3 prescribes: 'This act shall continue in force until such date as his majesty may by order in council declare to be the date on which the emergency that was the occasion of the passing of this Act came to an end.' This act was eventually repealed in 1990 with the Import and Export Control Act 1990, and was one of the last major pieces of the emergency legislation introduced at the beginning of the Second World War to remain in use until that time. See HC Deb 29 November 1990 vol 181 cols 1059–63.

159 Thomas Tayler, *The Law Glossary: Being a Selection of the Greek, Latin, Saxon, French, and Italian Sentences, Phrases and Maxims* (Martin & Marshall 1833) 56.

> it would be very unfortunate if the public were to receive the impression that the continuance of the state of emergency had become a sort of statutory fiction which was used as a means of prolonging legislation initiated under different circumstances and for different purposes.[160]

A pure sunset clause demands that parliamentary procedure begins *ab initio*. In conclusion, the hybrid clauses combining a sunset clause with a Henry VIII clause limit parliamentary intervention and, in practice, negate the effect of the sunset clause.

In light of the above concerns, Parliament enacted the Terrorism Prevention and Investigation Measures Act in 2011. According to this Act, although Parliament delegates to the Secretary of State the authority to revive the special anti-terrorism powers, it simultaneously imposes upon them the burden to lay the relevant order before Parliament for approval.[161]

The taxonomy[162] of current sunset clause usage has shown that a variety of constructions is possible, with different impacts on legislation. As mentioned earlier, a pure or proper sunset clause causes the law to expire on a specific date and the legislature becomes responsible for renewing the legislation with a new Act, should this be desired. Furthermore, the amalgam of a sunset clause with a Henry VIII clause reverses the benefits for the legislature within the separation of powers, such as Parliament's enhanced position to supervise the executive, because the renewal process is delegated to the executive under a specific timetable.

Conclusions

'Rule of law' is a manifold term. Different conceptions map the different perspectives on the rule of law. However, it is clear that the principles of the rule of law affect the form, the construction and the inclusion or abolition of a sunset clause.

My argument comes to bear upon its conclusion thus: in applying the formal constructions of the rule of law to sunset clauses, there are three main concerns. First, whether the temporary character of the laws disrupts stability and inhibits the legislative process; second, whether the expiration date increases uncertainty; and, finally, whether the process of renewal complies with parliamentary procedure.

Despite the fact that the temporary nature of the legislation is incongruent with the concepts of stability and continuity, inasmuch as it provides the system with flexibility, it is nonetheless acceptable. Furthermore, the pragmatic application of such clauses in areas with need for flexibility has shown that time limitation can be the means to regulate occasional and temporary issues. Suffice to repeat the role of sunset clauses in the making of the Act of Union which demanded a sharp and flexible approach. However, legislators have to be selective in the use of such clauses, as their extensive use might consume excessive amounts of legislative time and overburden Parliament.

160 *Willcock v Muckle* (1951) 2 KB 844, 853.

161 Terrorism Prevention and Investigation Measures Act 2011, s 21: '2. The Secretary of State may, by order made by statutory instrument (a) repeal the Secretary of State's TPIM powers; (b) at any time revive the Secretary of State's TPIM powers for a period not exceeding 5 years; [. . .] 4. An order under this section may not be made unless a draft of it has been laid before Parliament and approved by a resolution of each House. [. . .] 6. An order that contains such a declaration (a)must be laid before Parliament after being made; and (b) if not approved by a resolution of each House before the end of 40 days beginning with the day on which the order was made, ceases to have effect at the end of that period.'

162 See Ch 1.

Concerning the expiration of the law and its renewal, the construction of a sunset clause inevitably varies. The variety of constructions depends on particular circumstances such as the historical timing and the substance of the law. In principle, expiration dates based upon a future condition disrupt legal certainty. In addition, the construction of sunset clauses coupled with Henry VIII clauses gives the impression of a non-forceable termination.

8 Sunset clauses and substantive rule of law

Silent enim leges inter arma. (In times of war, the law falls silent.)

Cicero, *Pro Tito Annio Milone* 4.11

Sunset clauses and the substance of the law

The substantive conception of the rule of law refers to the content of the law and depends on its compatibility with human rights and/or a theory of justice.[1] Craig points out that:

> certain substantive rights are said to be based on, or derived from, the rule of law. The concept is used as the foundation for these rights, which are then used to distinguish between 'good' laws, which comply with such rights, and 'bad' laws, which do not.[2]

The interaction of such laws, good or bad, with sunset clauses takes place when good or bad laws are subject to a sunset clause, or alternatively, when a new law subject to a sunset clause overrides a good law or a bad law.

Within this context, good law[3] is not simply the need to ensure the technical quality of all legislation, as its content should also enshrine the substantive elements of the rule of law; bad laws are those that produce unjust and unfair results, and over and above that, limit the force and the scope of good laws.

1 Paul Craig, 'Formal and Substantive Conceptions of the Rule of Law: An Analytical Framework' (1997) PL 467, 480. See Brian Z. *Tamanaha On the Rule of Law: History, Politics, Theory* (CUP) 91.

2 Paul Craig, 'Formal and Substantive Conceptions of the Rule of Law: An Analytical Framework' (1997) PL 467, 480.

3 In *Leviathan*, Thomas Hobbes ponders the meaning of 'good law', which is 'To the care of the Sovereign, belongeth the making of Good Laws. But what is a good law? By a Good Law, I mean not a just law: for no law can be unjust. The law is made by the sovereign power, and all that is done by such power, is warranted, and owned by every one of the people; and that which every man will have so, no man can say is unjust. It is in the laws of a Commonwealth, as in the laws of gaming: whatsoever the amesters all agree on, is injustice to none of them. A good Law is that, which is needfull, for the good of the people, and withal perspicuous.': Thomas Hobbes, *Leviathan* (first published 1651, Forgotten Books 2008) 236. Moreover, in 1789 Edmund Burke famously observed that 'Bad laws are the worst sort of tyranny': Edmund Burke, *Speech of Edmund Burke at the Guildhall in Bristol Previous to the late Election in the City* (London 1780) 34.

Indeed, the rule of law prioritises the need to maintain 'good law'.[4] Accordingly, the aim of the legislator is to draft and enact just and watertight legislation.[5] In theory, sunset clauses are an ideal tool in the toolbox of law makers to experiment and introduce innovative legislation[6] that will keep pace with the changes in the society and mirror its needs.[7] To this end, the enactment of temporary laws permits legislators to review their past enactments and to evaluate them according to their practice, as well as to experiment on innovative policies. As this suggests, such temporary laws enhance the enactment of innovative legislation, improve the quality of the laws and remove obsolete statutes, which is desirable and in line with the constant need to maintain good legislation. In UK practice, though, it will be seen that this theory is implemented only in very few cases, such as the early termination of censorship in early modern Britain and, more recently, the abolition of the death penalty.

Sunset clauses in times of emergencies

Defining emergencies

Rousseau observed that in times of emergencies, 'the inflexibility of the laws, which keeps them from bending to events, can in some cases render them pernicious, and through them cause the ruin of a State in crisis'.[8] This remark became more relevant in light of terrorism. The term emergency legislation or emergency laws connotes legislation which regulates emergencies, as set out in section 1 of the Civil Contingencies Act.[9] The definition of this term, though, was a concern of the Select Committee on the Constitution.[10] Among several approaches, the most notable is the definition proposed by the Hansard Society, explaining that emergency legislation:

> [c]an be said to broadly fall into two categories: a) special legislation that is needed in order to tackle an emergency of national or international scope and importance in which human welfare, the environment or national security may be threatened [. . .]. b) legislation that is needed to cover a broader range of domestic situations in which the emergency does not meet the threshold of a national public emergency (as defined by the Civil Contingencies Act) but which is deemed by the Government to pose a threat to

4 In fact, the Select Committee on the Constitution characterised the 'need to maintain good law' as a constitutional principle. See Select Committee on the Constitution, *Fast-track Legislation: Constitutional Implications and Safeguards* (HL 2008–9, 116-II) [16].

5 Sir John Laws argues that one of the components of the rule of law is fairness: 'The third elementarily [fairness], requires that like cases be treated alike. It demands also an insistence on fair procedures'. See Sir John Laws, 'The constitution: morals and rights' (1996) PL 622, 630.

6 About sunset clauses and their utility to introduce experimental legislation see Sofia Ranchordás, *Constitutional Sunsets and Experimental Legislation: A Comparative Perspective* (Elgar 2014).

7 The ability of sunset clauses to reconcile law with the social norms is expressed by Roger Brownsword and Jeffrey Wale discussing the issue of the medicalisation of assisted suicide: Roger Brownsword and Jeffrey Wale, 'Compromise Medicalisation', in Catherine Stanton, Sarah Devaney, Anne-Maree Farrell and Alexandra Mullock (eds), *Pioneering Healthcare Law* (Routledge 2016) 303.

8 Rousseau, *The Social Contract and other Later Political Writings* (Victor Gourevitch, CUP 1997) 138.

9 Civil Contingencies Act 2004, s 1.

10 See Select Committee on the Constitution, *Fast-track Legislation: Constitutional Implications and Safeguards* (HL 2008–9, 116-I); Select Committee on the Constitution, *Fast-track Legislation: Constitutional Implications and Safeguards* (HL 2008–9, 116-II). For the elements of the definition see Clive Walker, *The Anti – Terrorism Legislation* (2nd edn, OUP 2009) 6.

> the good governance of the country (or a region thereof) and its political, legal, administrative or economic condition, or the health of the public, sufficient to justify the fast-tracking of legislative measures outside normal parliamentary procedures.[11]

By its very nature, emergency legislation is considered, first, as exceptional.[12] This is because legislative decisions are made under conditions of social pressure and substantial uncertainty.[13] Second, emergency legislation is considered transitional,[14] because the legislation aims to restore normality. Third, it is considered controversial, as the adopted measures have an impact on human rights.[15] Thus emergency legislation is, commonly, temporary.

Contemporary uses in emergency legislation

The principal mechanism by which the duration of an act can be limited is the sunset clause. Indeed, a series of UK emergency Acts are limited in time by the inclusion of such a clause.[16] In addition to sunset clauses, Parliament has used the Henry VIII clause, including in a series of Acts adopted during the Second World War,[17] which gave plenary power to the executive to repeal the Act. Subsequently, a new clause was introduced in an act regarding the prevention of terrorism,[18] and this was a combination of a sunset clause and a Henry VIII clause.

In the Prevention of Terrorism Act (Temporary Provisions) 1976, for instance, there was an expiry date due to a sunset clause, coupled with the inclusion of a Henry VIII clause, and thus the minister could renew it without significant parliamentary intervention. In practice, the combination of a sunset clause with a Henry VIII clause resulted in the neutralisation of the sunset clause, as in practice the Acts were renewed without parliamentary interference. The fact that emergency legislation remained in force for many years after the end of the

11 Select Committee on the Constitution, *Fast-track Legislation: Constitutional Implications and Safeguards* (HL 2008–9, 116-II) 5.

12 Select Committee on the Constitution, *Fast-track Legislation: Constitutional Implications and Safeguards* (HL 2008–9, 116-II) 5.

13 John E Finn, 'Sunset Clauses and Democratic Deliberation: Assessing the Significance of Sunset Provisions in Anti-terrorism Legislation' (2010) 48 Columbia Journal of Transnational Law 442, 450.

14 Oren Gross, 'Chaos and Rules: Should Responses to Violent Crises Always Be Constitutional?' (2003) 112 Yale Law Journal 1014, 1073.

15 Given the preceding analysis, Lord Goodhart remarked during the debate of anti-terrorism legislation that '[w]e believe, in principle, that emergency legislation – unless it is very simple indeed – should have a sunset clause. That is why, for example, the Football Disorder Bill, which was enacted a couple of years ago, is coming back next week in a new form of primary legislation. We believe that is the right course for that legislation, and even more the right course for this Bill. The more contentious a provision, the sooner the sun should set on it – and aspects of this Bill are very contentious.' See HL Deb 10 December 2001 vol 629 col 1201.

16 Prevention of Violence Act 1939, s 5; Northern Ireland (Temporary Provisions) Act 1972, s 1(5); Imprisonment (Temporary Provisions) Act 1980, s 8(1); Prevention of Terrorism (Temporary Provisions) Act 1989, s 27(5).

17 Import, Export and Customs Powers (Defence) Act 1939, s 9(3).; Unemployment Insurance (Emergency Powers) Act 1939, s 4(3); Administration of Justice (Emergency Provisions) Act 1939, s 11(2); Administration of Justice (Emergency Provisions) (Northern Ireland) Act 1939, s 12(2); Courts (Emergency Powers) Act 1943, s 14(3).

18 Prevention of Terrorism Act (Temporary Provisions) 1974, s 12, and Prevention of Terrorism Act (Temporary Provisions) 1976, s 17. The latter Act contained a twelve-month sunset clause, however by the inclusion of the Henry VIII clause, the Secretary of State had the power to renew it and invalidate the sunset clause.

emergency was a cause for parliamentary concern. The thoughts of the Marquess of Reading, comparing two emergency Acts, the former having a Henry VIII clause, and the latter having a sunset clause, are worthy of note:

> That Act [National Registration Act 1939] was, as I have said, to be brought to an end by Order-in-Council when the emergency terminated, and one might well have imagined that the carrying out of that statutory suicide pact was inescapable. Nevertheless, simply for administrative convenience the Government continued to reprieve the victims. It is worth bearing in mind that there was a National Registration Act in the 1914–18 War and that that Act contained the terse and peremptory clause as to its termination that it should continue in force "during the continuance of the present war and no longer." With the official termination of that war on August 31, 1921, after the prolonged peace negotiations, that National Registration Act ceased upon the midnight, without pain to itself or grief to anyone else.[19]

The difference between a sunset clause and a Henry VIII clause is the degree of parliamentary scrutiny, as a Henry VIII clause empowers the minister to renew or repeal the legislation without parliamentary deliberation.[20] As a result, the inclusion of a sunset clause in emergency legislation is considered to be a safeguard, since, where one is used, Parliament has frequent opportunities to debate the continuance of the Act and review its merit.[21] It also enables Parliament to reconsider its enactments, which is especially important when it is considered that emergency legislation is adopted as part of a fast track procedure.[22] For example, it is noteworthy that during the debates for the adoption of the Anti-terrorism, Crime and Security Act 2001, it was stated that 'given the nature of the Bill, it is impossible to say that it should be passed without a proper review being established'.[23]

A few days after 9/11, and just before the adoption of the anti-terrorism legislation in the US, Ackerman explicitly supported the idea of a two-year sunset clause in US legislation.[24] Finn, however, disagreed in this respect.[25] The difference between the two was that Ackerman emphasised the opportunity afforded to the legislature to review legislation, while

19 HL Deb 26 July 1951 vol 172 col 1339.

20 The Henry VIII clause is defined by the House of Lords Select Committee on the Scrutiny of Delegated Powers in its report of 2009 as 'a provision in a Bill which enables primary legislation to be amended or repealed by subordinate legislation, with or without further Parliamentary scrutiny'. See Delegated Powers and Regulatory Reform Committee, *Guidance for Departments on the Role and Requirements of the Committee* (HL Nov 2009) [16]. These clauses were so named from the Statute of Proclamations 1539, which gave King Henry VIII power to legislate by proclamation. See Committee on Ministers' Powers, Report (Cmd 4060 1932) 61. For more detailed analysis on these clauses see NW Barber, Alison L Young, 'The Rise and Prospective Henry VIII Clauses and their Implications for Sovereignty' (2003) PL 112.

21 Joint Committee on Human Rights, *Anti-terrorism, Crime and Security Act Statutory Review and Continuance of Part 4* (2003–4, HL 38, HC 381) 2.

22 Select Committee on the Constitution, *Fast-track Legislation: Constitutional Implications and Safeguards* (HL 2008–9, 116-I) 198.

23 Privy Counsellor Review Committee, *Anti – Terrorism, Crime and Security Act 2001 Review* (HC 2003–4, 100) 444.

24 Bruce Ackerman, 'Sunset can put a Halt to Twilight of Liberty' September 20, 2001 available at <http://articles.latimes.com/2001/sep/20/local/me-47757> accessed February 16, 2014.

25 John E Finn, 'Sunset Clauses and Democratic Deliberation: Assessing the Significance of Sunset Provisions in Antiterrorism Legislation' (2010) 48 Columbia Journal of Transnational Law 442, 502.

Finn concentrated on its effectiveness, claiming that it was not a successful mechanism. Gersen has shown that the level of attention paid by the legislature depends on the circumstances, and thus the success of sunset clauses, as review mechanisms vary.[26]

In the UK a series of reports urges legislators to use sunset clauses in emergency legislation. The cornerstone is a report submitted by Jellicoe reviewing the operation of the Prevention of Terrorism (Temporary Provisions) Act 1976, which, although it contained a sunset clause, also had a Henry VIII clause and thus could be renewed by the Secretary of State without parliamentary deliberation. One of his main recommendations was the 'requirement for periodic full re-enactment by Parliament' with a 'maximum life span of five years without the possibility of further extensions'.[27]

In addition, several memoranda submitted before the Select Committee on the Constitution support the use of such a clause. The Hansard Society recommended that 'wherever possible sunset clauses should be incorporated into emergency legislation, and particularly in relation to legislation that impacts upon civil liberties',[28] and the Better Governance Initiative states that 'it is characteristic of such legislation in that it has a sunset clause and Parliament therefore has the opportunity to vote on whether the situation still requires its renewal.'[29] However, the memorandum submitted by the Leader of the House of Commons and the Leader of the House of Lords argued that 'the case for sunset or renewal provisions must be considered on its merits in relation to each bill, having regard to all the relevant circumstances',[30] while the memorandum submitted by Dickson reasoned that the renewal requirement 'gave the impression of being effective and transparent but, in the end, was not'[31] and was an inadequate safeguard 'against the perpetuation of bad laws'.[32]

Moreover, the report from the Privy Counsellor Review Committee expressed its 'support for the principle of making emergency legislation subject to periodic review and renewal by Parliament',[33] and the Joint Committee on the Draft Civil Contingencies Bill proposed the inclusion of a sunset clause in the relevant bill.[34] Recently, in 2006, the Law Commission made it clear that 'emergency legislation should always be subject to post-legislative scrutiny, particularly where it affects civil liberties'.[35]

Furthermore, in the international arena, a UN report on the Promotion and Protection of Human Rights while Countering Terrorism supports the use of sunset clauses and, citing

26 Jacob E Gersen, 'Temporary Legislation' (2007) 74 Chicago Law Review 247, 277.

27 Home Office, *Review of the Operation of the Prevention of Terrorism* (Temporary Provisions) Act 1979 (Cm 8803, 1983) 14; also known as the Jellicoe Report.

28 Select Committee on the Constitution, *Fast-track Legislation: Constitutional Implications and Safeguards* (HL 2008–9, 116-II) 4.

29 Select Committee on the Constitution, *Fast-track Legislation: Constitutional Implications and Safeguards* (HL 2008–9, 116-II) 2.

30 Select Committee on the Constitution, *Fast-track Legislation: Constitutional Implications and Safeguards* (HL 2008–9, 116-II) 129.

31 Select Committee on the Constitution, *Fast-track Legislation: Constitutional Implications and Safeguards* (HL 2008–9, 116-II) 87.

32 Select Committee on the Constitution, *Fast-track Legislation: Constitutional Implications and Safeguards* (HL 2008–9, 116-II) 84.

33 Privy Counsellor Review Committee, *Anti – Terrorism, Crime and Security Act 2001 Review* (HC 2003–4, 100) 13.

34 Joint Committee on the Draft Civil Contingencies Bill, *Draft Civil Contingencies Bill* (2002–3, HL 184, HC 1074) [201]

35 Law Commission, *Post-Legislative Scrutiny: A Consultation Paper* (Law Com No 178, 2006) [7.59].

Walker,[36] remarks that 'to be effective, it is important that independent review mechanisms be based on statutory terms of appointment, linked to the work of relevant parliamentary committees and accompanied by adequate resourcing.'[37] It states that:

> periodic parliamentary review and sunset clauses also enable the Legislature to consider whether the exercise of powers under counter-terrorism laws has been proportionate and thus whether, if they continue, further constraints on the exercise of such powers should be introduced, and/or whether the overall operation of counter- terrorism laws calls for their modification or discontinuance.[38]

The recent application of sunset clauses during the financial and banking crisis of 2008 merits further consideration. In order to deal with the problem of the Northern Rock bank and prevent its collapse,[39] the government adopted the Banking (Special Provisions) Act.[40] The Act gave draconian and wide-ranging powers to the executive,[41] including the power to nationalise banks through secondary legislation, but these powers were limited by an annual sunset clause.[42] On 21 February 2009 the powers conferred on the executive expired, but the Act nonetheless remains in force unless it is repealed by order as prescribed in the Banking Act 2009.[43]

The crucial role of sunset clauses in emergencies can be further explored by focusing on anti-terrorism legislation, which is a fundamental subset of emergency legislation.[44] The emergency legislation enacted in the aftermath of 9/11 and the subsequent terrorist attacks by al-Qaeda in Spain and London attracted the interest of politicians and academics throughout the world.[45] Few governments now rely on their pre-9/11 emergency legislation, and most governments, such as the UK, Canada[46] and the US,[47] have enacted new anti-terrorism

36 Clive Walker, 'The United Kingdom's Anti-terrorism laws: Lessons for Australia', in Andrew Lynch, Edwina MacDonald and George Williams (eds), *Law and Liberty in the War on Terror* (Federation Press, 2007) 189.

37 UNHCR Report of the Special Rapporteur on the Promotion and Protection of Human Rights and Fundamental Freedoms while Countering Terrorism (22 December 2010) UN Doc A/HRC/16/51 [19].

38 UNHCR Report of the Special Rapporteur on the Promotion and Protection of Human Rights and Fundamental Freedoms while Countering Terrorism (22 December 2010) UN Doc A/HRC/16/51 [20].

39 HL Deb 21 February 2008 vol 699 col 276.

40 Banking (Special Provisions) Act 2008.

41 Roman Tomasic, 'The rescue of Northern Rock: nationalisation in the shadow of insolvency' (2008) 1 Corporate Rescue and Insolvency 109.

42 Banking (Special Provisions) Act 2008, s 2(8).

43 Banking Act 2009, s 262(1).

44 Regarding the definition of terrorism see Home Department, *The Definition of Terrorism* (Cm 7052, 2007).

45 See John E Finn, 'Sunset Clauses and Democratic Deliberation: Assessing the Significance of Sunset Provisions in Antiterrorism Legislation' (2010) 48 Columbia Journal of Transnational Law 442; John Ip, 'Sunset Clauses and Counterterrorism Legislation' (2013) PL 74.

46 In Canada, the Privy Council Office issued a guide to law making according to which legislators should use sunset clauses with caution 'since these provisions may result in a gap of legal authority if the new legislative regime cannot be brought into force in time': see Privy Council Office, *Guide to Making Federal Acts and Regulations* (2nd edn, Government of Canada, Privy Council Office 2001) 91. In the aftermath of 9/11, though, the Parliament passed Bill C-36, the Anti-terrorism Act (SC 2001, c 41), which was incorporated into the Criminal Code as 'Part II.1 – Terrorism'. A sunset clause was included in the bill (section 83.32) sunsetting sections 83.28, 83.29 and 83.3 concerning preventative arrest and investigative hearing powers after a five-year period.

47 In the US, a statute enacted in 2001 in response to the 9/11 attacks, the 'USA Patriot Act', contained in section 224 a sunset clause providing that a series of sections shall cease to have effect on 31 December 2005. For more details see Ch 5.

legislation, or at least updated their existing statutes so as to meet the challenges of the 21st century. Significantly, sunset clauses are a common feature of this legislation.

The new anti-terrorism legislation in the UK, the US and Canada prompted two academic articles[48] on the subject of sunset clauses. The articles aimed to evaluate the use of sunset clauses as a post-legislative vehicle for scrutiny. Their principal conclusion was that even if sunset clauses may have the potential to be an effective review mechanism, they failed to meet the challenges of anti-terrorism policies.[49] With regard to the UK legal order, despite these articles, relatively little attention has been paid, first, to legislation where the sunset clause amendment failed, and, second, to the inclusion of Henry VIII clauses alongside sunset clauses. Thus, the analysis below will present a full account of anti-terrorism legislation where a sunset clause was debated, and will evaluate the critical elements supporting or opposing their use.

Just one year before 9/11, in 2000, the UK enacted the Terrorism Act[50] with the aim of adopting permanent measures against terrorism.[51] A partial sunset clause was introduced by the government, but it referred only to Part VII[52] of the Act, which was related to Northern Ireland. According to the Home Secretary, the government incorporated this in the bill:

> because the Emergency Provisions Act that covers Northern Ireland is due to expire next August. It was felt appropriate to bring these matters together. It is the fervent wish of hon. Members on both sides of the House and of the people of Northern Ireland that the emergency provisions should be withdrawn as soon as possible.[53]

The attacks of 9/11 were the catalyst for the Anti-terrorism, Crime and Security Act, which amended the Terrorism Act of 2000[54] and introduced the indefinite detention of foreign suspects of terrorism without trial.[55] When the bill was introduced in the House of Commons on 12 November 2001, the section concerning indefinite detention was subject to a fifteen-month sunset clause, together with a Henry VIII clause.[56] There was strong

48 See John E Finn, 'Sunset Clauses and Democratic Deliberation: Assessing the Significance of Sunset Provisions in Antiterrorism Legislation' (2010) 48 Columbia Journal of Transnational Law 442; John Ip, 'Sunset Clauses and Counterterrorism Legislation' (2013) PL 74;

49 Finn states: 'Whether sunset clauses work depends instead upon whether they deliver the informational, distributive and deliberative benefits they promise. Our study suggests that in many case sunsets do offer informational and distributive benefits, but these benefits can, sometimes, lead to merely modest deliberative benefits': see John E Finn, 'Sunset Clauses and Democratic Deliberation: Assessing the Significance of Sunset Provisions in Antiterrorism Legislation' (2010) 48 Columbia Journal of Transnational Law 442, 501. Ip, in addition, points out: 'This article has examined the effectiveness of sunset clauses by looking at specific examples that have been enacted in the counterterrorism legislation of the US, Canada and the UK since the 9/11 terrorist attacks. The article then evaluated the effectiveness of sunset clauses in both a substantive and procedural sense. The number of occasions of substantive success is few and that there are significant barriers to procedural success as well': see John Ip, 'Sunset Clauses and Counterterrorism Legislation' (2013) PL 74.

50 Terrorism Act 2000.

51 HC Deb 14 December 1999 vol 341 col 154.

52 Terrorism Act 2000, s 112.

53 HC Deb 14 December 1999 vol 341 col 153.

54 Anti-Terrorism, Crime and Security Act 2001, s 2.

55 Anti-Terrorism, Crime and Security Act 2001, s 23.

56 Anti-Terrorism, Crime and Security Bill [49] s 28(1) prescribed that: 'Sections 21 to 23 shall, subject to the following provisions of this section, expire at the end of the period of 15 months beginning with the day on which this Act is passed', and (2) prescribed that: 'The Secretary of State may by order (a)

opposition in the Commons. In particular, a member of the Select Committee expressed his disagreement with the Henry VIII clause, stating:

> that despite all the semi-sunset clauses that the Home Secretary has included in the Bill to enable us to review aspects of it, I believe that we are moving too fast. If we cannot properly scrutinise legislation, we shall serve neither the House nor the country well.[57]

Moreover, a Labour MP and member of the Select Committee on Home Affairs stated:

> As we all know, the history of anti-terrorism legislation is that when it is introduced, it is represented as temporary and as a response to some immediate crisis, but it has a habit of becoming permanent. I have therefore tabled – as have others, probably – a sunset clause which requires the Government to come back to Parliament after five years to go through the entire legislative process to obtain the powers that they seek in Part 4. We picked five years – others may choose a shorter or a longer period – because there is a precedent for it.[58]

The Home Secretary contended that 'in any case, the derogation has a five-year life and is automatically a sunset clause',[59] bearing in mind section 16 of the HRA.[60] A five-year sunset clause was supported by several MPs,[61] which was proposed by the Home Affairs Select Committee.[62] Consequently, sections 21 to 23 were to 'by virtue of this subsection cease to have effect at the end of 10th November 2006'.[63]

Furthermore, in 2004 the government introduced the Civil Contingencies Act, and a political debate took place within Westminster regarding the issue of sunsetting either a part of the Act or the Act as a whole.[64] Both sides expressed solid arguments. Eventually, a thirty-day clause was incorporated sunsetting the emergency regulations,[65] but in the end, the

---

repeal sections 21 to 23; (b) revive those sections for a period not exceeding one year; (c) provide that those sections shall not expire in accordance with subsection (1) or an order under paragraph (b) or this paragraph, but shall continue in force for a period not exceeding one year'.

57 HC Deb 19 November 2001 vol 375 col 77.

58 HC Deb 19 November 2001 vol 375 col 62.

59 HC Deb 19 November 2001 vol 375 col 28.

60 Human Rights Act 1998, s 16: '(1)If it has not already been withdrawn by the United Kingdom, a designated derogation ceases to have effect for the purposes of this Act – (a) in the case of the derogation referred to in section 14(1)(a), at the end of the period of five years beginning with the date on which section 1(2) came into force; (b) in the case of any other derogation, at the end of the period of five years beginning with the date on which the order designating it was made. (2)At any time before the period – (a) fixed by subsection (1)(a) or (b), or (b)extended by an order under this subsection, comes to an end, the Secretary of State may by order extend it by a further period of five years.'

61 HC Deb 21 November 2001 vol 375 col 397.

62 Home Affairs Select Committee, *The Anti-Terrorism, Crime and Security Bill 2001* (HC 2001–2, 351) [41].

63 Anti-Terrorism, Crime and Security Act 2001, s 29(7).

64 See Joint Committee on the Draft Civil Contingencies Bill, *Draft Civil Contingencies Bill* (2002–3, HL 184, HC 1074); HC Deb 16 November 2004 vol 426 col 1364. Ruth Kelly, the Minister for the Cabinet Office, stated that the government had reconsidered the issues of sunsetting and reporting on the use of Part 2 of the Bill which had been a concern raised, but had denied the sunsetting of the Act itself as not appropriate because the need to be able to respond to the most serious emergencies would not disappear after a given period.

65 Civil Contingencies Act 2004, s 26(1)(a).

government imposed its will and this political decision led to rejection of a clause sunsetting the Act as a whole.

The following year, in 2005, the UK government introduced another piece of anti-terrorism legislation, the Prevention of Terrorism Act 2005, so as to comply with the Supreme Court (at that time the House of Lords) decision in *A v Secretary of State for the Home Department*.[66] The House of Lords held that the indefinite detention of foreign suspects for terrorism without trial under the Anti-Terrorism, Crime and Security Act was incompatible with the Convention for the Protection of Human Rights and Fundamental Freedoms.[67] It is noteworthy that the measure of indefinite detention was reviewed twice by an order of the Secretary of State,[68] which inevitably raises concerns about the effectiveness of sunset clauses when combined with Henry VIII clauses, since parliamentary control is thereby diminished.[69] Suffice to mention here a remark by Lord Lloyd of Berwick, who criticised the executive because it ignored the reports in favour the repeal of the indefinite detention measure:

> In December 2003, the committee under the chairmanship of the noble Lord, Lord Newton, recommended that Part 4 of the 2001 Act should be repealed and replaced as a matter of urgency. But that was not done while there was still time to do it; for some reason, the Government waited until they were forced into action by the decision of the Law Lords on 16 December.[70]

Nevertheless, the new legislation, the Prevention of Terrorism Act, as a response to the House of Lords decision, contained again a hybrid clause comprising a sunset clause and a Henry VIII clause. Sections 1 to 9 were stipulated to expire after a year,[71] while the Secretary of State may renew them with an order for a period less than a year, to be approved by both Houses.[72]

Initially, the bill did not contain a sunset clause at all,[73] and was subject to severe criticism in the Lords.[74] As Walker mentions:

> [the Prevention of Terrorism Act 2005] did not get off to a good start. The exceptionally rapid legislative process was the subject of highly rancorous debate which was said

66 *A v Secretary of State for the Home Department* (2004) UKHL 56.

67 HL Deb 22 February 2005 vol 669 col 1102.

68 The Anti-terrorism, Crime and Security Act 2001 (Continuance in force of sections 21 to 23) Order 2003 SI 2003/691; The Anti-terrorism, Crime and Security Act 2001 (Continuance in force of sections 21 to 23) Order 2004 SI 2004/751.

69 In practice, the Home Secretary appointed an independent committee according to section 122 of the Act to review the legislation in April 2002 with the aim of reporting to Parliament by December 2003. Despite the fact that the Independent Committee expressed its objection to indefinite detention, the legislation was renewed. See Privy Counsellor Review Committee, Anti–terrorism, Crime and Security Act 2001 Review (HC 2003–4, 100).

70 HL Deb 01 March 2005 vol 670 col 161.

71 Prevention of Terrorism Act 2005, s 13(1)

72 Prevention of Terrorism Act 2005, s 13(4)

73 See Prevention of Terrorism HC Bill (2004–2005) [61].

74 HL Deb 01 March 2005 vol 670 col 132.

> to have "demeaned" Parliament as well as becoming the catalyst for the most severe bout of disagreement between Houses of Commons and Lords in modern history.[75]

The Lords proposed the inclusion of an annual sunset clause which would empower Parliament to scrutinise the bill as a whole.[76] Eventually, a sunset clause was agreed, and the Prime Minister stated:

> Yes, it is true that we have agreed on a sunset clause. Why? Because it is important. If people have these concerns, and I understand them, let us test it over the year. Let us see if the worries that people have are justified, or not. That is a reasonable thing to put forward. We have an independent review of the system – Lord Carlile will also report on it – but let us send out a signal from the House that, when it comes to defeating terrorism, we are going to give the police the powers that they need and back them.[77]

The structure of the sunset clause in the Prevention of Terrorism Act 2005 was followed in 2006 in the Terrorism Act adopted as a response to the bombings in London in July 2005,[78] which extended the length of the previous detention period. However, the Joint Committee on Human Rights criticised the new structure of the sunset clause, comparing the simple sunset clause in the Canadian Anti-Terrorism Act with that in the Prevention of Terrorism Bill 2005, and stated:

> The contrast between the two types of provision can be seen by comparing the amount of parliamentary scrutiny of the renewal of the Canadian Anti Terrorism Act with that of the UK Prevention of Terrorism Act 2005. In Canada, there have been detailed hearings before Committees of both the House of Commons and the Senate, examining the operation of the legislation and practice and the evidence of the continued need for it. In the UK, by comparison, there was a single debate of one hour in each House before the renewal of that part of the Prevention of Terrorism Act 2005 which authorises the making of control orders.[79]

The government response to the report was that all future terrorism legislation should have a five-year duration and should require renewal by parliamentary legislation.[80]

As seen in the historical chapters and from the preceding discussion, sunset clauses were used extensively in emergency legislation. This practice is explained by the nature of emergencies. Given that emergency legislation is often adopted under exigencies of time and without appropriate consideration from the legislative branch, the sunset clause enhances legislative oversight. Moreover, where special powers are granted to the executive, the expiration date provides the legislature with an opportunity to reconsider the delegated powers.

75 Clive Walker, 'Keeping Control of Terrorists without Losing Control of Constitutionalism' (2007) 59 Stanford Law Review 1395, 1408.

76 HL Deb 01 March 2005 vol 670 col 203.

77 HC Deb 9 November 2005 vol 439 col 298.

78 Terrorism Act 2006, s 25.

79 Joint Committee on Human Rights, *Counter – Terrorism Policy and Human Rights: Prosecution Pre – Charge Detention* (2005–6, HL 240, HC 1576) 166.

80 Home Department, *The Government reply to the Twenty-Fourth Report from the Joint Committee on Human Rights, Counter Terrorism Policy and Human Rights* (Cm 6920, 2006) 30.

A sunset clause might also be used as an effective apparatus in order to pass controversial measures, might prevent the normalisation of extreme measures in the legal order and might provide the opportunity to the legislature to evaluate its measures.

Focusing on the use of sunset clauses in the UK, it is important to consider legislation where a sunset clause is included and also where it is rejected. The sunset clauses to limit the duration of the Terrorism Act 2000 and the Civil Contingencies Act 2004 were, as a whole, denied. The common element between these Acts was that they were not adopted with a fast track procedure and the government aimed to provide a permanent legal framework. Nonetheless, both contained a partial sunset clause – the former because it adopted extreme measures the compatibility of which with the rule of law was impugned, and the latter because it gave special emergency powers to the executive which were related to concerns about the possibility of abuse (hence the sunset of executive orders).

The reports reviewing anti-terrorism legislation had a significant impact on the drafting of sunset clauses. The main focus was on the renewal process and the level of parliamentary scrutiny. The executive tends to draft sunset clauses with the least possible parliamentary review, and this was criticised by numerous reports. Nonetheless, the impact of the reports concerning whether to extend sunset clauses varies. The report of the Privy Counsellor Review Committee (the Newton Committee) urged the government to replace Part 4 of the Anti-terrorism, Crime and Security Act,[81] which was due to expire but was renewed twice following orders from the Secretary of State. The government ignored the recommendation, and eventually the House of Lords ruled that that part was incompatible with the HRA.

In light of the preceding analysis, it is evident that sunset clauses seek to increase legislative oversight, bureaucratic responsiveness and regulatory efficiency,[82] while also attempting to minimise the impact of draconian measures. Last but not least, such clauses aim to address a procedural deficit in the fast track process, which is to make certain that the legislation is properly discussed and debated at a later stage. Due to the nature of contingencies, emergency legislation is passed using a quick procedure through Parliament, so-called fast track legislation.[83] Therefore, the use of sunset clauses, as a form of post-legislative scrutiny, is vital, and offers safeguards in relation to such procedures.[84]

Nevertheless, the most common use of sunset clauses in emergency legislation is in conjunction with a Henry VIII clause. The combination of a sunset clause and a Henry VIII clause, even if in principle it prescribes an expiration date, vests in the executive the power to renew the legislation for a specific period of time. Furthermore, it appears that the executive favours the use of sunset clauses coupled with Henry VIII clauses, while the legislature endorses the use of sunset clauses.

By using sunset clauses coupled with Henry VIII clauses, parliamentary scrutiny is limited, and such enactments fail to expire. Yet both negatives consequences are caused mainly by

81 Privy Counsellor Review Committee, *Anti – Terrorism, Crime and Security Act 2001 Review* (HC 2003–4, 100) 25.

82 Jacob E Gersen, 'Temporary Legislation' (2007) 74 Chicago Law Review 247, 260.

83 The House of Lords has explicitly considered as fast track legislation governmental bills that received their second and third reading on the same day. See Select Committee on the Constitution, *Fast-track Legislation: Constitutional Implications and Safeguards* (HL 2008–9, 116-I) [18]. According to the report submitted by the Lords on fast track legislation, over thirty bills were recorded in the past twenty years which have been fast tracked through Parliament.

84 Select Committee on the Constitution, *Fast-track Legislation: Constitutional Implications and Safeguards* (HL 2008–9, 116-I) [208].

the Henry VIII clause. Sunset clauses, by contrast, in principle enhance the role of the legislature, as shown in the previous chapter,[85] while their evaluation pertaining to the rule of law depends on a number of combined elements, such as the right at stake and the amount of time restricted.

Sunset clauses and the models of reaction

Regardless of the system of government, an emergency has proven to be the Achilles' heel of many a democracy. The dilemma posed during an emergency is enshrined in the words of Abraham Lincoln, who pondered, 'is there, in all republics, this inherent, and fatal weakness? Must a government of necessity, be too strong for the liberties of its own people, or too weak to maintain its own existence?'[86] The means are justified by the ends, and in Posner's and Vermeule's words, 'civil liberties are compromised because the protection of human rights interferes with effective response to the threat'.[87]

Likewise, Posner has remarked that in a state of emergency, a conflict arises between liberty and public safety.[88] Lord Pearce, moreover, has pointed out that 'the flame of individual right and justice must burn more palely when it is ringed by the more dramatic light of bombed buildings',[89] and Justice Jackson, in his dissenting opinion in *Terminiello v City of Chicago*,[90] said that in a state of emergency:

> the choice is not between order and liberty. It is between liberty with order and anarchy without either. There is danger that, if the Court does not temper its doctrinaire logic with a little practical wisdom, it will convert the constitutional Bill of Rights into a suicide pact.[91]

Broadly speaking, during emergencies the priority of the government is to defend the polity from internal or external peril, and the exigencies of the emergency occasionally require the suspension of several liberties. Cicero set the principle in a state of emergency, saying *salus populi suprema lex esto.*[92] Even constitutional provisions are recorded[93] which allow the executive to suspend certain constitutional rights, creating gaping loopholes.[94] Nowadays the suspension of several liberties is 'institutionalised' and it is called derogation. Section 14 of the HRA provides that the Secretary of State has the power to make a

85 See Ch 5.
86 Speeches and Letters of Abraham Lincoln: 1832–1865 (ReadHowYouWant 2008) 257.
87 See Eric A Posner, *Adrian Vermeule Terror in the Balance: Security, Liberty, and the Courts* (OUP 2007) 12.
88 Richard A Posner, *Not a Suicide Pact* (OUP 2006) 1.
89 *Conway v Rimmer* (1968) AC 910, 982 (HL).
90 (1949) 337 US 1(US SC).
91 (1949) 337 US 1, 37 (US SC).
92 For further discussion on this principle see Andrew Roy Dick, *A Commentary on Cicero: De Legibus* (University of Michigan Press 2004) 457.
93 The official translation of the article 48 of the Greek Constitution is the following: 'In case of war or mobilization owing to external dangers or an imminent threat against national security, as well as in case of an armed coup aiming to overthrow the democratic regime, the Parliament, issuing a resolution upon a proposal of the Cabinet, puts into effect throughout the State, or in parts thereof the statute on the state of siege, establishes extraordinary courts and suspends the force of the provisions of articles 5 paragraph 4, 6, 8, 9, 11, 12 paragraphs 1 to 4 included, 14, 19, 22 paragraph 3, 23, 96 paragraph 4, and 97, in whole or in part.' See Constitution of the Hellenic Republic 1975 art 48.
94 Janet Koven Levit, 'The Constitutionalization of Human Rights in Argentina: Problem or Promise' (1999) 37 Columbia Journal Transnational Law 281, 298.

'designated derogation order',[95] which is in accordance with the framework of the European Convention of Human Rights.[96]

In liberal constitutional theory,[97] there are two traditional strategies used to face emergency situations. The first one is the 'business as usual model',[98] according to which the polity faces the peril with appropriate legislation from its legal arsenal related to war and crime. The second one is the 'accommodation model',[99] in accordance with which the polity departs from its ordinary legislation, as it is inadequate to respond to the needs of the state of emergency, and adopts specific modifications to face the exact peril.[100]

The use of sunset clauses is, thus, compatible with the accommodation model. In times of crisis, like wars and other major emergencies such as terrorism, executive power is bolstered and rights and liberties are restricted temporarily. One such proponent of the use of sunset clauses in combination with an increasing super-majority vote is Ackerman. He proposes that the emergency legislation should expire in a short period, unless it is approved by the majority for a short period again. Further reauthorisation should take place according to a super-majority requirement which will increase each time.[101]

The environment of panic which occurs after an emergency necessitates an immediate parliamentary reaction so that something is seen to be, and is in fact, done.[102] As Donohue reports, 'no politician wants to be seen as responsible for the next, possibly more lethal attack'.[103] Under the circumstances of panic, parliamentary enactments may not be able to benefit from the appropriate consultation period, so the inclusion of a sunset clause works

95 Human Rights Act 1998, s 14.

96 Convention for the Protection of Human Rights and Fundamental Freedoms (adopted 4 November 1950, entered into force 3 September 1953) 213 UNTS 221, art 15. Regarding the legal framework of the derogation in the ECHR see Rosalyn Higgins, 'Derogations under Human Rights Treaties' (1976) 48 British Yearbook of International Law, 281; Joan F Hartman, 'Derogation from Human Rights Treaties in Public Emergencies' (1981) 22 Harvard International Law Journal 1, 4.

97 In constitutional theory, a fruitful discussion is intrigued by the early ideas of Carl Schmitt according to which during emergencies the rule of law has no place as the powers of the sovereign are endless. Carl Schmitt, *Political Theology: Four Chapters on the Theory of Sovereignty* (George Schwab tr, University of Chicago Press 2005) 5.

98 One of the proponents of this model is Dyzenhaus. See David Dyzenhaus, *The Constitution of Law: Legality in a Time of Emergency* (CUP 2006).

99 One proponent of the accommodation model is Ackerman. See Bruce Ackerman, 'The Emergency Constitution' (2004) 113 Yale Law Journal 1029.

100 Gross and Tushnet propose a third one – the 'extra-legal measures model' – which is a model focused on the judicial management of the crisis. For further discussion of these models, see Oren Gross, 'Chaos and Rules: Should Responses to Violent Crises Always Be Constitutional' (2003) 112 Yale Law Journal 1011; Mark Tushnet, 'Defending Korematsu?: Reflections on Civil Liberties in Wartime' (2003) 2003 Wisconsin Law Review, 273. For criticism over Gross' model see David Dyzenhaus, 'The State of Emergency in Legal Theory', in Michael Yew Meng Hor, Victor Vridar Ramraj and Kent Roach (eds), *Global Anti-Terrorism Law and Policy* (CUP 2009) 65; Bruce Ackerman, 'The Emergency Constitution' (2004) 113 Yale Law Journal 1029, 1041.

101 See Bruce Ackerman, 'The Emergency Constitution' (2004) 113 Yale Law Journal 1029, 1047. This proposal is criticized by Posner and Vermeule: see Eric A Posner and Adrian Vermeule, *Terror in the Balance; Security, Liberty, and the Courts* (OUP 2007) 163.

102 David Cole, 'No Reason to Believe: Radical Skepticism, Emergency Power, and Constitutional Constraint' (2008) 75 University of Chicago Law Review 1329, 1343. This was the case of the fast track adoption of the Prevention of Terrorism (Temporary Provisions) Act 1974.

103 Laura K Donohue, *The Cost of Counterterrorism* (CUP 2008) 12.

as a protection against this deficiency.[104] In addition, another aspect of an emergency situation relates to the cognitive difficulties that arise when legislating in such a hustle, as it is commonly accepted that 'fear distorts human decision-making'.[105]

Without doubt, according to the theoretical understanding of the 'business as usual model' and the 'extra-legal measures model', as long as the inclusion of sunset clauses permits legislators to enact controversial laws that decrease the level of human rights protection, the use of sunset clauses is not desirable given that such clauses sweeten the pill of controversial legislation.

Sunset clauses and the de-juridification in emergencies

The extensive use of sunset clauses in emergency legislation gave rise to the presumption that with such clauses the adoption of controversial legislation hindering the substantive elements of the rule of law is facilitated. There have been concerns pertaining to the rule of law due to the strategic decision of policy makers in times of crisis to suspend rights, guarantees and legal procedures, which enshrine democratic core values, what is termed as de-juridification in times of emergency.[106]

Indeed, during emergencies, security is inversely proportional, in other words, weighs more in the minds of policy makers than human rights protection, and institutional guarantees and procedures. Consequently, the compatibility of such temporary accommodations with the rule of law is impugned. But, of greater concern, the use of such clauses is questionable when they are used in a state of normality, which cannot be regarded as times of stress.[107]

To begin with, emergencies require centralisation of decision making, effective and prompt decision making and, consequently, executive action.[108] Hence, the special emergency powers given to the executive at the expense of the legislature, albeit temporary, raise concerns about the possibility of abuse, what was exemplified notably with the activation of article 48 of the Weimar Constitution, ultimately diminishing the democratic character of the polity.

On the top of that distortion of the separation of powers, the suspension of guarantees such as the habeas corpus remedies has a side effect diminishing the role of the courts.[109] Examples are tracked in historic depth,[110] with the most notable being the case *Ex parte*

104 John E Finn, 'Sunset Clauses and Democratic Deliberation: Assessing the Significance of Sunset Provisions in Antiterrorism Legislation' (2010) 48 Columbia Journal Transitional Law 442, 456; John Ip, 'Sunset Clauses and Counterterrorism Legislation' (2013) PL 74, 86.

105 Ip, 'Sunset Clauses and Counterterrorism Legislation' (2013) PL 74, 83.

106 Antonios Kouroutakis and Sofia Ranchordás, 'Snoozing Democracy: The De-juridification of Emergencies' (2016) 25 Minnesota Journal of International Law 29.

107 An example is the derogation from human rights treaties in situations where the existence of an emergency is arbitrary. That was the case of Greece when in 1967 it adopted a royal decree invoking article 15 of the European Convention of Human Rights and suspended a number of constitutional provisions. See *Greek Case* (1969) 12 YB 1.

108 Peter M Shane, 'Executive Branch Self-Policing in Times of Crisis: The Challenges for Conscientious Legal Analysis' (2011–2012) 5 Journal of National Security Law and Policy 507.

109 Antonios Kouroutakis, Sofia Ranchordás, 'Snoozing Democracy: The De-juridification of Emergencies' (2016) 25 Minnesota Journal of International Law (forthcoming).

110 Regarding the UK, numerous cases are discussed in Chapter 3, for instance the successive Habeas Corpus Suspension Acts under George III. During the same period in the US, in 1798, President Adams' administration adopted an emergency framework, the Alien and Sedition Acts, to suppress the Republican critics during the Quasi War with France. This framework was constituted by four laws, two among

Merryman,[111] about the suspension powers of the President and the unequivocal marginalisation of the court's decision.[112]

But a pragmatic approach on the topic, defending the suspension of habeas corpus, was spelled out by Dicey, who pointed out that:

> the so-called 'suspension of the Habeas Corpus Act' bears, it is true, a certain similarity to what is called in foreign countries 'suspending the constitutional guarantees.' But, after all, a statute suspending the Habeas Corpus Act falls very far short of what its popular name seems to imply; and though a serious measure enough, is not, in reality, more than a suspension of one particular remedy for the protection of personal freedom. The Habeas Corpus Act may be suspended and yet Englishmen may enjoy almost all the rights of citizens.[113]

Despite the fact that the writ of habeas corpus is a remedy which secures the effectiveness of a right, in case a habeas corpus suspension Act is coupled with an indemnity Act, this combination denies any relief to the people deprived from writ of habeas corpus.[114]

Moreover, the enactment of temporary emergency legislation with impact on civil liberties in favour of security can lead to the undermining of individual rights. These views are fortified by the words of Justice Brennan, who emphatically remarked: 'After each perceived security crisis ended, the United States has remorsefully realized that the abrogation of civil liberties was unnecessary. But it has proven unable to prevent itself from repeating the error when the next crisis came along.'[115]

Bringing together the principles of security and human rights protection, practice in the UK and at an international level has shown that the most common model to face emergencies is the accommodation model. In this model, the rationale is that such clauses are not beyond the rule of law but part of it. As Ackerman remarks, in times of crisis 'the challenge is to provide it [regime] with the tools for an effective short run response without doing unnecessary long – run damage'.[116] To an extent sunset clauses provide the common ground to accommodate both security and rule of law concerns. In reality, the accommodation being sought is not between the governmental interest for security and the rights of the individual, but between the rights of the community for safety and the rights of the individual.

---

them temporary due to a sunset clause (An Act in addition to the Act entitled 'An Act for the Punishment of Certain Crimes against the United States' (c 74 1 stat 596), the expiration of which was on 3 March 1801 (section 4). The second one was 'An Act Concerning Aliens' (c 58 1 stat 570), which included a two-year sunset clause from the passing of the Act). See Alexander DeConde, *The Quasi – War: The Politics and Diplomacy of the Undeclared War with France 1797–1801* (Charles Scribner's Sons 1966).

111 *Ex parte Merryman*, 17 F. Cas. 144 (C.C.D. Md. 1861).

112 For more details about the conflict between President Lincoln and the US Supreme Court Chief Justice Roger Brooke Taney, see Arthur T Downey, *The Conflict between the Chief Justice and the Chief Executive: Ex Parte Merryman* (2006) 31 Journal of Supreme Court History, 262.

113 AV Dicey, 'Contrast between the English Constitution and Foreign Constitutions', in JWF Allison (ed), *Introduction to the Study of the Law of the Constitution Vol I* (OUP 2013) 115, 118.

114 For more analysis see Ch 3.

115 William J Brennan, Jr, 'The Quest to Develop a Jurisprudence of Civil Liberties in Times of Security Crises' (1988) 18 Israeli Yearbook on Human Rights 11.

116 Bruce Ackerman, 'The Emergency Constitution' (2004) 113 Yale Law Journal 1029, 1040.

Hence, a common element of emergency legislation restricting human rights is the sunset clause. In fact, sunset clauses are highly recommended in emergency legislation that impacts upon human rights.[117] Thus, on these occasions the benefits of increased security outweigh the negative aspects of constraints upon liberty.

There are several arguments that support the inclusion of sunset clauses in emergency legislation, and especially in legislation restricting human rights and suspending guarantees and procedures. To begin with, there is a notion of temporariness, as the emergency is a temporary event. The Romans used to say that *necessitas est lex temporis et loci* (necessity is the law of a particular time and place).[118] In addition, Greatly remarks that:

> the reason for that [time limit] would be that it would keep the issue alive and there would be a need for reports and it would maintain the sense of the urgency and the importance and one hopes the temporary nature of the crisis that provoked these powers.[119]

As the adoption of security measures with the limitations on liberties and the distortions in the normal functions of liberal democracy is the common practice in emergency situations, it is plain that sunset clauses smooth the consequences of such decisions. Suffice to mention here criticism made by an MP in relation to the Anti-terrorism, Crime and Security Bill, namely: 'in my view, the sunset clause only makes Part 4 less bad than it was'.[120]

Moreover, the environment of panic, the cognitive difficulties in enacting emergency laws and the concern of legislators in relation to the balance between security and liberties is enshrined in the statement of Senator Clinton regarding the USA Patriot Act Reauthorization Conference Report. She said:

> [B]ut even in the immediate aftermath of the September 11th tragedy, Congress recognized that in its haste to give law enforcement these expanded powers, there was a risk that this new authority was coming at the expense of constitutionally guaranteed rights and liberties. And so in the wisdom of both Republican and Democratic legislators, several provisions of the Patriot Act included four-year sunsets, allowing Congress the opportunity to revisit whether the Patriot Act strikes the proper balance between securing our safety and ensuring our freedom.[121]

The inclusion of such clauses in legislation, for instance restricting human rights, was occasionally a concern of MPs, the Commons and the Lords. For instance, in 1915 an MP criticised the temporary adoption of the Price of Coal (Limitation) Bill, saying that:

117 See Select Committee on the Constitution, *Fast-track Legislation: Constitutional Implications and Safeguards* (HL 2008–9, 116-II) [11].

118 John Bouvier, *A Law Dictionary, Adapted to the Constitution and Laws of United States of America* (GW Childs 1870) 139.

119 Home Affairs Select Committee, *The Anti-Terrorism, Crime and Security Bill 2001* (HC 2001–2, 351) [38].

120 HC Deb 21 November 2001 vol 375 col 394.

121 Senator Hillary Rodham Clinton, 'USA Patriot Act Reauthorization Conference Report' (16 Dec 2005, Congressional Record, S13713)

> this Bill is of a temporary character to meet a special and urgent national emergency. It is difficult, however, to retrace a step of this sort if once it is taken, and I urge the House not to adopt a policy of the nature proposed in this Bill without very serious consideration, or in any haphazard fashion. To say the least the Bill is an alarming interference with the hitherto free right to contract, and it is a violation of the principle of Free Trade.[122]

In emergency situations it is possible that legislators could conspire to pass draconian legislation with a time limitation that would otherwise have been opposed.[123] Finn remarks that 'we should expect that some opponents of emergency legislation will favor sunsets as the second-best option to voting against antiterrorism legislation altogether'.[124] Those sceptical of such clauses criticise them because they permit the normalisation of the extraordinary and, second, because they fail to provide safeguards against unwise emergency legislation. Gross remarks:

> [H]owever, as already noted, temporary arrangements in this area have a peculiar tendency to become entrenched over time and thus normalized and made routine. Time-bound emergency legislation is often the subject of future extensions and renewals [. . .]. It is commonplace to find on the statute books legislative acts that had originally been enacted as temporary emergency or counterterrorism measures, but that were subsequently transformed into permanent legislation. Furthermore, the longer that emergency legislation, broadly understood, remains on the statute books, the greater the likelihood that extraordinary powers made available to government under this legislation will become part of the ordinary, normal legal system.[125]

Second, a sunset clause is not an efficient tool to protect individual rights and restore guarantees and institutional procedures in emergencies. Finn argues that although sunset clauses offer information and distributive benefits, they fail to offer deliberative benefits.[126] Finn's argument is based on the fact that many sunset clauses fail to expire, and thus the restriction on liberties in the end remains.[127]

But, limitations to the use of sunset clauses exist. First, legislators cannot use such clauses to limit non-derogable rights. Second, the polity must face an imminent danger like an emergency. Third, any restriction upon individual rights has to survive the proportionality test in case of a challenge before the courts. Fourth, such restrictions should not violate any obligation under international law.

122 HC Deb 19 July 1915 vol 73 col 1197.

123 John E Finn, 'Sunset Clauses and Democratic Deliberation: Assessing the Significance of Sunset Provisions in Antiterrorism Legislation' (2010) 48 Columbia Journal Transitional Law 442, 454.

124 John E Finn, 'Sunset Clauses and Democratic Deliberation: Assessing the Significance of Sunset Provisions in Antiterrorism Legislation' (2010) 48 Columbia Journal Transitional Law 442, 454.

125 Oren Gross, 'Chaos and Rules: Should Responses to Violent Crises Always Be Constitutional' (2003) 112 Yale Law Journal 1011, 1090.

126 John E Finn, 'Sunset Clauses and Democratic Deliberation: Assessing the Significance of Sunset Provisions in Antiterrorism Legislation' (2010) 48 Columbia Journal Transitional Law 442, 501.

127 John E Finn, 'Sunset Clauses and Democratic Deliberation: Assessing the Significance of Sunset Provisions in Antiterrorism Legislation' (2010) 48 Columbia Journal Transitional Law 442, 501 495.

As regards the first limitation on the use of sunset clauses, the ECHR prescribes that states cannot derogate from specific rights;[128] the non-derogable rights are the right to life (except in respect of lawful deaths from lawful acts of war), freedom from torture, the right to be free from slavery, and the right not to be subject to retrospective laws. These rights are absolute and no sunset clause can suspend their force.

Second, a state of exception is a precondition and compelling justification for the government's adoption of sunset clauses suspending the rights of individuals.[129] It is for the political branches of the government, executive and legislature to declare an emergency, and the judiciary will be wary of interfering with this conclusion.[130]

While the judiciary is reluctant to assess political issues such as the existence and the extent of an emergency, the courts' role is nonetheless central. Article 15 of the ECHR prescribes that any measures taken should be 'strictly required by the exigencies of the situation'.[131] Proportionality is the principle through which the balance between competing values is adjudicated.[132] The main question before the courts is whether the exigency justifies the suspension of specific rights, whether the means undertaken are rationally connected to the objective and, finally, whether these means are no more than is necessary to accomplish the objective. Thus the question of proportionality of the emergency legislation may be linked to the duration of the emergency.

The evaluation of the compatibility of sunset clauses through proportionality requires a de facto analysis, case by case. There are several important variables: the imminent emergency, the legislative objective, the severity of the derogating measure, the right at stake and the amount of time restricted. The impact on the rule of law is different when there is a short-term sunset clause as compared with a long-term one, and it is also different to restrict freedom of religion, on the one hand, and habeas corpus, on the other hand.

The final limit to the use of sunset clauses derives from the obligations of the government under international law. Thus, according to the International Covenant on Civil and Political Rights, no derogation is permitted as long as it has a discriminatory result.[133] This fourth caveat was also discussed in *A v Secretary of State for the Home Department*.[134] The court found that the measure of indefinite detention of non-nationals was discriminatory in breach of article 14 of the ECHR.[135]

Sunset clauses permit legislators to suspend human rights protection temporarily, while subjecting their action to a modicum of judicial control. However, ex post intervention by the courts is not always sufficient to contain the damage to the rule of law. Is it quixotic to

128 Convention for the Protection of Human Rights and Fundamental Freedoms (adopted 4 November 1950, entered into force 3 September 1953) 213 UNTS 221, art 15 (2).

129 Convention for the Protection of Human Rights and Fundamental Freedoms (adopted 4 November 1950, entered into force 3 September 1953) 213 UNTS 221, art 15(1).

130 Regarding the deference that the courts recognize to the executive in times of emergencies see David Dyzenhaus, *The Constitution of Law: Legality in a Time of Emergency* (CUP 2006) ch 4.

131 Convention for the Protection of Human Rights and Fundamental Freedoms (adopted 4 November 1950, entered into force 3 September 1953) 213 UNTS 221, art 15.

132 For further discussion on proportionality in UK law, see Paul Craig, *Administrative Law* (7th edn, Sweet and Maxwell 2008) [21–010]ff.

133 International Covenant on Civil and Political Rights (16 December 1966, entered into force 23 March 1976) 999 UNTS 171, art 4.

134 (2004) UKHL 56.

135 Convention for the Protection of Human Rights and Fundamental Freedoms (adopted 4 November 1950, entered into force 3 September 1953) 213 UNTS 221, art 14.

discuss human rights protection in a state of emergency? Is Cicero's saying, *salus populi suprema lex esto*, still contemporary, or is it outmoded? Sunset clauses do not per se provide answers to these questions.

That being said, the major criticism of sunset clauses in emergency legislation is that they fail to expire and cause the normalisation of extreme measures. Indeed, review clauses and long-term sunset clauses or sunset clauses coupled with Henry VIII clauses do not enhance the rule of law: the former weaken parliamentary intervention, and the latter do not mitigate the impact on individual rights. Therefore, it is suggested that legislators at the preliminary stage of policy making, when adopting emergency laws with sunset clauses, should integrate the duration of sunset clauses into their thinking, thereby best serving the rule of law.

Sunset clauses in times of normality

The problem of non-expiration

The interaction of sunset clauses with the substantive elements of the rule of law is not contained in crisis moments. Several laws, temporary in nature, are recorded in times of normality and raise a number of implications, especially when such temporary legislation affects human rights legislation. There are two distinct categories of temporary laws in times of normality. First, laws that are adopted in times of crisis and their force is extended in times beyond the exigency, and second, laws that are enacted in times of normality.

Given that times of crisis and times of normality are apart by a very thin dividing line, the first implication is relevant to the continuity of emergency legislation when the state of emergency is not present. In the case *A v Secretary of State for the Home Department*,[136] comparable issues arose before the court. As was mentioned above, the legislature reacted to the events of 9/11 by enacting the Anti-terrorism, Crime and Security Act, sections 21–23 of which delegated the power to the Secretary of State to indefinitely detain non-national suspects of international terrorism. Pursuant to section 28 of the Act, the indefinite detention policy without trial of foreign persons suspected of terrorism offences was subject to periodic reviews, and subject to a sunset clause until 10 November 2006, unless renewed.

Pursuant to that law, the government detained nine non-UK nationals who challenged the lawfulness of their detention. The case was brought before the House of Lords. The appellants claimed that there was no 'public emergency threatening the life of the nation' which excused the adoption of the emergency measures.[137] Lord Bingham, while addressing that claim, stated the position as follows:

> Assuming, as one must, that there is a public emergency threatening the life of the nation, measures which derogate from article 5 are permissible only to the extent strictly required by the exigencies of the situation, and it is for the derogating state to prove that that is so. The reasons given by SIAC do not warrant its conclusion [. . .]. The European Court does not approach questions of proportionality as questions of pure fact: see, for example, Smith and Grady v United Kingdom, above. Nor should domestic courts do so. The greater intensity of review now required in determining questions of proportionality, and the duty of the courts to protect Convention rights, would in my

136 (2004) UKHL 56.
137 (2004) UKHL 56 [16].

> view be emasculated if a judgment at first instance on such a question were conclusively to preclude any further review. So would excessive deference, in a field involving indefinite detention without charge or trial, to ministerial decision. In my opinion, SIAC erred in law and the Court of Appeal erred in failing to correct its error.[138]

Hence the majority decision took into consideration the extent of the emergency, and the proportionality test was applied. The court found that the measure of the indefinite detention was disproportionate. Lord Hope lingered over the long duration of the clause in combination with the possibility of renewal and stated:

> The effects on the individual of a derogation that deprives him of his right to liberty will vary according to the nature, and above all the length, of the emergency. It will usually be impossible to say when an emergency arises how long it will last. But in some cases it may be perfectly obvious from the outset that it will last for a very long time, perhaps indefinitely. That seems to be the situation in this case.[139]

The court's approach to the issue was, however, predicated on the issue being a question of law, not merely a question of fact. Hence it did not examine the state of emergency as a fact and consequently failed to examine evidence about the existence or not of the emergency.

A series of US Supreme Court cases decided in the aftermath of First World War are especially significant given that they addressed this topic as a point of fact. In October 1919, Congress passed the Rent Law,[140] regulating rent control in the District of Columbia and having a limited duration of two years. The constitutionality of this statute was challenged on due process grounds, and the US Supreme Court upheld the statute. Justice Holmes, who delivered the ruling of the court, explicitly held that:

> No doubt it is true that a legislative declaration of facts that are material only as the ground for enacting a rule of law, for instance, that a certain use is a public one, may not be held conclusive by the Courts. But a declaration by a legislature concerning public conditions that, by necessity and duty, it must know, is entitled at least to great respect. In this instance, Congress stated a publicly, notorious and almost worldwide fact.[141]

In 1921, Congress renewed the preceding Act before its expiration with a one-year sunset clause,[142] and this Act was continued with a subsequent Act until 22 May 1924.[143] It thus appears that this Act, originally purported to expire in 1921, had been extended by successive Acts until the middle of 1924, a period of more than four years. Another case was brought before the US Supreme Court, and the legal action was based on several grounds, the most important being that the emergency justifying interference with private rights had come to an end in 1922.[144]

138 (2004) UKHL 56 [44].
139 (2004) UKHL 56 [122].
140 41 Stat 80.
141 *Block v Hirsh* (1921) 256 US 135, 154 (US SC).
142 42 stat 200.
143 42 stat 543.
144 *Chastleton Corp v Sinclair* (1924) 264 US 543 (US SC).

Once again, Justice Holmes delivered the opinion. This time, however, the court's approach was different. Justice Holmes settled the jurisdiction of the court, stating that 'a Court is not at liberty to shut its eyes to an obvious mistake when the validity of the law depends upon the truth of what is declared', and in addition that 'a law depending upon the existence of an emergency or other certain state of facts to uphold it may cease to operate if the emergency ceases or the facts change, even though valid when passed'.[145] As a consequence, the US Supreme Court on 21 April 1924 remanded the case to the lower court, as 'obviously the facts should be accurately ascertained and carefully weighed, and this can be done more conveniently in the Supreme Court of the District than here',[146] and thus the door to invalidate the Act was left ajar.

Regardless of the fact that on 17 May 1924 Congress pointed to the continuance of the Rent Law until 22 May 1925,[147] on 3 November 1924 the Court of Appeal invalidated the Act, holding that:

> It of course is unnecessary for us to attempt to add to the reasoning of the Supreme Court, but we may say with propriety that, if the emergency in question is not at an end, then this legislation may be extended indefinitely, and that which was 'intended to meet a temporary emergency' may become permanent law.[148]

Thus in 1924 the US Supreme Court laid down a more precise framework concerning the nature of the emergency expiry date and the degree of the courts' intervention. The US Supreme Court treated the expiry date and the state of emergency as questions of fact, and as soon as the case was brought before its jurisdiction it questioned whether 'the conditions that justified the measures are, in fact, present'.[149] Considering Justice Holmes's dicta, Vermeule characterised the invalidation of legislation with sunset clauses before the expiry date as 'ex post sunsetting', in contrast to the 'ex ante sunsetting' of legislation, which occurs when legislation sunsets due to the lapse of time.[150]

Likewise, an example which is relevant to this discussion but does not refer to emergencies is drawn from the entrenched problem of racial discrimination in voting in the US. The US Supreme Court struck down in 2012 the Voting Rights Act, a law that was first adopted in 1965 and was reauthorised a number of times.[151] With the Voting Rights Act, Congress aimed to limit the states' authority to adopt voting procedures that result in the denial of the right to vote on account of race and colour. In particular, it required a number of states to obtain federal permission before adopting any voting law.[152] When the Act was reauthorised in 2006 with a 25-year life span,[153] a challenge was brought before the US Supreme Court. The court held that the conditions that originally justified such extraordinary measures were no longer present.[154]

145 *Chastleton Corp v Sinclair* (1924) 264 US 547 (US SC).
146 *Chastleton Corp v Sinclair* (1924) 264 US 549 (US SC).
147 43 stat 120.
148 *Peck v Fink* (1924) 2 F.2d 912, 913 (DC Cir).
149 Adrian Vermeule, 'Holmes on Emergencies' (2008) 61 Stanford Law Review 163, 192.
150 Adrian Vermeule, 'Holmes on Emergencies' (2008) 61 Stanford Law Review 163, 189.
151 For more details see below text to n 188.
152 Pub L No 89–110, 79 Stat 437 (1965) s 4 and 5.
153 An act to amend the Voting Rights Act of 1965 Pub L No 109–246, 120 Stat. 577 (2006).
154 *Shelby County v. Holder*, (2013) 570 U.S. ___(US SC).

All told, it is apparent that in a number of occasions, legislators failed to let laws subject to sunset clauses expire. This is problematic because it entrenches extraordinary measures in times that there is no need. In addition, this makes apparent that the review processes of temporary laws within the legislature are not tailored enough to the distinctive character of sunsets in order to efficiently review temporary laws and let them expire when the circumstances of enactment are no longer present.

Sunset clauses and controversial law making

In times of normality, where there is no special need for special and extraordinary measures and political and legislative routine is the norm, the enactment of laws derogating from existing standards and rules is questionable. For instance there was recently a use of a sunset clause in 2003 when Parliament enacted the Fire Service Act according to which the power was conferred to the Secretary of State to interfere with collective bargaining.[155] This law was subject to a two-year sunset clause,[156] and the clause was used to pass legislation in a state of normality which would not otherwise have been enacted.

Lord Rooker argued that the existence of the sunset clause smoothed the consequences, saying:

> I draw noble Lords' attention to the fact that the powers in the Bill are time-limited to two years so the issue will not be around for ever. If the powers in the Bill are not activated after two years, they fall.[157]

Lord Campbell of Alloway's criticism is worthy of note. He compared the sunset clause to the sword of Damocles and stated:

> My Lords, I am the third Member on the Back Benches in this House – this makes all three – who is wholly unable to support the Bill. The convention being that on Second Reading we do not turn down a Government Bill, save in wholly exceptional circumstances, I ride by convention, but I want the noble Lord, Lord Rooker, to understand that I merely defer to convention and that I am totally opposed to the Bill. What is a sunset clause, for a start? It is a sword of Damocles to dangle over those workmen, so that if they do not toe the Government line – the imposed resolution of the Government – the sword drops.[158]

Without doubt, such use of sunset clauses as means to depart from standard rules and procedures, although it might be desirable to meet political ends, is not always legally justified unless it aims to regulate a temporary or transitory issue. Suffice to mention here that a series of private bills were submitted in Parliament to temporarily withdraw the UK from the

155 Fire Services Act 2003, s 1(1)(a).

156 Fire Services Act 2003, s 1(7). The provision was objected to by the Human Rights Committee, which concluded that 'the Fire Services Bill, as it stands at present, gives rise to a significant risk of a violation of Article 6 of the European Social Charter and of Article 8 of ILO Convention No 151'. See Joint Committee on Human Rights Scrutiny of Bills: *Further Progress Report* (2002–3, HL 119, HC 765) [1.6].

157 HL Deb 19 June 2003 vol 649 col 1017.

158 HL Deb 19 June 2003 vol 649 col 1017.

European Convention of Human Rights,[159] but all of them failed to complete their passage through Parliament before the end of the session.

Likewise, in the US, controversy was raised when sunset clauses were used in tax legislation. More specifically, the Economic Growth and Tax Relief Reconciliation Act 2001 was stated to expire on 31 December 2010,[160] and the Jobs and Growth Tax Relief Reconciliation Act 2003 was set to expire on 31 December 2008.[161]

Both Acts stimulated academic literature in the US regarding the effectiveness of such a clause in tax cuts and its compatibility with budget rules.[162] Commentators pointed out that the sunset clause failed to represent the true cost of the tax cuts, and was in principle contrary to budget rules.[163] In addition, such clauses created uncertainty in the Tax Code[164] and highlighted the lack of policy commitment.[165] Finally, sunset clauses permitted the legislature to gain benefits from the lobbyists at the expiration date.[166]

In opposition, it was argued that sunset clauses in tax legislation did in fact reveal the cost of the continuation of the legislation and indeed enhanced fiscal restraint.[167] Moreover, it is claimed that sunset clauses in tax cuts created an immediate stimulus to invest,[168] and that they raised accountability, since they permitted constituents to track the votes of their legislators when they adopted, renewed or allowed sunset legislation to expire.[169]

Focusing on the budget rules and the true cost of the sunset clause, Altshuler and Dietz argue that sunset clauses 'complicate and compromise the value of information provided by

159 See European Convention on Human Rights (Temporary Withdrawal) (2010–2 HC Bill 308); British Bill of Rights and Withdrawal from the European Convention on Human Rights Bill (2014–15 HC Bill 59).

160 Pub L No 107–16, 115 Stat 38, (2001) 901.

161 Pub L No. 108–27, 117 Stat 752 (2003) 303.

162 Regarding the Budget Rules in the US see Rudolph G and Penner C, 'Eugene Steeple Budget Rules' (2004) 57 National Tax Journal 547.

163 See William G Gale and Peter R Orszag, 'Sunsets in the Tax Code' (2003) 99 Tax Notes 1553, 1557; Elizabeth Garrett, 'Accounting for the Federal Budget and Its Reform' (2004) 41 Harvard Journal on Legislation 187, 196; Rebecca M Kysar, 'The Sun Also Rises: the Political Economy of Sunset Provisions in the Tax Code' (2006) 40 Georgia Law Review, 335, 390; Manoj Viswanathan, 'Sunset Provisions in the Tax Code: a Critical Evaluation and Prescriptions for the Future' (2007) 82 New York University Law Review 656, 658.

164 William G Gale and Peter R Orszag, 'Sunsets in the Tax Code' (2003) 99 Tax Notes 1553, 1557; Rebecca M Kysar, 'The Sun Also Rises: the Political Economy of Sunset Provisions in the Tax Code' (2006) 40 Georgia Law Review 335, 393; Elizabeth Garrett, 'Accounting for the Federal Budget and Its Reform' (2004) 41 Harvard Journal on Legislation 187, 196;

165 Rebecca M Kysar, 'The Sun Also Rises: the Political Economy of Sunset Provisions in the Tax Code' (2006) 40 Georgia Law Review 335, 394.

166 William G Gale and Peter R Orszag, 'Sunsets in the Tax Code' (2003) 99 Tax Notes 1553, 1558; Rebecca M Kysar, 'The Sun Also Rises: the Political Economy of Sunset Provisions in the Tax Code' (2006) 40 Georgia Law Review 335, 393; Manoj Viswanathan, 'Sunset Provisions in the Tax Code: a Critical Evaluation and Prescriptions for the Future' (2007) 82 New York University Law Review 656, 658.

167 George K Yin, 'Temporary – Effect Legislation, Political Accountability, and Fiscal Restraint' (2009) 84 New York University Law Review 174, 181.

168 Darrel S Cohen, Dorthe-Pernille Hansen and Kevin A Hassett, 'The Effects of Temporary Partial Expensing on Investment Incentives in the United States' (2002) 55 National Tax Journal 557, 565

169 George K Yin, 'Temporary – Effect Legislation, Political Accountability, and Fiscal Restraint' (2009) 84 New York University Law Review 174, 204 (asserting that 'extension of a temporary law requires legislative action whereas continuation of a permanent one does not').

the tax expenditure reporting'.[170] This conclusion was based on the premise that tax expenditure analysis regards sunset clauses or their expiration as permanent features, without considering the possibility of their renewal and the policy proposals. This outcome is thus premised on an assumption which might be very different from the realised account.[171] In part, this explains why conflicting opinions were expressed by scholars in relation to the compatibility of sunset clauses with budget rules.

Promoting good laws

The other side of the coin is when such clauses are used in a way to promote good laws, and as a result their use is beneficial and has positive interaction with the substantive elements of the rule of law. Suffice to mention here two cases: the first is the termination of censorship in early modern Britain, and the second is the abolition of the death penalty in the UK. In both cases, the change in legislation did not happen overnight, but progressively with the use of sunset clauses.

During the reign of William III, it is significant that the Licensing Press Act of 1662[172] expired. It was revived for seven years in 1685,[173] and the last time it was renewed was in 1692, for one year.[174] However, during the Parliament of 1695, the House of Lords aimed to include the Licensing and Press Act in a general act with the title 'an Act for continuing, and making perpetual, several Laws therein mentioned', so as to make it perpetual. However, the Commons declined to renew the Act.[175]

According to the *House of Lords Journal*, at the joint conference the Commons presented eighteen reasons why the Act should not be renewed.[176] Indeed, it was the first time that a detailed account of temporary legislation was considered while the termination or the renewal of legislation was evaluated. As Thomson remarks, the Commons pointed out that the Licensing Act was 'absurd' and 'inequitable', even though there is no reference to the freedom of the press.[177]

Based on this development, Ihalainen claims that 'Britain had a comparatively free press after 1695, which supported the emergence, mobilisation and expression of the views of the people'.[178]

Pertaining to capital punishment, still in 1965, the death penalty was in the criminal codes of the UK and its abolition was a controversial issue. That same year, a bill abolishing the

170 Rosanne Altshuler and Robert Dietz, 'Reconsidering Tax Expenditure Estimation' (2011) 64 National Tax Journal 459, 462,

171 Rosanne Altshuler and Robert Dietz, 'Reconsidering Tax Expenditure Estimation' (2011) 64 National Tax Journal 459, 478 (concluding that 'As a result of sunsets, the AMT, and other complications of current law, reading a tax expenditure table across time requires fairly sophisticated knowledge of U.S. tax policy and is a bit like reading tea leaves').

172 14 Car II c 33 [An Act for preventing the frequent Abuses in printing seditious treasonable and unlicensed Bookes and Pamphlets and for regulating of Printing and Printing Presses].

173 1 Jac II c 17 [An Act for Reviveing and Continuance of severall Acts of Parlyament therein mentioned].

174 4&5 Gul&Mar c 24 s 14 [An Act for reviving continuing and explaining several Laws therein mentioned [that] are expired and neare expiring].

175 *Journal of the House of Commons Vol XI* (1803) 305.

176 *House of Lords Journal 1691–1696 Vol XV* (1767–1830) 544.

177 Mark A Thomson, *A Constitutional History of England 1642 to 1801* (Methuen 1938) 298.

178 See Pasi Ihalainen, *Agents of the People: Democracy ad Popular Sovereignty in British and Swedish Parliamentary and Public Debates, 1734–1800* (Brill, 2010) 62.

death penalty was introduced by a British Labour MP, Samuel Sydney Silverman, and was entirely endorsed by the Labour Government.[179] A consensus was formed regarding the experimental character of the bill, and Henry Brooke, a Conservative MP who introduced the sunset clause, stated:

> it seems to me that if the Bill becomes law, in five years' time we shall all know a great deal more than we do today, and we shall have had the benefit of the Report of the Royal Commission on the Penal System, which may help us with the terribly difficult problem of sentencing, on which we have spent so much time.[180]

Finally the bill passed,[181] and in 1969 the Home Secretary, James Callaghan, proposed a motion to make the Act permanent,[182] in spite of the opposition who aimed at least to keep the act temporary.[183]

Finally, an interesting application of sunset clauses is recorded to remedy, via regulation or deregulation, certain legal areas of pragmatic injustice. For the purpose of this discussion, pragmatic injustice exists when the reality is far from the ideal which is prescribed in the law books.[184] This is the case, for instance, with the race inequalities in the US and the gender inequality on a global scale. Currently, although equality is the default rule and it is emphatically recognised in constitutional and international documents, law in action is far from the ideal.

The underlying concept is that public institutions (such as governments or universities), due to path dependance,[185] preserve some injustices or they are unable to correct them. Having said that, a temporary policy may have a drastic remedial effect and bridge the gap between the reality and the ideal.[186] This point here is within the context of paternalism, and the focus is policies that limit or define the authority of institutions.[187] This, in practice, is exemplified with the affirmative action policies and with the Voting Rights Act of 1965 that targeted the racially discriminatory voting tests or devices of certain US states.

The former is related to the affirmative action policies adopted initially in the US. In essence, affirmative action policies aim to regulate and correct a given deficiency; as soon as the deficiency is eliminated, such policies have no reason to stay in force, thus a sunset clause is desirable to make them expire. Nonetheless, when affirmative action was introduced in the US, it was not presumed as temporary and thus did not contain any sunset clause. Yet the sunset clause was implied by Justice O'Connor when she mentioned that 'we expect

179 HC Deb 13 July 1965 vol 716 col 358.
180 HC Deb 13 July 1965 vol 716 col 444.
181 Murder (Abolition of Death Penalty) Act 1965.
182 HK Deb 16 December 1969 col 793 col 1151.
183 HL Deb 17 December 1969 vol 306 col 1138.
184 Roscoe Pound, 'Law in books and law in action' (1910) 44 American Law Review 12.
185 About the meaning of the term path dependance, see Tom Ginsburg, Jonathan S Masur and Richard H McAdams, 'Libertarian Paternalism, Path Dependence, and Temporary Law' (2014) 81 Chicago Law Review 291 fn 2.
186 Ginsburg, Masur and McAdams in the same way argue that '[i]f the problem is path dependence, a temporary law will often be both necessary and sufficient to move behavior to the more efficient outcome [. . .] [because] temporary law offers a new "starting" point, resetting the system to allow the emergence of the equilibrium with the lowest smoking levels'.: see Tom Ginsburg, Jonathan S Masur and Richard H McAdams, 'Libertarian Paternalism, Path Dependence, and Temporary Law' (2014) 81 Chicago Law Review 291, 296.
187 Interestingly, Thompson justifies paternalism given that it is temporary. See Dennis F Thompson, *Political Ethics and Public Office* (Harvard University Press 1987) 154–5

that 25 years from now, the use of racial preferences will no longer be necessary to further the interest approved today'.[188]

On the other side of the Atlantic, in the UK such policies were implemented with a sunset clause. Specifically, in 2002, Parliament adopted the Sex Discrimination (Election Candidates) Act, endorsing affirmative action policies in order to eliminate inequalities in the numbers of male and female candidates standing for election. The Act contained a sunset clause due to expire in 2015,[189] but the expiration date was later extended through to 2030 by the Equality Act 2010.[190]

The latter example is the Voting Rights Act of 1965,[191] which was one of the landmark Acts during the US Civil Rights Movement and was re-enacted several times in 1970,[192] 1975,[193] 1982,[194] 1992[195] and 2006.[196] This Act, which was repeatedly renewed, in essence prohibits certain states from amending their voting procedures without federal supervision.[197] This law targeted the states that were using voting procedures (test of devices, literacy tests etc.) with a discriminatory impact and with the result of denying the right of some citizens to vote on account of race.

This law provoked debate as to its constitutionality since it was claimed that it was incompatible with core principles of federalism given that it violated state autonomy and the principle of equality of states. It was challenged before the US Supreme Court, and the divergent views were enshrined in the text of the majority and dissenting opinions of the decision *South Carolina v Katzenbach*.[198] The court ruled in favour of the constitutionality of the law, acknowledged that such law aims to suspend policies in the voting procedures that perpetuate discrimination, and, in particular, Justice Warren for the majority stated:

> The Act suspends new voting regulations pending scrutiny by federal authorities to determine whether their use would violate the Fifteenth Amendment. This may have been an uncommon exercise of congressional power, as South Carolina contends, but the Court has recognized that exceptional conditions can justify legislative measures not otherwise appropriate.[199]

That said, sunset clauses may have a positive impact on the rule of law. By adopting extraordinary policies of temporary nature, they permit the law and policy makers to correct deficiencies due to path dependence and effectuate constitutional norms such as equality and prohibition of discrimination.

188 *Grutter v Bollinger et al* (2003) 539 US 306, 343 (US SC).
189 Sex Discrimination (Election Candidates) Act 2002, s 3.
190 Equality Act 2010, s 105(3).
191 Pub L No 89–110, 79 Stat 437 (1965).
192 An Act to extend the Voting Rights Act of 1965 with respect to the discriminatory use of tests and devices Pub L No 91–285, 84 Stat. 314 (1970).
193 An act to amend the Voting Rights Act of 1965 to extend certain provisions for an additional seven years, to make permanent the ban against certain prerequisites to voting, and for other purposes. Pub L No 94–73, 89 Stat. 400 (1975).
194 An act to amend the Voting Rights Act of 1965 to extend the effect of certain provisions, and for other purposes Pub L No 97–205, 96 Stat 131 (1982).
195 Voting Rights Language Assistance Act of 1992 Pub L No 102–344, 106 Stat 921 (1992).
196 An act to amend the Voting Rights Act of 1965 Pub L No 109–246, 120 Stat. 577 (2006).
197 For further details about the recent US Supreme Court see above text to n 151.
198 383 U.S. 301 (1966).
199 383 U.S. 334 (1966).

Sunset clauses and constitutional design

Examining the application of sunset clauses is beyond the primary scope of this book, but the use made of such clauses in countries with a written and codified constitution reveals a significant recognition of the use of sunset clauses in constitutional documents. Legislatures around the globe have relied on constitutional provisions containing sunset clauses and on constitutional provisions ordering the legislator to include sunset clauses in ordinary legislation.

Jackson, discussing constitution making, explores the idea of 'transitional constitution making' by adding a sunset clause and points out that:

> they [transitional constitutions] may shed new light on the advantages and disadvantages of constitutional 'sunset' – clauses – that is, requirement of reconsideration in plenary form after a set period of years, far enough into the future to allow time for the development of some authoritative institutions of politics and governance.[200]

There are several constitutional documents that are recorded as temporary in nature. These constitutions are often categorised as transitional and are commonly created as a result of a major national crisis.[201] Historically, the first temporary or transitional constitutions are recorded in the US after the War of American Independence, namely the Constitution of South Carolina and the Constitution of New Hampshire. Both constitutions were temporary in nature due to the end of the political crisis between the UK and the colonies. The inclusion of the sunset clauses in the preamble was in accordance with the resolution passed by the Continental Congress after the effort of Adams.[202]

The Constitution of South Carolina prescribed in the preamble that:

> [. . .] whereas the judges of courts of law here have refused to exercise their respective functions, so that it is become indispensably necessary that during the present situation of American affairs, and until an accommodation of the unhappy differences between Great Britain and America can be obtained, (an event which, though traduced and treated as rebels, we still earnestly desire,) some mode should be established by common consent, and for the good of the people, the origin and end of all governments, for regulating the internal polity of this colony.[203]

The Constitution of North Carolina prescribed in the preamble as well that:

> [. . .] for the preservation of peace and good order, and for the security of the lives and properties of the inhabitants of this colony, we conceive ourselves reduced to the necessity of establishing A FORM OF GOVERNMENT to continue during the present unhappy and unnatural contest with Great Britain.[204]

200 Vicki C Jackson, 'What's in a Name? Reflections on Timing, Naming, and Constitution – Making' (2008) 49 William and Mary Law Review 1249, 1282.

201 Kai Peter Ziegler, 'Democratic Republic of Congo: The Transitional Constitution of April 1, 2003' (2005) 3 International Journal of Constitutional Law 662.

202 Terry W Lipscomb, 'The South Carolina Constitution of 1776' (1976) 77 South Carolina Historical Magazine, 138, 139; Clark Bell, 'New Hampshire: Early Judicial History' (1099–1900) 17 Medico – Legal Journal 457, 458.

203 Constitution of South Carolina 1776.

204 Constitution of New Hampshire 1776.

In the more modern era, the preamble of the Constitution of the Republic of South Africa in 1993, also known as the 'Interim Constitution', prescribed that 'in order to secure the achievement of this goal, elected representatives of all the people of South Africa should be mandated to adopt a new Constitution in accordance with a solemn pact recorded as Constitutional Principle', and in chapter 5 a two-year sunset clause was included.[205]

The use of sunset clauses was discussed before the adoption of the US Constitution. Thus Jefferson, who is named as the US progenitor of sunset laws,[206] was concerned with the perpetuity of the constitution, suggesting its sunset after nineteen years, writing to Madison that:

> on similar ground it may be proved that no society can make a perpetual constitution, or even a perpetual law. The earth belongs always to the living generation. [. . .] Every constitution, then, and every law, naturally expires at the end of 19 years. If it be enforced longer, it is an act of force and not of right.[207]

Eventually, a sunset clause was included in article 1, section 9 of the US Constitution:

> the Migration or Importation of such Persons as any of the States now existing shall think proper to admit, shall not be prohibited by the Congress prior to the Year one thousand eight hundred and eight, but a Tax or duty may be imposed on such Importation, not exceeding ten dollars for each Person.[208]

In Europe, two recent constitutions, the German Constitution and the French Constitution, even if they do not contain a sunset clause to 'sunset' the whole document, endorse sunset clauses either sunsetting special authority or imposing an obligation on the legislator to include such clauses when law with specific content is enacted.[209] Thus, the German Constitution contains several sunset clauses, especially regarding the state of emergency. Article 81, entitled 'Legislative emergency', provides in clause 3 that:

205 Constitution of the Republic of South Africa, 1993, ch 5, art 73(1). Nonetheless, not all interim constitutions contain a sunset clause. For instance the interim Constitution of Albania in 1991, although it prescribes in article 44 that 'the provisions of this law operate till the adoption of the Constitution of the Republic of Albania, whose draft will be worked out by the special commission charged by the People's Assembly', does not contain a sunset clause. See Law on Major Constitutional Provisions of Albania 1991, art 44(1).

206 Guido Calabresi, *A Common Law for the Age of Statutes* (Lowboy Exchange 1999) 59

207 Paul Leicester Ford (ed), *The Writings of Thomas Jefferson Vol V* (GP Putnam's Sons 1895) 121, [Letter from Thomas Jefferson to James Madison (September 6, 1789)]. See also Jacob E Gersen, 'Temporary Legislation' (2007) 74 Chicago Law Review 247, 252.

208 Constitution of the United States, art I, s 9 cl 1. In art 1, s 8, there is an indirect sunset clause, as Congress is prescribed to appropriate the funds for the military maximum of two years. Thus, all appropriation Acts regulating the funds for the army shall contain a sunset clause with a maximum duration of two years. See Constitution of the United States, art I, s 8 cl 12: 'The Congress shall have the power [. . .] To raise and support Armies, but no Appropriation of Money to that Use shall be for a longer Term than two Years.'

209 Interestingly, in 1975 the draft constitution for the State of Texas contained a sunset clause provision. According to the sunset clause, all statutory agencies were subject to a ten-year lifespan unless renewed. Eventually the draft constitution was rejected for reasons not related to the sunset clause: see Janice C May, 'Texas Constitutional Revision' (1977) 66 National Civic Review 64, 67; Anthony R Licata, 'Zero – Base Sunset Review' (1977) 24 Harvard Journal of Legislation 505, 511.

> During the term of office of a Federal Chancellor, any other bill rejected by the Bundestag may become law in accordance with paragraphs (1) and (2) of this Article within a period of six months after the first declaration of a state of legislative emergency. After the expiration of this period, no further declaration of a state of legislative emergency may be made during the term of office of the same Federal Chancellor.[210]

Article 81 of the German Constitution regulates what might be called a 'legislative state of emergency'. Such a state of emergency happens when there is a crisis in government, for instance if the government and the Parliament no longer work together and there is a blockage. The essence of this rule is that under certain conditions and within temporal limits, the legislative power of the Bundestag (the first, 'directly elected' chamber) is suspended. Instead, the Bundesrat (second chamber, representing the Länder, to which the government of the Land send a representative), which usually only has the right to participate in certain matters, takes over that function.[211]

Furthermore, Article 115k, entitled 'Rank and duration of emergency provisions', provides in clause 1 that '[l]aws enacted in accordance with Articles 115c, 115e, and 115g, as well as statutory instruments issued on the basis of such laws, shall suspend the operation of incompatible law so long as they are in effect. This provision shall not apply to earlier law enacted pursuant to Articles 115c, 115e or 115g.' Clause 2 provides that '[l]aws adopted by the Joint Committee, as well as statutory instruments issued on the basis of such laws, shall cease to have effect no later than six months after the termination of a state of defence'. Clause 3 states that '[l]aws containing provisions that diverge from Articles 91a, 91b, 104a, 106 and 107 shall apply no longer than the end of the second fiscal year following the termination of a state of defence [. . .]'.[212]

Article 115k regulates legislative acts in relation to defence (i.e. military attack). The first paragraph regulates the rank of such laws within the German legal system, and the second and third paragraphs regulate how long these acts are valid. The article addresses the so-called laws for the case of defence, article 115c. These laws, which may be enacted at any time, are dependent on the existence of the state of defence, and only apply as long as the state of defence exists. Likewise, article 115e refers to emergency laws enacted by a joint committee of the Budestag and Bundesrat, which acts in cases of 'real emergency' and addresses all decrees or bylaws which are enacted by the minister or government based on these emergency laws.[213]

The article distinguishes between laws that have a sunset clause within them and those that do not, but declares that they apply until further notice. It only regulates their sunset in the case of emergency laws, since the other cases are seen as normal laws and so the normal rules apply. These laws sunset not later than six months after the end of the state of defence, but 'not later' means that they can also sunset earlier, either because the law itself contained a sunset clause or because the sunset is later enacted. However, the later sunset means real sunset: it must lead back to the normal state of affairs; if not, then the sunset clause of article 115k, clause 3 leads to the expiration of this rule.[214]

210 Basic Law for the Federal Republic of Germany art 81, ss 2, 3.
211 Theodor Maunz and Gunter Dürig (eds), *Grundgesetz Kommentar Vol VI* (Verlag CH Beck) [1].
212 Basic Law for the Federal Republic of Germany, art 115k, ss 2, 3.
213 Theodor Maunz and Gunter Dürig (eds), *Grundgesetz Kommentar Vol VII* (Verlag CH Beck) [1–7].
214 Theodor Maunz and Gunter Dürig (eds), *Grundgesetz Kommentar Vol VII* (Verlag CH Beck) [39–48].

Article 38 of the French Constitution, entitled '*ordonnances*' (ordinances in English), prescribes that:

> [i]n order to implement its programme, the Government may ask Parliament for authorisation, for a limited period, to take measures by Ordinance that are normally the preserve of statute law. Ordinances shall be issued in the Council of Ministers, after consultation with the Conseil d'État. They shall come into force upon publication, but shall lapse in the event of failure to table before Parliament the Bill to ratify them by the date set by the Enabling Act. They may only be ratified in explicit terms. At the end of the period referred to in the first paragraph herein above Ordinances may be amended solely by an Act of Parliament in those areas governed by statute law.

Article 74–1 prescribes that:

> In the Overseas territorial communities referred to by Article 74 and in New Caledonia, the Government may, in matters which remain within the power of the State, extend by Ordinance, with any necessary adaptations, the statutory provisions applying in mainland France, or adapt the statutory provisions applying, to the specific organisation of the community in question, provided statute law has not expressly excluded the use of this procedure for the provisions involved. Such Ordinances shall be issued in the Council of Ministers after receiving the opinion of the relevant Deliberative Assemblies and the Conseil d'État. They shall come into force upon publication. They shall lapse if they are not ratified by Parliament within eighteen months of their publication.

Article 38 authorises the French Parliament to delegate the power to the Council of Ministers under a *loi d' habilitation* (enabling act) to issue ordinances in an area of law which is reserved for ordinary law passed by the Parliament according to article 34 of the French Constitution.[215] However, Parliament shall include a sunset clause in the *loi d'habilitation*, and as a consequence the Council of Ministers shall present all ordinances enacted according to the *loi d'habilitation* to Parliament for ratification before the expiration of the sunset clause, otherwise they expire.[216] The first law enacted according to this procedure was in 1960 authorising the government to take certain measures relating to the maintenance of law and order in Algeria, and it lapsed one year after its promulgation as it was not ratified by Parliament.[217]

It is noteworthy that the ordinances of article 38 were not used exclusively to regulate emergency situations. A variety of issues were regulated, such as adoption of European directives[218] and the codification of law.[219] On the other hand, article 74–1, which is a recent clause adopted during the last amendment process of 2008, recognises the adoption of ordinances with subject matter restricted to overseas territorial communities and states

215 Philippe Malaire and Patrick Morvan, *Introduction General* (Defrenois 2009) 98.

216 Philippe Malaire and Patrick Morvan, *Introduction General* (Defrenois 2009) 98.

217 Loi n° 60–101 (4 Février 1960), art 2.

218 See Marc Guillaume, 'Les Ordonnances: Tuer ou Sauver La Loi? Pouvoirs' (2005) 114 Revue Française d'études Constitutionnelles et Politiques, 117, 120.

219 See Cecile Castaing, 'La ratification implicite des ordonnances de codification' (2004) 58 Revue Française de Droit Constitutionnel 275, 281.

explicitly that the sunset clause in these ordinances shall not exceed eighteen months after their promulgation.

According to a report issued by the French Senate, during the first thirty years of use of the procedural rules of article 38 (1960–90), twenty-five enabling acts were adopted, on the basis of which one hundred and fifty-eight ordinances were adopted and only about thirty of these ordinances were explicitly ratified, while until 2007 sixty-seven enabling acts were adopted, on the basis of which three hundred and twenty-five ordinances were adopted and only two hundred and twenty-seven of these ordinances were explicitly ratified.[220]

It can be seen from the preceding examples that sunset clauses have been widely used in parliamentary legislation and in constitutional documents. The use of such clauses has been motivated either by the desire to test the quality of the entire Constitution, or by rule of law concerns, in order to promote just or effective legislation. They are part of a broader practice noted by Dixon and Ginsburg, who analyse the practice of drafters to leave things undecided and to defer decision making to the future.[221] In so doing, drafters use mechanisms such as 'deliberate forms of constitutional vagueness, flexible amendment thresholds, mandatory periods of constitutional review and constitutional sunset clauses'.[222] Finally, constitutional drafters may employ sunset clauses in order to entrench constitutional provisions.[223]

Conclusions

The connection between sunset clauses and the substantive dimension of the rule of law is most problematic when such clauses are used temporarily to suspend rights, procedures and guarantees. As a matter of fact, the temporary erosion of civil liberties, the deactivation of the courts and the distortion of the separation of powers with the centralisation of powers in hands of the executive is more common practice of governments worldwide during a state of emergency.

Legislators rely on sunset clauses to accommodate the needs of such emergencies because sunset clauses are compatible with the urgent and transitional character of the exigency. From the pragmatic uses of sunset clauses in emergency legislation, it can be argued that such clauses perform multiple purposes and serve many functions, not necessarily restricted to temporal considerations. To begin with, when emergency legislation is enacted according to a fast track procedure, such clauses permit legislators to reconsider their enactments at a future point, without the time pressure under ordinary conditions. In addition, sunset clauses can mitigate the impact of extreme measures, provided that they are used subject to the conditions and limits discussed in this chapter.

A fortiori, the use of sunset clauses strengthens the right of the community for peace and safety, but such clauses are not panacea. According to the proponents of the 'business as usual model' and the 'extra-legal measures model', sunset clauses do not promote the rule

220 Les Documents de Travail du Sénat, 'Les Ordonnances, Série Etudes Juridiques, Bilan au 31 Décembre 2007' (n EJ4) 5, 6.

221 See Rosalind Dixon and Tom Ginsburg, 'Deciding not to decide: Deferral in Constitutional Design' (2011) 9 International Journal of Constitutional Law 636.

222 Rosalind Dixon and Tom Ginsburg, 'Deciding not to decide: Deferral in Constitutional Design' (2011) 9 International Journal of Constitutional Law 636, 646.

223 See Richard Albert, Temporal Limitations in Constitutional Amendment (March 21, 2016). 21 Review of Constitutional Studies, 2016, Forthcoming; Boston College Law School Legal Studies Research Paper No. 390. Available at SSRN: http://ssrn.com/abstract=2749288

of law, and what is perceived as a mechanism of introducing new policies and enhancing legislative oversight transforms into a menace to the rule of law. The questionable utility of sunset clauses pertaining to liberties and institutional guarantees is exacerbated when legislators utilise such clauses in times of normality. Such unnecessary use enhances the negative stereotype surrounding the utility of temporary laws and marginalises the benefits that derive from the enactment of temporary laws.

Furthermore, the use of sunset clauses entrenches and bolsters the rule of law when it is used for deductive purposes such as to test the application of a law, to raise the accountability of new agencies, to make law more efficient and to reconcile injustices. In other words, temporary legislation allows experimentation, as it provides a mechanism through which policy choices can be applied and tested, and for bold legislation when it is needed. It is noteworthy that a series of important laws – such as the first bankruptcy law, laws governing income taxation, and even the abolition of the death penalty – were initiated with sunset clauses. Also, it is noteworthy that important policies such as affirmative action and the abolition of racial discrimination in voting were implemented with sunset clauses.

Finally, in constitutional design, such clauses can satisfy a number of purposes. They permit constitution drafters to adopt interim provisions and leave some decisions to be made by future drafters. In addition, the constitutional drafter might prescribe the framework of temporary law making and decide when and under which special circumstances ordinary legislation shall be temporary.

9 Epilogue

> Yesterday's law is not binding to-day; but silence is taken for tacit consent, and the Sovereign is held to confirm incessantly the laws it does not abrogate as it might.
>
> Jean-Jacques Rousseau, *On the Social Contract*, Book 3 XI

This book has examined the constitutional value of sunset clauses. In so doing, it has demonstrated that sunsets are incorporated in, or their use is relevant to, important constitutional documents. It has shown not only that such clauses affect cornerstones of the UK Constitution (such as the separation of powers, parliamentary sovereignty and the rule of law), but also that concerns with regard to executive and legislative politics justify the enactment of such clauses. The study was presented in three parts: the positive, the historical and the normative.

The positive law part (Chapter 1) of the book analysed the current use of temporary legislation and contested the widespread view that either the use of sunset clauses is infrequent, or legislators adopt such legislation only to regulate temporary needs. More precisely, the positive part elaborated on the definition of, meaning of and components of sunset clauses, identified their major classifications and showed that, nowadays, the texts of legislation are replete with such clauses. Sunset clauses are not used exclusively in emergency legislation or in the regulation of temporary or transitory issues, but also in quotidian policies, for instance in economic policies, and in constitutional documents.

The historical part of the book (Chapters 2,3 and 4) provided a detailed examination of the first uses of sunset clauses. It illustrated the usage of such clauses, which has previously gone largely unnoticed. Contrary to the modern belief that such clauses are a device employed by the legislative branch to offset the comparative advantage of the executive, it was revealed that such clauses were initially used by the monarch to safeguard their institutional advantage. The historical analysis provided an account of the complex evolution of law making powers and of the role that such clauses played, and still play, in the evolution of the law.

The use of sunset clauses has proven to be a long-standing practice in English legislative history, and their origin can be traced to the late medieval period. It is evident that sunset clauses were a constant feature in the statute book, ever since the first Parliaments. Indeed, such clauses were used as soon as the Commons was involved in the legislative process from the period of Edward III. One of the most interesting findings of their early use was the willingness of the monarch to enact such clauses. In particular, in the late medieval period sunset clauses were used by the King to limit the duration of statutes.

Later, the Commons and the Lords were also willing for such clauses to be included in legislation, and this is further exemplified by the frequent presence of sunset clauses in contemporary legislation. At the turn of the 16th century, they were seen as an expression of consensus, and in the 17th century onwards they were more of a parliamentary mechanism.

Hence, sunset clauses have been a constant feature in the balance of powers between the monarch and Parliament, but their utility was heavily dependent on the balance of powers. Interestingly, sunset clauses were used quite commonly in a variety of historical circumstances. Important events are associated with sunset provisions, for instance the Lancastrian constitutional experiment, the Civil War and the Acts of Union.

The first two parts of the book served to underline the importance of sunset clauses through different historical periods and provided a springboard for the formulation of a normative theory concerning the interaction between sunset clauses and important elements of constitutional theory, namely the separation of powers (Chapter 5), parliamentary sovereignty, constitutional dialogues (Chapter 6) and the rule of law (Chapters 7 and 8).

The development of the use of sunset clauses reveals the main reasons that legislators include them in legislation (Chapter 5): limited consensus in the majority party or a coalition government (unlike their early 16th century use), experimentation, lack of information and time pressure. Building on this historical and positive analysis on sunset clauses, the normative part of the book demonstrates that such clauses are used in order to satisfy separation of powers concerns. The abuse of delegated powers can be moderated through their time limitation, while their use effectuates a transfer of powers from the executive to the legislature.

It is also argued that their current function depends upon the separation of powers and the role of the legislature, and nowadays is less of a mechanism to claim sovereignty. Depending on the separation of power model, such clauses play a role in the system of checks and balances. On the one hand, they impact the institutional relationship between the executive and the legislative branches; on the other hand, they influence the interaction between the legislature and the courts.

After the establishment of the Human Rights Act 1998 (Chapter 6), such clauses enhance the legislative role with respect to judicial decisions and facilitate the dialogue between the UK Supreme Court and the political branches of the government. In addition, a neglected aspect of such clauses is their utility to affect future Parliaments by interfering with their legislative agenda setting. However, they create space for the electorate to participate in and influence the law making process.

The normative analysis also contains a critique of sunset clauses from the rule of law perspective. It evaluates such clauses from the perspective of flexibility and certainty (Chapter 7) and discusses how the construction of the clause can provide more certain legislative outcomes. Without doubt, the need to review constantly temporary laws burdens the legislative process and eventually outweighs the benefits from their use. Most importantly, it is argued that sunset clauses should not be used in combination with Henry VIII clauses given that this combination in essence results in the neutralisation of the sunset clause.

The inclusion of such clauses in legislation also has an impact on the substantive conception of the rule of law (Chapter 8). Temporary laws restricting human rights and suspending institutional guarantees and procedures are more common during emergencies. Their extensive use may encapsulate the right of the community to peace and safety, but such clauses are not panacea. Undoubtedly, the constant failure of the parliamentary process reviewing laws subject to sunsets to let them expire means that the review process by the legislature is not tailored enough to the distinct character of sunsets. What is most problematic is the use of such clauses to suspend rights and guarantees in a state of normalcy.

However, this book has argued that such clauses can also be seen as an expression of the rule of law and can, in specific instances, promote the rule of law. This is exemplified by the inclusion of such clauses in affirmative action policies to heal pragmatic inequalities or the use of such clauses in constitutional design to promote better constitutional drafting.

Further, innovative legislation is initiated with a sunset clause, and thus the clause is an ingredient in the process of enacting new laws, controversial or experimental, for instance the adoption of income tax or the abolition of censorship and of the death penalty for ordinary crimes. As the examples suggest, such clauses enhance regulation, promote more efficient governance and expand the scope of human rights. Thus the rule of law and such clauses are not always antagonistic, but in fact can complement each other.

A detailed examination of statute books has shown that sunset clauses are in 'the legal DNA' of the UK. If history repeats itself, law makers in the UK have much to learn from the past applications of sunset clauses. Sunset clauses are not simply a mechanism for transitional legislation, or an instrument to facilitate executive decision making in times of crises by suspending procedures, rights and guarantees. Their use echoes the demand for particular sets of values to be embodied in legislation and in the legislative process as a whole. Sunset clauses are also used where legislators aim to enhance the rule of law, reinforce the separation of powers and, finally, spur the dialogue between different branches of the government.

Time and timing in constitutional law is an area that for many years did not attract the interest of researchers. The examination of the constitutional value of sunset clauses explores only one dimension pertaining to the significance of time in constitutional theory. Sunset clauses in constitutional documents and ordinary legislation illustrate how constitutional drafters, policy makers and legislators can form and transform the duration of laws and set the time framework.

The ultimate goal of this book is not to approve or disapprove the use of sunset clauses, but, paraphrasing Carl Schmitt in his study on the concept of sovereignty, to suggest, with a rhetorical hyperbole perhaps, that in a state of normalcy, 'Sovereign is he who decides the lifespan of law'. This was apparent during the first Parliaments in England, and in the contemporary era it is illustrated when the duration of law becomes a controversial issue.

This book has therefore sought to shed light on the development and application of sunset clauses in the UK legal order, the ways in which such clauses have played an integral part in the evolving constitutional order and their value in the constitutional system.

Bibliography

Ackerman B, *We the People: Foundations* (Harvard University Press 1991)
——— *We the People: Transformations* (Harvard University Press 1998)
——— 'The New Separation of Powers' (2000) 113 Harvard Law Review 633
——— 'The Emergency Constitution' (2004) 113 Yale Law Journal 1029
Adams B, 'Sunset: A Proposal for Accountable Government' (1976) 28 Administrative Law Review 511
Adams GB, *Constitutional History of England* (Jonathan Cape 1965)
Agamben G, *State of Exception* (Kevin Attell tr, University of Chicago Press 2005)
Allan TRS, *Law, Liberty and Justice: The Legal Foundations of British Constitutionalism* (OUP 1995)
——— 'Constitutional Dialogue and the Justification of Judicial Review' (2003) 23 Oxford Journal of Legal Studies 563
Allison JWF, *English Historical Constitution: Continuity, Change and European Effects* (CUP 2007)
Altshuler R and Dietz R, 'Reconsidering Tax Expenditure Estimation' (2011) 64 National Tax Journal 459
Anderson S, 'Public Law', 490–525 in William Cornish, J Stuart Anderson, Ray Cocks, Michael Lobban, Patrick Polden and Keith Smith (eds), *The Oxford History of the Laws of England Vol XI* (OUP 2010)
Anson WR, *The Law and Custom of the Constitution Vol I* (5th edn, Clarendon Press 1935)
Aristotle, *Politics* (Aeterna Press London 2015)
Armingeon K, 'The Effects of Negotiation Democracy: A Comparative Analysis' (2002) 41 European Journal of Political Research 81
Bacon F, *The Elements of the Common Laws of England* (printed for C and J Rivington 1826)
Bagehot W, *The English Constitution* (2nd edn, Chapman & Hall 1873)
Baldwin JF, *The Kings' Council in England during the Middle Ages* (Clarendon Press 1913)
Barber NW and Young AL, 'The Rise and Prospective Henry VIII Clauses and Their Implications for Sovereignty' (2003) PL 112
Barendt E, 'Separation of Powers and Constitutional Government' (1995) PL 599
Barnett H, *Constitutional and Administrative Law* (5th edn, Cavendish Publishing 2004)
Beckett J, *The Rise and Fall of Grenvilles* (Manchester University Press 1994)
Bell C, 'New Hampshire: Early Judicial History' (1099–1900) 17 Medico – Legal Journal 457
Bellamy JG, *The Law of Treason in England in the Later Middle Ages* (CUP 2004)
Benin FAR, *Bennion on Statutory Interpretation* (5th edn, Lexis Nexis 2008)
Bessette Joseph M, 'Deliberative Democracy: The Majority Principle in Republican Government', 102–16 in Robert A Goldwin and William A Schambra (eds), *How Democratic Is the Constitution?* (American Enterprise Institute for Public Policy Research 1980)
Bingham T, *The Rule of Law* (Allen Lane 2010)
Black's Law Dictionary (Bryan A Garner ed, 8th edn, Thomson West 2004)

Blackstone W, *Commentaries on the Law of England Vol I* (Clarendon Press 1765)
Bogdanov V, *The New British Constitution* (Hart Publishing 2009)
Bouvier J, *A Law Dictionary, Adapted to the Constitution and Laws of United States of America* (GW Childs 1870)
Bradley AW and Ewing KD, *Constitutional and Administrative Law* (14th edn, Pearson Education 2007)
Brennan WJ Jr, 'The Quest to Develop a Jurisprudence of Civil Liberties in Times of Security Crises' (1988) 18 Israeli Yearbook on Human Rights 11
Brown AL, 'The Commons and the Council in the Reign of Henry IV' (1964) 79 English Historical Review 1
——— *The Governance of Late Medieval England 1272–1461* (Stanford University Press 1989)
Brownsword Roger and Wale Jeffrey, 'Compromise Medicalisation', 292–303 in Catherine Stanton, Sarah Devaney, Anne-Maree Farrell and Alexandra Mullock (eds), *Pioneering Healthcare Law* (Routledge 2016)
Buckland WW, *Roman Law & Common Law: A Comparison in Outline* (2nd edn, CUP 1952)
Burke E, *Speech of Edmund Burke at the Guildhall in Bristol Previous to the Late Election in the City* (Printed for J Dodsley 1780)
Burnet G and Burnet T, *Bishop Burnet's History of His Own Time Vol II* (Thomas Ward 1724–1734)
Calabresi G, *A Common Law for the Age of Statutes* (Lowboy Exchange 1999)
Calendar of Patent Rolls, Richard II Vol I (HMSO 1895–1909)
Cameron A, 'The Giving of Livery and Retaining in Henry VII (1974) 18 Renaissance and Modern Studies 17
Casper G, 'An Essay in Separation of Powers: Some Early Versions and Practices' (1989) 30 William and Mary Law Review 213
Castaing C, 'La ratification implicite des ordonnances de codification' (2004) 58 Revue Française de Droit Constitutionnel 275
Castles AC, 'The Judiciary and Political Questions: The First Australian Experience, 1824–1825' (1975) 5 Adelaide Law Review 294
Cavill PR, 'Debate and Dissent in Henry VII's Parliaments' (2006) 25 Parliamentary History 160
Chrimes SB, 'House of Lords' and House of Commons' in the Fifteenth Century' (1934) 49 English Historical Review 494
——— *English Constitutional Ideas in the Fifteenth Century* (CUP 1936)
——— *Henry VII* (University of California Press 1972)
Cicero MT, *The Orations of Marcus Tullius Cicero*, (CD Yonge ed, George Bell & Sons 1891)
Clayton R, 'Judicial Deference and "Democratic Dialogue", the Legitimacy of Judicial Intervention under the Human Rights Act 1998' (2004) PL 33
Cobbett's Parliamentary History of England Vol I (Hansard 1806)
Cobbett's Parliamentary History of England Vol II (Hansard 1807)
Cobbett's Parliamentary History of England Vol VIII (Hansard 1813)
Cobbett's Parliamentary History of England Vol XI (Hansard 1810)
Cobbett's Parliamentary History of England Vol XII (Hansard 1811)
Cobbett's Parliamentary History of England Vol XV (Hansard 1813)
Cobbett's Parliamentary History of England Vol XVI (Hansard 1813)
Cobbett's Parliamentary History of England Vol XVII (Hansard 1813)
Cobbett's Parliamentary History of England Vol XXXII (Hansard 1818)
Cobbett's Parliamentary History of England Vol XXXVI (Hansard 1820)
Cohen DS, Hansen DP and Hassett KA, 'The Effects of Temporary Partial Expensing on Investment Incentives in the United States' (2002) 55 National Tax Journal 557
Cohen J, 'The History of Imprisonment for Debt and Its Relation to Development of Discharge in Bankruptcy' (1982) 3 Journal of Legal History 153

——— 'Deliberation and Democratic Legitimacy', 67–92 in James Bohman and William Rehg (eds), *Deliberative Democracy: Essays on Reason and Politics* (MIT Press 1997)
Coke E, *The Fourth Part of the Institutes of the Laws of England: Concerning the Jurisdiction of the Courts* (Printed for E and R Brooke 1797)
——— *The First Part of the Institutes of the Laws of England Vol I* (19th edn, J & WT Clarke 1832)
Cole D, 'No Reason to Believe: Radical Skepticism, Emergency Power, and Constitutional Constraint' (2008) 75 University of Chicago Law Review 1329
Collier D, Hidalgo FD and Maciuceanu AO, 'Essentially Contested Concepts: Debates and Applications' (2006) 11 Journal of Political Ideologies 211
Cornish W, 'Empire's Law', 234–54 in William Cornish, J Stuart Anderson, Ray Cocks, Michael Lobban, Patrick Polden and Keith Smith (eds), *The Oxford History of the Laws of England Vol XI* (OUP 2010)
Costa P, 'The Rule of Law: A Historical Introduction', 73–152 in Pietro Costa and Danilo Zolo (eds), *The Rule of Law; History Theory and Criticism* (Springer 2007)
Cox B, 'Origin and Growth of Income Tax' (1919) 1 Journal Comparative Legislation and International Law 42
Craig PP, 'Sovereignty of the United Kingdom, Parliament after Factortame' (1991) Yearbook of European Law 221
——— 'Formal and Substantive Conceptions of the Rule of Law: An Analytical Framework' (1997) PL 467
——— 'Public Law, Political Theory and Legal Theory' (2000) PL 211
——— *Administrative Law* (7th edn, Sweet and Maxwell 2008)
——— 'Political Constitutionalism and the Judicial Role: A Response' (2011) 9 International Journal of Constitutional Law 112
——— and DeBurca G, *EU Law: Text, Cases, and Materials* (5th edn, OUP 2011)
Davies KG (ed), *Calendar of State Papers Colonial, America and West Indies Vol 45* (HM Stationery Office 1994, Digital version at British History Online)
Davis LA, 'Review Procedure and Public Accountability in Sunset Legislation: An Analysis and Proposal for Reform' (1981) 33 Administrative Law Review 393
Dean D, 'Pressure Groups and Lobbies in the Elizabethan and Early Jacobean Parliaments' (1991) 11 Parliaments, Estates and Representation 139
——— *Law-making and Society in Late Elizabethan England* (CUP 1996)
Dearlove J and Saunders P, *Introduction to British Politics* (2nd edn, Polity Press 1991)
DeConde A, *The Quasi-War: The Politics and Diplomacy of the Undeclared War with France 1797–1801* (Charles Scribner's Sons 1966)
Dicey AV, *Introduction to the Study of the Law of the Constitution Vol I* (JWF Allison ed, OUP 2013)
Dick AR, *A Commentary on Cicero: De Legibus* (University of Michigan Press 2004)
Dickinson HT, *Liberty and Property: Political Ideology in Eighteenth-Century Britain* (Weidenfeld and Nicolson 1977)
Dixon R and Ginsburg T, 'Deciding Not to Decide: Deferral in Constitutional Design' (2011) 9 International Journal of Constitutional Law 636
Donohue LK, *The Cost of Counterterrorism* (CUP 2008)
Douglass A, 'The Authorship of the Disputed Federalist Papers' (1944) 1 William and Mary Quarterly 97
Dworkin R, *A Matter of Principles* (OUP 1985)
Dyzenhaus D, 'Schmitt v. Dicey: Are States of Emergency Inside Or Outside the Legal Order?' (2006) 27 Cardozo Law Review 2005
——— *The Constitution of Law: Legality in a Time of Emergency* (CUP 2006)
——— 'The State of Emergency in Legal Theory', in Michael Yew Meng Hor, Victor Vridar Ramraj and Kent Roach (eds), *Global Anti-Terrorism Law and Policy* (CUP 2009) 65–89

Elster Jon, 'Deliberation and Constitution Making', 97–122 in Jon Elster (ed), *Deliberative Democracy* (CUP 1998)

Elton GR, *Reform and Renewal, Thomas Cromwell and the Common Weal* (CUP 1973)

——— *Studies in Tudor and Stuart Politics and Government Vol II* (CUP 1974)

——— *The Parliament of England: 1559–1581* (CUP 1986)

Evans MW, 'The Budget Process and the Sunset Provision of the 2001 Tax Law' (2003) 99 Tax Notes 405

Ewing KD, 'The Human Rights Act and Parliamentary Democracy' (1999) Modern Law Review 79

Fagan Frank, *Law and the Limits of Government Temporary versus Permanent Legislation* (Elgar 2013)

Farnsworth A, *Addington: Author of the Modern Income Tax* (Stevens & Sons 1951)

Finch V, *Insolvency Law, Perspectives and Principles* (CUP 2002)

Finn JE, 'Sunset Clauses and Democratic Deliberation: Assessing the Significance of Sunset Provisions in Antiterrorism Legislation' (2010) 48 Columbia Journal of Transnational Law 442

Firth CH and Rait RS (eds), *Acts and Ordinances of the Interregnum 1642–1660* (HMSO 1911)

Fisher Louis, *Constitutional Dialogues: Interpretation as Political Process* (Princeton University Press 1988)

Ford TPL (ed), *The Writings of Thomas Jefferson Vol 5* (GP Putnam's Sons 1895)

Friedman Barry, 'Dialogue and Judicial Review' (1993) 91 Michigan Law Review 577

Fryde EB and Miller E (eds), *Historical Studies of the English Parliament Vol I* (CUP 1970)

Fuller LL, *The Morality of Law* (Yale University Press 1969)

Gale WG and Orszag PR, 'Sunsets in the Tax Code' (2003) 99 Tax Notes 1553

Gallie WB, 'Essentially Contested Concepts' (1956) 56 Proceedings of the Aristotelian Society 167

Ganz G, 'Delegated Legislation: A Necessary Evil or a Constitutional Outrage', 60–82 in Peter Leyland and Terry Woods (eds), *Administrative Law Facing the Future: Old Constraints and New Horizons* (Blackwell 2003)

Gardbaum S, 'The New Commonwealth Model of Constitutionalism' (2001) 49 American Journal of Comparative Law 707

Gardiner SR, *Debates in the House of Commons in 1625* (Camden Society 1873)

——— *The First Two Stuarts and the Puritan Revolution* (2nd edn, Longmans Green 1877)

——— *History of England from the Accession of James I to the Outbreak of the Civil War 1603–1642 Vol V* (Longmans Green 1883)

——— *The Constitutional Documents of the Puritan Revolution 1625–1660* (Clarendon Press 1906)

Garrett E, 'Accounting for the Federal Budget and Its Reform' (2004) 41 Harvard Journal on Legislation 187

——— Graddy E and Jackson HE (eds), *Fiscal Challenges: An Interdisciplinary Approach to Budget Policy* (CUP 2008)

Gensen JE, 'Temporary Legislation' (2007) 74 Chicago Law Review 247

——— and Posner EA, 'Timing Rules and Legal Institutions' (2007) 121 Harvard Law Review 543

Ginsburg Tom, Masur Jonathan S and McAdams Richard H, 'Libertarian Paternalism, Path Dependence, and Temporary Law' (2014) 81 Chicago Law Review 291, 296

Given-Wilson C (ed), *The Parliamentary Rolls of Medieval England 1275–1504 Vol VIII* (Boydell Press 2005)

Golden GK, *Emergency Measures: Crisis and Response in the Roman Republic* (ProQuest 2011)

Goldsworthy J, *The Sovereignty of Parliament: History and Philosophy* (Clarendon Press 1999)

Gould LS, 'The Congressional Response to Duro v. Reina: Compromising Sovereignty and the Constitution' (1994) 28 University of California Davis 53

Gray HL, *The Influence of the Commons on Early Legislation* (Harvard University Press 1932)

Greenburg D (ed), *Craies on Legislation* (8th edn, Sweet and Maxwell 2004)

Grinnell CE, *Poor Debtor Law of Massachusetts* (Little Brown and Company 1883)

Gross FB, *The Theory and Practice of Statutory Interpretation* (Stanford University Press 2009)

Gross O, 'Chaos and Rules: Should Responses to Violent Crises Always Be Constitutional' (2003) 112 Yale Law Journal 1011

Guillaume M, 'Les Ordonnances: Tuer ou Sauver La Loi? Pouvoirs' (2005) 114 Revue Française d'études Constitutionnelles et Politiques 117

Habermas Jurgen, 'Popular Sovereignty as Procedure', 35–66 in James Bohman and William Rehg (eds), *Deliberative Democracy: Essays on Reason and Politics* (MIT Press 1997)

Hakewill W, *The Manner How Statutes Are Enacted in Parliament by Passing of Bills, Collected Many Years Past Out of the Journals of the House of Commons* (Printed for John Benson 1641)

Hale, Sir Matthew, *The History of the Pleas of the Crown Vol I* (Printed by E and R Nutt and R Gosling 1736)

Harper A, 'Finance Act Notes: Annual Investment Allowance etc – Sections 74–76 and Schedule 24' (2008) British Tax Review 480

Harrison GA, 'Innovation and Precedent: A Procedural Reappraisal of the 1625 Parliament' (1987) 102 English Historical Review 51

Harriss GL, *King, Parliament and Public Finance in Medieval England to 1369* (Clarendon Press 1975)

Hart HLA, *The Concept of Law* (Paul Craig ed, 3rd edn, OUP 2012)

Hartman JF, 'Derogation from Human Rights Treaties in Public Emergencies' (1981) 22 Harvard International Law Journal 1

Hayek FA, *The Road of Selfdom* (Routledge & Sons 1944)

Hayton D, 'Contested Kingdoms 1688–1756', 35–70 in Paul Langford (ed), *The Eighteenth Century* (OUP 2002)

Henderson EF (ed), *Select Historical Documents of the Middle Ages* (University Press of the Pacific 2004)

Hickman TR, 'Constitutional Dialogue, Constitutional Theories and the Human Rights Act 1998' (2005) Public Law 306

Higgins R, 'Derogations under Human Rights Treaties' (1976) 48 British Yearbook of International Law 281

Hill B, 'Parliament, Parties and Elections 1688–1760', in HT Dickinson (ed), *A Companion to Eighteenth-Century Britain* (Blackwell Publishing 2002)

Hinton RWK, 'The Decline of Parliamentary Government under Elizabeth I and the Early Stuarts' (1957) 13 Cambridge Historical Journal 116

Hobbes T, *Leviathan* (first published 1651, Forgotten Books 2008)

Holdsworth WS, *A History of English Law Vol VI* (Methuen 1924)

——— *A History of English Law Vol X* (Methuen 1938)

——— *A History of English Law Vol XI* (Methuen 1938)

——— *A History of English Law Vol IV* (3rd edn, Methuen 1945)

——— *A History of English Law Vol XIII* (Methuen 1952)

Holloway SWF, 'The Apothecaries' Act, 1815: A Reinterpretation Part 1 The Origin of the Act' (1966) 10 Medical History 107

Homes OW, 'The Path of the Law' (1897) 10 Harvard Law Review 457

Huber JD, Shipan CR and Pfahler M, 'Legislatures and Statutory Control of Bureaucracy' (2001) 45 American Journal of Political Science 330

Hulme H, 'Charles 1 and the Constitution', in William Appleton Aiken and Basil Duke Henning (eds), *Conflict in Stuart England: Essays in Honour of Wallace Notestein* (New York University Press 1960)

Hume David, *Essays, Moral, Political and Literary* (Eugene F. Miller ed, Liberty Fund 1987)

Ilbert C, *Legislative Methods and Forms* (Clarendon Press 1901)

Inderwick FA, *The Interregnum AD 1648–1660: Studies of the Commonwealth, Legislative, Social, and Legal* (S Low, Marston, Searle and Rivington 1891)
Ip J, 'Sunset Clauses and Counterterrorism Legislation' (2013) PL 74
Jackson VC, 'What's in a Name? Reflections on Timing, Naming, and Constitution – Making' (2008) 49 William and Mary Law Review 1249
Jacobson GC, 'A House and Senate Divided: The Clinton Legacy and the Congressional Elections of 2000' (2001) 116 Political Science Quarterly 5
Jansson M and Bidwell WB (eds), *Proceedings in Parliament 1625* (Yale Center for Parliamentary History 1987)
Javits JK and Klein GJ, 'Congressional Oversight and the Legislative Veto: A Constitutional Analysis' (1977) 52 New York University Law Review 455
Jennings WI, *Principles of Local Government Law* (University of London Press 1931)
——— *The Law of the Constitution* (5th edn, University of London Press 1959)
Jensen M (ed), *English Historical Documents* (Eyre & Spottiswoode 1955)
Jones JR, 'Parties and Parliament', 48–70 in JR Jones (ed), *The Restored Monarchy 1660–1688* (MacMillan 1979)
Jones WJ, *Politics and the Bench, the Judges and the Origins of the English Civil War* (George Allen & Unwin 1971)
Journal of the House of Commons 1547–1629 Vol I (1802)
Journal of the House of Commons 1667–1687 Vol 9 (1802)
Journal of the House of Commons 1693–1697 Vol 11 (1803)
Journal of the House of Lords 1509–1577 Vol I (1767–1830)
Journal of the House of Lords 1620–1628 Vol III (1767–1830)
Journal of the House of Lords 1666–1675 Vol XII
Journal of the House of Lords 1685–1691 Vol XIV (1767–1830)
Journal of the House of Lords 1691–1696 Vol XV (1767–1830)
Journal of the House of Lords 1756–1760 Vol XXIX (1767–1830)
Kadens E, 'The Pitkin Affair: A Study of Fraud in Early English Bankruptcy' (2010) 84 American Bankruptcy Law Journal 483
Kaiser A, 'Types of Democracy: From Classical to New Institutionalism' (1997) 9 Journal of Theoretical Politics 419
Katz SN (ed), *The Oxford International Encyclopaedia of Legal History Vol 5* (OUP 2009)
Kearney RC, 'A Survey and Analysis of the State Experience' (1990) 50 Public Administration Review 49
Keir DL, *The Constitutional History of Modern Britain 1485–1937* (3rd edn, Adam and Chales Black 1946)
Kemp B, *King and Commons 1660–1832* (MacMillan 1957)
Ketcham R (ed), *Selected Writings of James Madison* (Hacket Publishing 2006)
Kingsford CL (ed), *Chronicles of London* (Clarendon Press 1905)
Kouroutakis Antonios and Ranchordás Sofia, 'Snoozing Democracy: The De-juridification of Emergencies' (2016) 25 Minnesota Journal of International Law 29
Kysar RM, 'The Sun Also Rises: the Political Economy of Sunset Provisions in the Tax Code' (2006) 40 Georgia Law Review 335
Lambert S, 'Procedure in the House of Commons in the Early Stuart Period' (1980) 95 English Historical Review 753
Langford P (ed), *Contested Kingdoms, 1688–1756: The Eighteenth Century 1688–1815* (OUP 2002)
Lapsey G, 'The Commons and the Statute of York' (1913) 28 English Historical Review 118
Larkin JF and Hughes P (eds), *Stuart Royal Proclamations Vol 1* (Clarendon Press 1973)
Laws J, 'The Constitution: Morals and Rights' (1996) PL 622
Lawson P, 'Grenville's Election Act: 1770' (1980) Historical Research 218
Leadam IS, *History of England* (Longmans Green 1909)

Lenman BP, 'Britain and India', 460–72 in HT Dickinson (ed), *A Companion to Eighteenth-Century Britain* (Blackwell Publishing 2002)

Levit JK, 'The Constitutionalization of Human Rights in Argentina: Problem or Promise' (1999) 37 Columbia Journal Transnational Law 281

Licata AR, 'Zero – Base Sunset Review' (1977) 24 Harvard Journal of Legislation 505

Lieberman D, *The Province of Legislation Determined: Legal Theory in Eighteenth Century Britain* (CUP 1989)

Lijphart A, *Patterns of Democracy, Government Forms and Performance in Thirty-Six Countries* (Yale University Press 1999)

Lintott A, *The Constitution of the Roman Republic* (Clarendon Press 1999)

Lipscomb TW, 'The South Carolina Constitution of 1776' (1976) 77 South Carolina Historical Magazine 138

Little P and Smith DL, *Parliaments and Politics during the Cromwellian Protectorate* (CUP 2007)

Locke J, *Two Treatises of Government* (J Whiston, W Strahan, J and F Rivington, L Davis, W Owen and 18 others 1772)

Lockyer R, *Buckingham the Life and Political Career of George Villiers, First Duke of Buckingham* (Longman 1984)

Lowi TJ, *The End of Liberalism, the Second Republic of the United States* (2nd edn, WW Norton & Company 1979)

Lyons W and Freeman PK, 'Legislation and the Legislative Process in Tennessee' (1984) 9 Legislative Studies Quarterly 151

Machiavelli N, *The Prince* (Peter Bondanella tr, OUP 1998)

MacKendrick RL and Bennett EL, *The Speeches of Cicero: Context, Law, Rhetoric* (Duckworth 1995)

Mackie JD, *The Earlier Tudors 1485–1558* (Clarendon Press 1952)

Mackworth H, *A Vindication of the Rights of the Commons of England* (Printed and sold by the booksellers of London and Westminster 1701)

Maitland FW, *The Constitutional History of England: A Course of Lectures* (HAL Fisher ed, CUP 1908)

Malaire P and Morvan P, *Introduction General* (Defrenois 3 de Paris 2009)

Maltzman F and Shipan CR, 'Change, Continuity and the Evolution of the Law' (2008) 52 American Journal of Political Science 252

Martineau H (tr), *The Positive Philosophy of Auguste Comte Vol I* (Calvin Blanchard 1858)

Marvel MK, 'Sunset: An Early Evaluation' (1984) 42 Public Choice 193

Masterman R, *The Separation of Powers in the Contemporary Constitution: Judicial Competence and Independence in the United Kingdom* (CUP 2011)

Matsushita M, Schoenbaum T and Mavroidis P, *The World Trade Organisation: Law, Practice and Policy* (2nd edn, OUP 2006)

Maunz T and Dürig G (eds), *Grundgesetz Kommentar Vol VI* (CH Beck 1991)

——— (eds), *Grundgesetz Kommentar Vol VII* (CH Beck 1994)

Maxwell PB, *On the Interpretation of Statutes* (4th edn, Sweet & Maxwell 1905)

May JC, 'Texas Constitutional Revision' (1977) 66 National Civic Review 64

McCarthy MT, 'Recents Developments: USA Patriot Act' (2002) 39 Harvard Journal on Legislation 435

McCoid JC, 'Discharge: The Most Important Development in Bankruptcy History' (1996) 70 American Bankruptcy Law Journal 163

McFarlane KB, *Lancastrian Kings and Lollard Knights* (Clarendon Press 1972)

McIlwain CH, 'Magna Carta and Common Law', 122–79 in Henry Elliot Malden (ed), *Magna Carta Commemoration Essays* (Lawbook Exchange 2005)

McKelvey RD, 'Intransitivities in Multidimensional Voting Models and Some Implications for Agenda Control' (1976) 12 Journal of Economic Theory 472

McKinley V, 'Sunrises without Sunsets. Can Sunset Laws Reduce Regulation?' (1995) 18 Regulation 57

Medley DJ, *English Constitutional History* (6th edn, Basil Blackwell 1925)

Mitchell SK, *Taxation in Medieval England* (Yale University Press 1951)

Mitchell WM, *The Rise of the Revolutionary Party in the English House of Commons 1603–1629* (Columbia University Press 1957)

Moe TM and Caldwell M, 'The Institutional Foundations of Democratic Government: A Comparison of Presidential and Parliamentary Systems' (1994) 150 Journal of Institutional and Theoretical Economics 171

Moir TL, *The Addled Parliament of 1614* (Clarendon Press 1958)

Montesquieu, *The Spirit of the Laws* (Anne Choler and others trs, CUP 1989)

Morgan A, 'American Law and the Desuetudo' (1916) 50 American Law Review 815

Mousourakis G, *The Historical and Institutional Context of Roman Law* (Ashgate Publishing 2003)

Mun T, *Englands Treasure by Forraign Trade or the Balance of Our Forraign Trade Is the Rule of our Treasure* (Printed by John Grismond 1664)

Muskie ES, 'Sunset Legislation, Restoring Public Confidence in Government' (1977) 4 Journal of Legislation 11

Myers AR, 'Parliamentary Petitions in Fifteenth Century Part II, Petitions of the Commons and Common Petitions' (1937) 52 English Historical Review 590

——— 'Parliament 1422–1509', 141–84 in RG Davies and JH Denton (eds), *The English Parliament in the Middle Ages* (Manchester University Press 1981)

North DC, *Understanding the Process of Economic Change* (Princeton University Press 2005)

Norton P, 'Parliamentary Oversight', 155–76 in Patrick Dunleavy, Andrew Gamble, Ian Holliday and Gillian Peele (eds), *Developments in British Politics* (MacMillan 1997)

Notestein W, *The House of Commons 1604–1610* (Yale University Press 1971)

Ogg D, *England in the Reigns of James II and William III* (Clarendon Press 1955)

O'Keefe C and Safirstein P, 'Fallen Angels, Separation of Powers, and the Saturday Night Massacre: An Examination of the Practical, Constitutional and Political Tensions in the Special Prosecutor Provisions of the Ethics in Government Act' (1982) 49 Brooklyn Law Review 113

Parquet D, *An Essay on the Origins of the House of Commons* (CUP 1925)

Penner RG and Steeple CE, 'Budget Rules' (2004) 57 National Tax Journal 547

Phillimore R, *Memoirs and Correspondence of Lord Lyttelton Vol II* (James Ridgway 1845)

Plucknett T, *Statutes and Their Interpretation in the First Half of the Fourteenth Century* (Lawbook Exchange 2005)

Pollard AF, *The Evolution of Parliament* (2nd edn, Longmans Green 1926)

Pollard AJ, 'Lancastrian Constitution Experiment Revised: Henry IV, Sir John Tiptoft, and the Parliament of 1406' (1995) 14 Parliamentary History 103

——— (ed), *The Wars of the Roses* (Macmillan 1995)

Popofsky LS, 'The Crisis over Tonnage and Poundage in Parliament in 1629' (1990) 126 Past and Present 44

Porritt E, *The Unreformed House of Commons, Parliamentary Representation before 1832 Vol I* (CUP 1909)

Posner EA and Vermeule A, 'Legislative Entrenchment: A Reappraisal' (2002) 111 Yale Law Journal 1665

——— and Vermeule A, 'Emergencies and Democratic Failure' (2006) 92 Virginia Law Review 1091

——— and Vermeule A, *Terror in the Balance; Security, Liberty, and the Courts* (OUP 2007)

Posner RA, *Not a Suicide Pact* (OUP 2006)

Post Robert and Siegel Reva 'Popular Constitutionalism, Departmentalism, and Judicial Supremacy' (2004) 92 California Law Review 1027

Powell E, *The Wool Trade* (OUP 1941)

——— 'The Strange Death of Sir John Mortimer: Politics and the Law of Treason in Lancastrian England', 83–97 in Rowena E Archer and Simon Walker (eds), *Rulers and Ruled in the Late Medieval England* (Hambledon Press 1995)
Price DR, 'Sunset Legislation in the United States' (1978) 30 Baylor Law Review 401
Radin M, 'Statutory Interpretation' (1929–1930) 43 Harvard Law Review 863
Ranchordás Sofia, *Constitutional Sunsets and Experimental Legislation: A Comparative Perspective* (Elgar 2014)
——— 'Sunset Clauses and Experimental Legislation: Blessing or Curse for Legal Certainty?' (2014) 35 Statute Law Review 1
Rawls John, *The Law of Peoples* (Harvard University Press 1999)
Raz J, 'The Rule of Law and Its Virtue' (1977) 93 LQR 195
——— *The Authority of Law Essays on Law and Morality* (2nd edn, OUP 2009)
Redneck S, 'The Early History of the Parliamentary Declaration of Treason' (1927) 42 English Historical Review 49
Riley PWJ, 'The Union of 1707 as an Episode in English Politics' (1969) 84 English Historical Review 498
Roberts JC and Chemerinsky E, 'Entrenchment of Ordinary Legislation: A Reply to Professors Posner and Vermeule' (2003) 91 California Law Review 1773
Robertson CG, *Select Statutes, Cases and Documents to Illustrate English Constitutional History* (4th edn, Methuen 1923)
Rockman BA, 'Legislative-Executive Relations and Legislative Oversight' (1984) 9 Legislative Studies Quarterly 387
Rosen MD, 'Multiple Authoritative Interpreters of Quasi – Constitutional Federal Law: Of Tribal Courts and the Indian Civil Rights Act' (2000) 69 Fordham Law Review 479
Rossiter C, *Constitutional Dictatorship, Crisis Government in the Modern Democracies* (Princeton University Press 1948)
Rousseau, *The Social Contract and Other Later Political Writings* (Victor Gourevitch, CUP 1997)
Ruigh RE, *The Parliament of 1624 Politics and Foreign Policy* (Harvard University Press 1971)
Rule J, 'Manufacturing and Commerce', 127–40 in HT Dickinson (ed), *A Companion to Eighteenth-Century Britain* (Blackwell Publishing 2002)
Russell C, 'Parliamentary History in Perspective: 1604–1629' (1976) 61 History 1
——— *Parliaments and English Politics: 1621–1629* (Clarendon Press 1982)
Russell MJ, 'I Trial by Battle and the Writ of Right' (1980) 1 Journal of Legal History 111
Rutt JT (ed), *The Diary of Thomas Burton Vol 2* (Published by H Colburn 1828)
Sainsbury WN (ed), *Calendar of State Papers Colonial, America and West Indies Vol 5* (HM Stationery Office 1984, Digital version at British History Online
Schmitt C, *Political Theology: Four Chapters on the Theory of Sovereignty* (George Schwab tr, University of Chicago Press 2005)
Schulz F, *History of Roman Legal Science* (Clarendon Press 1953)
Shane Peter M, 'Executive Branch Self-Policing in Times of Crisis: The Challenges for Conscientious Legal Analysis' (2011–2012) 5 Journal of National Security Law and Policy 507
Sharpe K, 'Introduction: Parliamentary History 1603–1629: In Or Out Or Perspective?', 1–42 in Kevin Sharpe (ed), *Factions and Parliament Essays on Early Stuart History* (Clarendon Press 1978)
Sheridan RB, 'The Molasses Act and the Market Strategy of et British Sugar Planters' (1957) 17 Journal of Economic History 63
Smith AGR, *The Emergence of a Nation State* (Logman 1984)
Southwick AB, 'The Source of Molasses Act' (1951) 8 William and Mary Quarterly 389
Speck WA, 'Britain and the Atlantic World', 447–59 in HT Dickinson (ed), *A Companion to Eighteenth-Century Britain* (Blackwell Publishing 2002)
Speeches and Letters of Abraham Lincoln: 1832–1865 (ReadHowYouWant 2008)

Stagg JCA (ed), *The Papers of James Madison* (Digital edn, University of Virginia Press 2010)
Stubbs W, *The Constitutional History of England in Its Origin and Development Vol I* (first published 1875, CUP 2011)
——— *The Constitutional History of England in Its Origin and Development Vol III* (first published 1878, CUP 2011)
Sullivan MA, 'False Alarms and Real Problems with Budget Gimmicks' (2003) 99 Tax Notes 1129
Sunstein CR, 'Interpreting Statutes in the Regulatory State' (1989) 103 Harvard Law Review 405
——— 'Deliberative Democracy in the Trenches' November 2, 2015, forthcoming, Daedalus, symposium on deliberative democracy, available at SSRN http://ssrn.com/abstract=2685195 or http://dx.doi.org/10.2139/ssrn.2685195
Sutherland LS, *The East India Company in Eighteenth Century Politics* (Clarendon Press 1952)
Swarland A, *The House of Lords in the Reign of Charles II* (CUP 2002)
Tachmes AI, 'Independent Counsels under the Ethics in Government Act of 1978: A Violation of the Separation of Powers Doctrine or an Essential Check on Executive Power' (1988) 42 University Miami Law Review 735
Tanner JR, *English Constitutional Conflicts of the Seventeenth Century 1603–1689* (CUP 1928)
Tayler T, *The Law Glossary: Being a selection of the Greek, Latin, Saxon, French, and Italian Sentences, Phrases and Maxims* (Martin & Marshall 1833)
The History and Proceedings of the House of Commons 1680–1695 Vol 2 (1742)
The Reports of that Reverend and Learned Judge Sir Richards Hutton (2nd edn, Richards and Edward Atkins 1682)
The Statutes of the Realm, Vol III (Tanner Richie Publishing 1817)
The Statutes of the Realm, Vol IV Part II (Tanner Richie Publishing 2007)
Thomas PDG, *The House of Commons in the Eighteenth Century* (Clarendon Press 1971)
Thompson Dennis F, *Political Ethics and Public Office* (Harvard University Press 1987)
Thomson MA, *A Constitutional History of England 1642 to 1801* (Methuen 1938)
Tomasic R, 'The Rescue of Northern Rock: Nationalisation in the Shadow of Insolvency' (2008) 1 Corporate Rescue and Insolvency 109
Tompkins A, 'The Rule of Law in Blair's Britain' (2007) 26 University of Queensland Law Journal 255
Tushnet MV, 'The Possibilities of Comparative Constitutional Law' (1999) 108 Yale Law Journal 1225
——— 'Defending Korematsu?: Reflections on Civil Liberties in Wartime' (2003) 2003 Wisconsin Law Review 273
Unger RM, *Law in Modern Society: Towards a Criticism of Social Theory* (Free Press 1976)
Unwin G, *Finance and Trade under Edward III* (Frank Cass & Co 1962)
Vermeule A, 'Emergency Lawmaking After 9/11 and 7/7' (2008) 75 University of Chicago Law Review 1155
——— 'Holmes on Emergencies' (2008) 61 Stanford Law Review 163
Vile MJC, *Constitutionalism and the Separation of Powers* (2nd edn, Liberty Fund 1998)
Viswanathan M, 'Sunset Provisions in the Tax Code: A Critical Evaluation and Prescriptions for the Future' (2007) 82 New York University Law Review 656
Wade HWR, 'The Basis of Legal Sovereignty' (1955) 13 Cambridge Law Journal 172
Wagner JA, *Encyclopedia of the Wars of the Roses* (ABC-CLIO 2001)
Waibel M, 'Debt Relief to Poor Countries: Rules v Discretion' (2010) Butterworths Journal of International Banking and Financial Law 295
Waldron J, 'Is the Rule of Law an Essentially Contested Concept (In Florida)' (2002) 21 Law and Philosophy 137
Walker C, 'Keeping Control of Terrorists without Losing Control of Constitutionalism' (2007) 59 Stanford Law Review 1395

——— 'The United Kingdom's Anti-terrorism Laws: Lessons for Australia', 181–98 in Andrew Lynch, Edwina MacDonald and George Williams (eds), *Law and Liberty in the War on Terror* (Federation Press 2007)

——— *The Anti-Terrorism Legislation* (2nd edn, OUP 2009)

Watson JS, *The Reign of George III 1760–1815* (Clarendon Press 1960)

Webb S, *The Manor and the Borough* (Logmans Green 1963)

Wicks E, *The Evolution of a Constitution* (Hart Publishing 2006)

Wilk K (tr), *The Legal Philosophies of Lask, Radbruch and Dabin* (Harvard University Press 1950)

Williams B, *The Whig Supremacy: 1714–1760* (Clarendon Press 1962)

Williams C (ed), *YB 1 Hen VI Vol 50* (SS 1933)

Williams EN, *The Eighteenth Century Constitution 1688–1815* (CUP 1960)

Wirszubski C, *Libertas as a Political Idea at Rome during the Late Republic and Early Principate* (CUP 1960)

Yin GK, 'Temporary – Effect Legislation, Political Accountability, and Fiscal Restraint' (2009) 84 New York University Law Review 174

Yorke P, *The Life and Correspondence of Philip Yorke, Earl of Hardwicke, Lord High Chancellor of Great Britain Vol II* (CUP 1913)

Young AL, *Parliamentary Sovereignty and the Human Rights Act* (Hart Publishing 2009)

Zagorin P, *The Court and the Country* (Routledge & Kegan 1969)

Ziegler KP, 'Democratic Republic of Congo: The Transitional Constitution of April 1, 2003' (2005) 3 International Journal of Constitutional Law 662

Zolo D, 'The Rule of Law: A Critical Reappraisal', 3–72 in Pietro Costa and Danilo Zolo (eds), *The Rule of Law: History Theory and Criticism* (Springer 2007)

Index

For Product Safety Concerns and Information please contact our EU representative GPSR@taylorandfrancis.com Taylor & Francis Verlag GmbH, Kaufingerstraße 24, 80331 München, Germany